Chicken Soup for the Soul®

Messages from Heaven

Chicken Soup for the Soul: Messages from Heaven
101 Miraculous Stories of Signs from Beyond, Amazing Connections, and Love that Doesn't Die
Jack Canfield, Mark Victor Hansen, Amy Newmark.

Published by Chicken Soup for the Soul Publishing, LLC   www.chickensoup.com
Copyright © 2012 by Chicken Soup for the Soul Publishing, LLC. All Rights Reserved.
No part of this publication may be reproduced, stored in a retrieval system or transmitted in any form or by any means, electronic, mechanical, photocopying, recording or otherwise, without the written permission of the publisher.

CSS, Chicken Soup for the Soul, and its Logo and Marks are trademarks of
Chicken Soup for the Soul Publishing LLC.

The publisher gratefully acknowledges the many publishers and individuals who granted Chicken Soup for the Soul permission to reprint the cited material.

Front cover photo courtesy of iStockphoto.com/Liliboas (© Lisa Thornberg). Back cover and interior photo courtesy of iStockphoto.com/horstklinker (© horstklinker).

Cover and Interior Design & Layout by Pneuma Books, LLC
For more info on Pneuma Books, visit www.pneumabooks.com

Distributed to the booktrade by Simon & Schuster. SAN: 200-2442

Publisher's Cataloging-in-Publication Data
(Prepared by The Donohue Group)
Chicken soup for the soul : messages from heaven : 101 miraculous stories of
  signs from beyond, amazing connections, and love that doesn't die / [compiled
  by] Jack Canfield, Mark Victor Hansen, [and] Amy Newmark.

    p. ; cm.

   Summary: A collection of 101 personal stories from people who have received
messages from loved ones who have passed away, whether in the form of signs, angels,
divine intervention, answered prayers, or other miraculous occurrences.
   ISBN: 978-1-935096-91-7

   1. Spiritualism--Literary collections. 2. Spiritualism--Anecdotes. 3. Supernatural--
Literary collections. 4. Supernatural--Anecdotes. I. Canfield, Jack, 1944- II. Hansen,
Mark Victor. III. Newmark, Amy. IV. Title: Messages from heaven

PN6071.S9 C45 2012
810.2/02/37   2011942715

PRINTED IN THE UNITED STATES OF AMERICA
on acid∞free paper
21 20 19 18 17 16 15 14 13 12   01 02 03 04 05 06 07 08 09 10

Chicken Soup for the Soul.

Messages from Heaven

101 Miraculous Stories of Signs from Beyond, Amazing Connections, and Love that Doesn't Die

**Jack Canfield
Mark Victor Hansen
Amy Newmark**

Chicken Soup for the Soul Publishing, LLC
Cos Cob, CT

Chicken Soup for the Soul
www.chickensoup.com

Contents

❶
~To Heaven and Back~

❷
~Miraculous Connections~

❸
~Signs from Beyond~

❹

~Dreams and Premonitions~

❺

~An Angel Told Me~

❻
~Love that Doesn't Die~

❼
~Saying Goodbye~

❽
~Heaven Sent~

❾

~Messengers and Angels~

❿

~Answered Prayers~

Chapter
1

Messages from Heaven

To Heaven and Back

An Escort to Heaven

Peace is not the absence of affliction, but the presence of God.
~Author Unknown

The doctor's words ricocheted through my mind: "Unfortunately, Jake didn't make it." I slammed the phone down in disbelief. Sobbing, I collapsed on the counter.

My fiancé grabbed my purse and rushed me to his truck. By the time we got to the hospital, the sight of my five-year-old son Garrett was a shock. The blood from the wounds on his face had already turned a crusty black. At first glance, it looked like all of his teeth had been knocked out from the impact.

"Hi Garrett," I said as I forced a smile and leaned down to kiss his forehead. "Where did you get this stuffed bear? He sure is cute."

"From the ambulance man," Garrett managed to say through his swollen jaw.

Like most young boys, Garrett was fascinated by emergency responders. His favorite TV program was *Rescue 911*. Before the show started, he would line up all of his electronic emergency vehicles on the carpet in front of the TV. His collection of fire trucks, police cars and ambulances were ready for action. I never imagined he would be a victim in his own episode.

Suddenly the curtains opened and the doctor entered the room. "We need to check for internal injuries. Since Garrett can't swallow the contrast dye, we'll need to insert a tube up his nose and down his throat to inject the dye for the X-ray. Would you like to stay in the room and hold his hand?"

"Of course." I gulped, fighting back tears. Never mind that I couldn't even watch my own blood being drawn.

The rest of the day was a blur. Between all the phone calls and the multitude of visitors I barely remember a thing except that an odd but welcome sense of peace began to settle on me. Later that day, the doctor gave us the first bit of good news.

"Garrett has a hairline fracture to his jaw but the X-rays show no internal injuries."

The swelling in Garrett's face prevented much of an expression, but I could tell he was trying to smile. He didn't want me to worry. Soon, he drifted off to sleep.

The next morning, I dropped little squirts of juice into Garrett's mouth with a baby eyedropper. "What's wrong, Mommy?"

"Nothing," I lied. Despite the peace I felt, the truth was I didn't have a clue how I was going to tell him about his two-year-old brother Jake.

"Why don't you wait until Garrett asks about Jake?" my friends advised. Initially, that sounded like a good plan, but four days later he still hadn't asked.

With the funeral approaching, my fiancé was concerned. "Do you want me to talk to him?" John asked.

"No." I sighed. "I have to do this myself."

Garrett's face brightened as I entered his room. "Look Mommy! Bruce brought me some more stuffed animals. And the Transformer I wanted—Optimus Prime."

"That's nice, honey." I hesitantly pulled up a chair to his bedside.

"Garrett," I began.

"Yeah, Mommy?"

My body felt suddenly paralyzed. "What would you say if I told you…," I stalled, gasping for air. "It's Jake. Jake didn't make it." Tears streamed down my face. I couldn't even look up.

"Mom, I already know."

"You already know?" My jaw dropped. "What do you mean, you already know?"

"After the accident, I got to go to heaven with Jake." Garrett swooped Optimus Prime into the air. He made gun sounds as he beat up his invisible enemies. "Jake got to go in but God told me it wasn't my time."

Suddenly I was on the edge of my seat. "What was heaven like?"

"Mommy!" Garrett's eyes squinted with apparent irritation. He set his Transformer down. A bewildered look spread across his face. "Mommy! I can't tell you that!"

"Why not?" I insisted.

"It's a surprise!"

"I'm sure God won't mind if you tell me, Garrett. He'll understand—I'm your mother."

"No, Mommy, I can't!"

"Why not?"

"Cuz. God told me it's a secret."

He went back to playing with his toys while I sat back in my chair flabbergasted. Garrett sure picked a good time to start keeping secrets. In the past he flunked confidentiality, but now his lips were locked.

The peace that Garrett felt magnified my own. We both spoke at Jake's funeral. I held the microphone while he shared his story about escorting his little brother to heaven in front of hundreds of attendees. In the days and weeks following his release from the hospital, I tried to squeeze details out of Garrett, but he never uttered another clue. His childlike trust amazed me, yet I fought skepticism. Did Garrett really take a trip to heaven or was his story a figment of his five-year-old imagination?

Preschoolers can make up some enchanting stories. If it was make-believe, however, it worked for him. He didn't grieve like the grief recovery books predicted. He never had a nightmare about the accident. And even though his biological father received a deferred sentence for negligent homicide for driving under the influence of several narcotics, Garrett held no bitterness toward his dad. Even so, I pried and pried to get him to open up about his trip to heaven.

Until I found the reason for his peculiar silence.

One day, I was reading my morning devotional and came across a story in the Bible about a man who had been to heaven. He couldn't describe what he saw because it was a secret. I was spellbound. In the book of Second Corinthians, the apostle Paul says that he was caught up in the "third heaven" where he heard inexpressible things—things that man was not permitted to tell.

Paul experienced the same kind of secret quest that Garrett had witnessed.

I lingered over the verses for a moment. What Garrett saw, he wasn't permitted to tell. It really was a secret. It wasn't a fairy tale—it was a faith tale.

I closed my Bible. My doubts had finally vanished. Who was I to contend with a divine mystery? Awestruck, I realized that his journey to heaven empowered him with peace in the midst of disaster. Never again will I doubt the faith of a child, nor God's ability to provide peace in the midst of tragedy.

Especially to his precious little children.

• • •

Jake's death changed my destiny. I started writing because of the peace and joy I experienced in the midst of sorrow. In a way, Jake's legacy lives on in me. As for Garrett—he is nineteen and although he still speaks little of his trip to heaven, his countenance of peace has never left. I know God has a strong purpose for the secret he entrusted with Garrett that day. As much as I long to understand more, one thing I know for sure—heaven is flowing with peace and joy, because Garrett came back with a lifetime supply.

~Christy Johnson

Make Sure You Come Too

A little faith will bring your soul to heaven, but a lot of faith will bring heaven to your soul.
~Author Unknown

This story was written and documented during our daughter Susan's illness and death years ago. Today I realize the impact these circumstances had on each member of our family. By faith we look forward one day to see Jesus, Susan and angels in Heaven.

•••

Our seven-year-old daughter Susan lies in the ICU drifting between some unknown place and reality. For a brief moment Susan opens her eyes, looks at me and asks, "Who was that man that was just here?"

"Do you mean Daddy?" I ask.

"No. Shhh, here he comes again." Susan closes her eyes and again is gone.

When she comes to the next time, I ask. "Suze, what does the man look like?"

"Just see for yourself," she says. "Here he comes again. I'm going back and fly." I glance around the room. No one is in sight.

I run for help. "Something is happening to Susan," I call out. "I think she's dying."

After taking her vital signs, the nurse says, "Look at her. Susan's radiant. Her eyes are glowing. She is fine."

Susan had been diagnosed with a malignant brain tumor several months before. I had fallen on my knees and prayed that night, "Are you there, God? If you hear me, please give our family strength for whatever we face." Everything I had learned in church for years no longer mattered. I needed to find God for myself.

Leaving the hospital this Sunday afternoon, I sense maybe God heard my cries. Susan had given me a message.

"Your daughter may never walk," the neurosurgeon tells us the day we take our little girl home.

In a few short weeks we watch Susan rise up to stand and practice taking one step at a time until she walks a straight line without help. Soon she pushes her crutches aside. "Get those things out of here. I'll do it myself," she shouts.

I sense my prayers are being heard. While bathing Susan one morning, she says, "Love is the splendid way of taking care of someone."

Uncertain of what I heard, I ask, "What did you say, Suzy?"

"Love is the splendid way of taking care of someone." Susan's messages stymie me, but they have spiritual implications.

Susan's physical body begins to fail after weeks of setbacks, but inwardly Susan grows more vibrant.

I search my grandmother's old Bible for answers to questions about God. I read scripture to Susan in the morning. When I read that Jesus is the light, she says, "We're following the light. Right, Mum?"

Are we following the light? I wonder. I continue petitioning God.

Weeks pass—weeks of treatments, germ-free tents, blood transfusions and a second surgery. Again Susan confounds the doctors by learning to walk once more. She never loses her ability to think or speak clearly. She appears well as she sits on the living room floor playing board games with her sister and brother. Suddenly she begins crying. "I want to go back and fly again."

"You wouldn't want to leave Michael, Kristen, Daddy and Mummy."

"Yes, I would," Susan says.

"But we would miss you," I say, hugging her close.

"Okay," Susan announces, hops up and returns to play. This idea of flying has never left Susan.

After twenty-one months of her illness, Susan's body falters for the third time. She loses her sight and use of her right arm and leg and lies paralyzed, but speaks fluently and is overflowing with joy.

"Mumzy-Poo," she shouts from her bed, using her favorite nickname for me and following it with a giggle. She raises her functional arm. With one pointed finger, she announces, "I'm having a birthday party soon. I'm inviting all my friends to my party next week. It's going to be the biggest party ever."

"It's only June 18th," I say. "Your birthday is July 3rd."

"That's too long to wait," she says. I try to pretend I never heard her.

But the next message, I hear clearly.

"The angels were in my room last night," she says matter-of-factly.

Trying to sound nonchalant, I ask, "What did they do?"

"They came down to me."

Remembering Susan's earlier claims of flying, I ask, "Where did the angels go?" Expecting a lengthy tale, I wait.

Susan smiles and points toward the ceiling. "They went up and were gone."

Angels! How do they relate to Susan's faith in God? The concept of angels in close proximity to Susan bothers me.

I justify Susan's encounter by telling myself that God knows what she needs. Maybe cherubs floating around entertain Susan and help her. But she isn't finished sharing with me.

"You know what, Mummy?"

"What?"

"I had a pair of wings once. They were orange. I'm getting a new pair real soon. This time they're going to be yellow." Light streams from her blind eyes. Does she expect me to receive this information happily? The idea of wings, flying, angels and any reference to these curious beings directly relating to Susan tear at my heart. Speechless, I hide my tears, but Susan senses my gravest fear.

"Come here, Mumzy," she commands. Flinging one arm around my neck in the strongest of embraces, she whispers a consolation. "My poor Mummy. Don't worry. It's okay." Silently I weep, comforted by my little girl.

On June 19th, I tiptoe into the bedroom. Susan appears to be sleeping soundly. She moves slightly. "Mummy," she says softly. "When they take me out of here tonight, make sure you come too."

"You're not going anywhere, Suze. Mummy will be right here beside you."

Her words hardly fade before she slips back to sleep.

I am awakened in the early morning on June 20th by a jolt. I glance over to see a contorted look on Susan's face. "Suze? Are you okay?" I ask, lightly brushing her forehead. "Suze, I'm here. Mummy's right here." No response. Again her body jerks. "Susan? Susan?" With each call I grow more frantic. Taking her hand and falling on my knees by the bedside, I pray.

With the rays of early morning light beaming downward, I kiss Susan goodbye in the ambulance. I kiss her one last time before letting go. As I bend to step onto the sidewalk, Phil climbs up to meet me. "She's gone," he whispers, as if he had known how this trip would end.

"Yes."

I wait on the pavement and watch Phil tenderly say his farewell to his precious princess before backing out to stand beside me in grief.

For days, weeks and years later, I remember Susan's messages. Each carries a comfort. Susan was right. "Just see for yourself," she had told me. God carried me through heartache, gave me strength and brought me to faith to see Christ for myself. He showed me a glimpse of what Heaven is like with angels flying.

Susan left us before her ninth birthday. I envisioned her enjoying her biggest birthday party ever with the angels. I think of her today with a new pair of yellow wings. I can almost see her face radiant, her eyes glowing in the light of the splendid love of Christ. Today I am reminded of Susan's last words to me on earth. "Make sure you come too," she said.

"I will make sure I come too, Suzy," I whisper.

~Phyllis Cochran

Walking Her Daughter to Heaven

An angel can illuminate the thought and mind of man by strengthening the power of vision.
~St. Thomas Aquinas

The phone rang. It was 11:30 p.m. My sister Yvonne was calling from Iowa, but why so late?

"Hello?" I said, half-asleep.

"Regina is in the emergency room. I don't know what's wrong. Just pray, right now. Get on your knees and pray. I'll call you when I know something. Someone is calling in," she said as she hung up.

Four minutes later, Yvonne called again. "She's gone!" she wailed. "Oh, my God! She's gone! What am I going to do now?"

Regina was one of my four sisters—a daughter, mother, wife and twin. She was forty-three years old when she died from a ruptured ovarian cyst. Her departure was so sudden, no one had an opportunity to say goodbye. In the hours and days that followed her passing, my family would experience an unbearable sadness. Yet in the flurry of confusion and despair, a miracle was unfolding—an unexpected glimpse into the realm of eternal life.

My brother-in-law called just after dawn the morning following Regina's death.

"Denise, you need to get over here. Your mom has been acting strange all morning," he said. When I asked what she was doing, he replied, "She's talking to Regina."

Twenty minutes later another sister, Kristen, and I arrived where the rest of our family had slept the night before. Mom was sitting at the kitchen table, slumped in the chair, head resting in her hands, crying. She lifted her head when we came in.

"Thank God you're here," she said. "This is one really screwed up dream. But it's over now."

She paused and looked around. "Where am I?" she asked. "How did I get here? Is someone gone?"

Regina's twin sister Yvonne tried to console her. "Mom, you're in Peoria. You and Dad flew here on an airplane because Regina has died."

"What? That's not possible," she said. "I was just with her." I looked at my other sisters, dumbfounded.

"Is someone gone?" Mom asked again, eyes searching the room for her daughters. "One, two, three, four," she said, counting.

"She's not here," I said softly. "Regina is gone, Mom. She died." Mom stared at me in disbelief.

Without warning, Mom's position and demeanor changed dramatically. She sat upright in the chair, fixed her eyes on something directly in front of her, and began talking. I didn't know what to do at first, because the dialogue was so strange. But as I listened intently, I realized that when Mom's behavior shifted, Regina was speaking through her.

"Quick," I said. "We need to write this down. Mom isn't crazy. I think she is telling us a story."

The following is an edited transcript of the words that Mom spoke over a two-hour period. The breaks in dialogue represent the times Mom's connection to Regina was temporarily lost and she would return to a state of confusion, repeating the same questions, not understanding where she was or why. It was during those "down" times we finally realized what was happening. Mom was traveling between dimensions. She was confused and disoriented, because she was experiencing two worlds simultaneously: the physical realm, and the ethereal. One of my sisters was able to write it all down. While all the words were spoken by my mother, it appeared that she was speaking for Regina half the time and also there was another unidentified voice.

Mom: Regina is right here and she is telling me, "Mom, hold my hand."

(Pause)

Mom: Where are we going?

Regina: We're going on a journey.

Mom: We're all together. Everything is going to be okay.

Regina: Mom, I woke up and you were the only one there.

Mom: Okay, come here, because we have to bring Regina back.

Regina: We're all in Peoria, because I am here.

Mom: I didn't know I was in Peoria.

(Pause)

Mom: I don't want anyone to go. I want to know about Regina's dreams.

Regina: Mom, you have to let go.

Mom: Okay, we'll go back to the beginning.

Regina: We have to find out where the heck this road is going. I think the spirits are calling.

Mom: The heck with the spirits.

Regina: Mom, I see everything.

Mom: Let's slow down. (Pause) Okay, let's go look at that light.

Regina: Mom, just walk with me.

BREAK

Mom: I don't want to let her go. She's not going anywhere.

Mom: Regina, how come I'm here?

Regina: Because you have to hear my story.

Mom: Why listen to your story?

Regina: Just listen, Mom.

BREAK

Regina: It's time for me to go. Mom, you have to pick up the light because I'm leaving.

Mom: If I need to keep telling the story, you need to stay here. I need to hear this so I don't forget it. Regina keeps saying we all need to see the light so we know who is telling the story.

Regina: Mom, do you know the story?

Mom: I want out of here. (She hears a voice.)

Voice: You need to talk to Regina about the light.

Regina: Because you have to remember.

BREAK

Voice: You have to remember the story, and just know you were here.

BREAK

Mom: Okay, I'm going to go with her now.

Startled, I screamed, "NO, MOM! You can't go with her! It's not your time!" My eyes were wild. "Everyone, hurry, call her back!"

Just then, Dad lunged across the table and smacked Mom's cheek.

"Suzanne, it's me, Mike. Please don't leave me. I'm not ready for you to go. I NEED YOU! Please don't go! Please wake up!" But Mom's eyes remained fixed, looking straight ahead.

Mom: I am holding Regina's hand tight, but I'm losing grip. Regina's hand is falling and the light is fading.

Suddenly Mom blinked her eyes. "Is the light still there?" I said softly, "Can you see Regina?"

"No," she said sadly. "She is gone and the light is gone." She started to cry. "Oh why did I have to do that? Why did I have to walk her to heaven?"

My father, who is normally not an emotional man, had displayed enormous gentleness and patience throughout this two-hour encounter. He wrapped his arms around Mom, as the rest of us joined my parents in a big group hug. While Mom didn't understand what had happened yet, the rest of us recognized that we had just witnessed a miracle, following an enormous family loss.

Mom prayed for weeks to the Blessed Mother to let her know Regina was okay. A few months after Regina's passing, three dancing fairies appeared to my mother as she was lying in bed, reading. As they danced at the foot of her bed, Regina appeared in full form and stood near the window. Mom said she looked beautiful. Mom woke up Dad, but he couldn't see what she could see. Regina and the fairies stayed for a minute, maybe two, and then they left.

Mom has never seen her again. But we're all convinced God gave her the privilege of walking her daughter to heaven, assuring all of us that Regina will one day be reunited with the rest of her family that misses her so much.

~Denise Bernadette Fleissner

Amazingly Fun

While we are mourning the loss of our friend, others are rejoicing to meet him behind the veil.

~John Taylor

Like many teens, Kyley used the word "amazing" to describe everything, from the chili cheese dog she had for lunch, to the bright pink shoelaces adorning her sneakers. What was different about my daughter was that every time she used that particular word, you knew she wholeheartedly meant it.

When Kyley died in a car accident five days before her seventeenth birthday, it was almost incomprehensible to me that someone with such a huge presence, someone who lived life with such enthusiasm, with such wonderment, could be gone so suddenly.

I took great care in planning a funeral service that reflected exactly who she was; it was a perfectly joyful celebration of her life and the tears were saved for later.

When the time came, I selected a headstone and began the search for the perfect inscription. My husband and I selected a poem for the back, but I wanted something more personal for the front.

I imagined asking Ky about Heaven. "How is Heaven, Kyley? What is it like?"

"Oh my gosh, Mom, Heaven is AMAZING!" would be her exuberant reply. And I had my inscription: Heaven is Amazing.

Shortly after her death, my husband and I both had very vivid, life-like dreams of Kyley. She'd appear, tell us how much she loved us, and then she'd be gone again. We came up with a way to describe the difference between the dreams we had of her. Standard, run-of-the-mill dreams were called "regular dreams" and the life-like dreams were referred to as "visits."

Although the visits were few, they sustained me during some of my darkest hours. So when one of her best friends called me unexpectedly months after Kyley died, I was excited to hear that she, too, had received a visit. I listened closely as she expressed her amazement over how real it had seemed. "It was like she was right there with me!" I smiled. I knew what she was talking about, and it made perfect sense to me that Kyley would visit the friend she loved so much. I was anxious to hear what my daughter was up to and I hung on every word her friend spoke.

"Before she left, I asked her what it was like… you know, in Heaven."

I caught my breath. "What did she tell you?" I asked, eagerly anticipating her obvious reply.

"She said it's fun; it's a lot of fun."

I thanked Ky's friend for sharing her dream as I felt my excitement give way to surprised disappointment.

My husband had been sitting next to me in eager anticipation. He looked at me, patiently waiting for the details of our daughter's visit. I shook my head. "It wasn't a visit, just a regular dream," I informed him. After all, if Kyley had actually been there visiting with her friend and answering questions about Heaven, would she really have used the word "fun" to describe her life there? I mean, if I had to think of a word to describe Heaven, "fun" didn't seem like it would be my first choice. Not coming from a sixteen-year-old whose favorite adjective was "amazing." It had to have just been a regular dream.

Days after her burial, my husband and I received a phone call from Kyley's father informing us that his son, Kyley's half-brother Luke, had been diagnosed with a rare, inoperable brain tumor. Nine months later, ten-year-old Luke was nearing the end of his journey and preparing to join his sister. My husband, who I married when

Kyley was only a baby and who legally adopted her, made the trip to the hospital with me for one last visit with Luke.

My husband and I visited with Kyley's father in the sitting area of Luke's hospice suite while her stepmother sat at her son's bedside in the adjoining room. We shared our experiences of Kyley's visits to us in dreams. I hoped it might somehow comfort them. I hadn't planned on it, but I started to relay the dream Kyley's friend had shared with me and I ended it just as she had, by telling them that Kyley had said Heaven is fun.

There was a sudden commotion in the room next to us and I heard Kyley's stepmother's voice. "What did you just say?" She appeared in the doorway and asked me again. "What did you just say?"

Startled, I answered her. "Kyley told her friend Heaven is fun... in a dream."

Luke's mother was excited as she talked. "Luke told me that Kyley came to him in a dream. He said it felt real, like she was right there with him. He said that his big sister told him not to be afraid.... Heaven is fun."

I caught my breath once again, this time in humble gratitude.

Luke and Kyley are together now, laughing, playing, and having so much fun.

~Melissa R. Wootan

Taking Bert Home

While we are sleeping, angels have conversations with our souls.
~Author Unknown

The metal springs squeaked as I rolled into bed at ten o'clock that Sunday night. Despite the sagging mattress, I sighed with contentment. I was tired in a good way. I'd gotten up early that morning, bathed and dressed my three-month-old daughter for church, and driven across town to pick up my uncle Bert. I was so glad he could come to service with us. Bert was a World War II veteran who had suffered several illnesses and operations lately. What a blessing that he was well enough to call and ask to come along to Sunday School.

My uncle Bert, Daddy's younger brother, had never married. He had lived on the farm with our family. He was like a second father to me, especially since my dad had died seven years before. Bert was all fun and no discipline. He let my sister and I dress him up in aprons and stockings and Mother's old black pumps. He took us berry picking and sliced off bits of carrots from the garden with his pocketknife. Bert was my best friend and my hero.

After Daddy died, I left the farm and got married. After several years my mother remarried. Bert remained on the farm until his health began to fail, and he came to live with my husband and me. When my daughter came along, the tiny four-room house was too small and Bert went to live across town with my mother and stepfather. I saw him often, talked to him on the phone daily, and was so happy my infant daughter had a chance to meet her great (really great) uncle.

On that Sunday night, I tossed restlessly and kept glancing at the clock. Ten-thirty came and went, and the clock hands approached eleven. I worried about the alarm going off at six. I doubled up my pillow and looked toward the window. Maybe if I ignored the clock, sleep would come. My eyes closed, I began to relax and neared dozing. Suddenly in the distance I could see two objects traveling toward me. When they got closer, I saw they were angels. They were so bright I hadn't noticed a third entity between them. Now I could see that it was Bert. When they reached my side, I was lifted from my bed and joined them in flight. Bert said not a word, but I could feel him telling me he loved me.

We traveled for a short time through the blackest night I had ever seen. Then, in the distance, I saw a glimmer of light. As we grew nearer, I saw a mountain with a bright light streaming from behind. Along a beach in front stood several people. I recognized my grandparents who were dressed in white robes tied loosely with a sash at the waist. Then I saw my dad. He was peering in our direction as if expecting to see something. He looked neither aged nor ravaged by illness. He appeared as he had in pictures when he was a younger, healthier man.

I was so happy to see Daddy that I could hardly contain myself. I felt an overpowering joy. I tried to wave and call out to him, but I could not get him to notice me. And as suddenly as I had been lifted into the air, I was returned to my bed. The vision was gone. The dim streetlight shined through the curtains, and I knew I was far away from where I had been just a moment ago.

Even though I knew my beloved Bert was gone, I felt complete peace and fell into an immediate and deep sleep. My daughter never awoke for a feeding that night and I did not wake until the phone rang just before six. My mother called to tell me Bert had passed away. "He died sometime this morning," she said. She had called the doctor when she found him unresponsive in his bed.

The death certificate listed his date of death as November 6,

1973. But that was wrong. After I had gone with Bert on his final journey and returned to my bed, I had opened my eyes and looked at the clock. It read 11:58. Still November 5th. And that is the date I commemorate every year—the date my beloved uncle Bert went to heaven and God, in his infinite love and mercy, allowed me to accompany him home.

~Shirley Nordeck Short

6

Hope

Is death the last sleep?
No—it is the last and final awakening.
~Sir Walter Scott

I took my mom to the ER one evening because she said she wasn't feeling well. When we got there, I went upstairs to the nursing supervisor's office to tell her that I wouldn't be at work the next day. I was in the elevator when I heard a code blue called in the ER, and I knew it was my mom.

Many times I had worked a code, so I knew exactly what to expect. The ER ward clerk was watching for me and she ushered me to the "quiet room." This is the room they take family members to tell them their loved one has passed away. I called my sister and told her she needed to come to the hospital.

It seemed like we waited for an eternity, when two of Mom's doctors came into the quiet room. I had worked at this hospital for five years; I knew both of these doctors very well and trusted their judgment. My mom's primary doctor had tears in his eyes when he told me she was gone. He explained that he tried everything, and asked me to get in touch with my dad. We needed to decide what funeral home we wanted to come pick up my mom's body. As long as I live, I will never forget my sister on her knees in that little room crying and praying.

While I was trying to get in touch with my dad, the doctor came back in. The nurse had found a heartbeat while removing the monitors. He told me not to expect much, that he didn't think she would make it through the night. Mom was on a ventilator and she would be moved to ICU. He then told me, "If by the grace of God she does live, she will be a vegetable. She went fifteen minutes without any oxygen to her brain." My sister and I spent the night with her in that hospital room. My mom had one seizure after another all night, and I felt so guilty for letting the doctors intubate her. I felt like I was making her suffer needlessly, and as a nurse I knew what she would face if she did survive. We would have to decide whether to insert a feeding tube to keep her alive or let her go.

The next morning, the doctor came in and seemed surprised my mom had lived through the night. But he still didn't offer me any hope.

After he left, I noticed my mom's eyelids fluttering. As I leaned over her bed, she opened her eyes and looked directly into mine. The nurse in me was thinking that her eyes looked clear and she didn't look like an oxygen-deprived patient. So I asked, "Mom, how are you feeling?" My mother was still intubated but she managed to mouth around that tube, "I've been better." I was overjoyed and shocked at the same time. The nurse in me knew this was impossible, but the spiritual person that I am was praising God.

Everyone at the hospital was in shock. The doctors called my mom "the miracle." Three days later, when mom came off the ventilator, she told everyone that would listen to her about her "trip." She talked about floating over her body and seeing the doctors and nurses working on her. She saw my sister and I in the quiet room, and she knew that my sister was on her knees crying and praying.

She talked about being in a black tunnel. She said to the right wall of this tunnel was a whirlpool—that was the gate to hell. She must have been in a wheelchair and someone was pushing her, she said, because she knew she wasn't walking. She talked about a light at the end of the tunnel. But when she got to the light, it wasn't a light but two big, shiny white doors—the pearly gates. She went through those doors and into a beautiful, peaceful place. She saw flowers she had never seen before, colors were vivid and prettier than "what we have here," and sidewalks sparkled. And, she said, "In heaven we get to wear our favorite clothes."

She told me my grandmother, her mother-in-law, walked toward her and was smiling. My grandmother never spoke to her. "She took me by the hand, smiled at me and shook her head no," Mom said. "And the next thing I remember, you were in my face asking me how I felt."

If I heard this story from anyone else, I would have thought it was a drug-induced hallucination. But this was from my momma, so I know in my heart this is exactly what happened to her. I am thankful that God let me experience this because it has brought me so much comfort. I hope by sharing this, it will also be a comfort to someone else.

~Brenda Louque

Chapter 2

Messages from Heaven

Miraculous Connections

7

Mom Knows Best

Faith is not without worry or care, but faith is fear that has said a prayer.
~Author Unknown

I lowered myself to the bathroom floor. The linoleum stuck to my knees while I steadied myself against the wall. I found the pills under the sink and forced handfuls of antacids into my mouth. The pain became more violent.

It was 1 a.m. and too late to call Dr. Hughes again. When I talked to him earlier, he thought it was gas pains.

"It's not uncommon after abdominal surgery. It can be pretty uncomfortable," Dr. Hughes had said.

"Ten days later?"

"Yes. Call me back if it gets worse. Come see me tomorrow."

I went downstairs and waited for the agony to subside. My husband, John, had to go to work in a few hours. Why disturb him now?

When I reached the living room, I collapsed into the recliner. Some invisible force held me to the chair — I couldn't move. I tried to call out, but no sound came. Then a flood of warmth and love spread through me and I no longer felt fear — I knew it was my mom. She had died eight years ago, but I often felt her presence — tonight, stronger than ever. Mom communicated but not in words. It was as if her thoughts transferred to mine.

"Tell Dr. Hughes you've got blood clots."

John found me resting in the recliner in the morning. "You're white as a ghost," he said.

"I need the doctor, but I can't get to the phone."

He brought me the cordless. "Let's call an ambulance."

"No, I have to see Dr. Hughes," I insisted, and waited for the doctor's office to answer. "Great, their message says they don't open till nine. Help me get dressed. I want to be ready when I reach them."

Nine o'clock brought more bad news.

"Dr. Hughes is in surgery until 1 p.m.," his nurse said.

"I talked with him last night. He said to come in today." I tried to keep my voice calm.

"Come in at noon. We'll work you in." And she disconnected.

"We can go right away?" John asked, grabbing his coat.

"No. Not until noon. They'll work me in."

"You'd better believe they'll work you in. Shouldn't we just head to the hospital?"

"I have to see Dr. Hughes. Besides, I'm feeling a little better."

"What do you think is wrong?"

"I'm afraid to tell you…"

He wouldn't let me finish. "You know you can tell me anything." John sat on the arm of my chair.

"You'll think I've lost my mind. I'm not so sure I haven't."

"I'll decide for myself." He stroked my hair and looked straight into my eyes.

"I have blood clots. At least that's what Mom told me last night."

"I believe you. And your mom. Now I know we need to get to the hospital right away."

"No. Mom said I need to tell Dr. Hughes."

•••

An extremely shaken nurse helped me to an examining room.

"Why didn't you tell me on the phone how serious this was?"

I knew I was in trouble when I couldn't lie back on the table. A bed of nails would've felt better.

Dr. Hughes finished early in surgery and rushed in to see me.

"I thought I told you not to go home and go to bed after surgery," he scolded me while he listened to my chest. "You've got yourself an old-fashioned case of pneumonia from inactivity after surgery."

"But I haven't been in bed. We've got a two-story house and my office is in the basement," I protested. "I've been working part-time since my first day home."

"That may be true, but you still have pneumonia. I'll order an X-ray to be sure, but we'll send you home with antibiotics. You'll be good as new in a few days."

•••

"Yep, pneumonia," Dr. Hughes said as he attached the film to the illuminated light box.

"I don't have pneumonia," I insisted. "I have blood clots."

"Are you a doctor?"

"No. My mom told me to tell you I have blood clots."

"Is she a doctor?" He asked with a wry smile.

"No. She's been dead for eight years."

He just stared at me with his hand on his chin. Then he made a phone call.

"I've got someone I need you to see. Her X-ray shows pneumonia. She's ten days post-op from abdominal surgery. But she's sure it's blood clots. I think we need to consider it."

Within minutes, I was in the Nuclear Medicine Department with radioactive dye forced through a vein in my arm.

"We'll know in about an hour or so," the tech said.

John pushed me in a wheelchair to the waiting area. After what seemed like an eternity, a dark-haired doctor in thick black glasses knelt down beside me. He reached over and gently clasped his hand on mine.

"Mrs. Hall, I'm Dr. Goheen. Dr. Hughes called and asked me to take a look at your test results. You have three blood clots in your lungs. I think there may be a nest of them ready to move at any time."

My body went numb. John stepped closer and put his hand on my shoulder. I took a deep breath.

"What do we do?" I asked.

"I'm sending you to the ER first," the doctor said. "You'll be staying with us for a week or so in intensive care. We'll evaluate from there."

A nurse took control of the wheelchair and John followed. An eager team greeted us. I traded my chair for a green-draped gurney and they set to work. An array of machines attached to my chest and arms kept rhythm with beeps and blips. The smell of alcohol swabs preceded countless blood draws. The technician labeled them STAT and disappeared through the curtains. Things moved so quickly my emotions didn't have time to process the severity of the situation.

"You're very lucky," said the nurse. "Your blood gasses are normal, your heart rate is fine, you're not short of breath, and your chest X-ray could be mistaken for pneumonia." He read the latest printout from my heart monitor. "You've got silent blood clots with no symptoms. They're easily overlooked and fatal. You've got a sharp doctor to catch these. He saved your life," the nurse said and called for transport upstairs.

"Strict bed rest," the intensive care nurse instructed, and started IV blood thinner through the automated pump attached to my left hand. "Pretend you're glued to those sheets. The doctor doesn't want those blood clots moving around. They've done enough damage," she said and adjusted the oxygen tubes in my nose. "I've got something here to help you sleep."

"Just be still and pray for morning," a voice intoned in my head.

• • •

The clatter of breakfast trays awakened me. I'd survived the night.

Later, Dr. Hughes stopped by. "Just passing through but I wanted to know if your mom had anything else she thought I should know about?"

~Carolyn Hall

Love You Forever

I cannot forget my mother. She is my bridge.
~Renita Weems

No one is ever ready to say goodbye to a parent, and I was no exception. When my mother suddenly passed away at the age of fifty-five, it was devastating. The only way I knew how to cope was to write. When it came time to write her eulogy, I welcomed the chance to honor her. After reading the eulogy at her funeral, I folded it neatly and tucked it between the pages of her favorite children's book, *Love You Forever*. When it was time to pay final homage to her, I felt satisfied as I placed my only copy of the book in her arms and helped to lower her casket.

Shortly thereafter though, I broke down. I could think of nothing but my mother. I missed her with every cell in my body. But most overwhelmingly, I could no longer grasp the concept of where she had gone. I found it impossible to believe that she was watching over me. If she were, I thought, then she would surely make her presence known. I pleaded with the Heavens to show me she was there, that she was still sending her love, and keeping a watchful eye. No such luck.

Weeks went by. I became depressed and broken, unable to fulfill simple tasks and care for myself. I stayed home. People came in and out, checking on me at all hours of the day. Family and friends tried to coax me out of the house, but all I wanted to do was hide. I wanted to hide from my harsh reality: I would never see or hear from my mother again. Finally, those who cared about me had had enough.

One night, my best friend and her partner came over with a plan to get me out of the house. I debated with them for over an hour, pleading for them to leave me alone. Two hours and a million excuses later, we finally compromised and I allowed them to take me on a quick trip to Target.

As we walked through the aisles my feet dragged. I didn't want to be there. I didn't want to be anywhere. Nonetheless, we perused the make-up, electronics, and home goods aisles. They were there to offer me an outlet, and I was only there to placate them. After several more minutes of mindless meandering I was done. I told them I had to go back home, that I needed to get out of there.

"Alright, but first we have to stop by the candy section. A little sugar will give you a pick-me-up," they reasoned.

I swallowed my pain and continued. I picked out a piece of candy just to avoid my friends' concerned stares. At the checkout, we dropped our items on the conveyor belt and waited in line. I looked at the merchandise arrayed at the checkout. At the top of a shelf, on top of the candy, hair ties, and hand sanitizer, sat a book, a copy of *Love You Forever*! I snatched the copy and skimmed the pages, enjoying the pictures of a mother cradling her child. Tears welled in my eyes.

"Ma'am? Ma'am? How would you like to pay for this?" the cashier asked.

I snapped back to reality, but ignored her question. "Why is this book here?" I demanded to know.

"I'm not sure, ma'am. Maybe someone was planning to buy it but chose not to in the end? They were probably just too lazy to put it back… It happens all the time, unfortunately. Thanks for pointing it out."

I felt compelled to know more, and am still not sure why I asked my next question.

"Where are the rest of the copies of this book?"

"Wow. You sure love that book. The rest are probably in our book section, but I'll scan it just to make sure. Sometimes when a book is on promotion it is moved."

She scanned it. The machine made a loud, shrill beep.

"Huh. That's weird. It's not scanning. Let me see..."

The few moments I waited felt like eternity. A ball of excitement mixed with anxiety formed in my stomach.

"I'm sorry, ma'am. This book isn't scanning because we have no other copies in-store. In fact, we haven't for a while. It says the last time we had this book in stock was two and a half years ago. I'm not really sure why it was sitting there... If you'd like to buy it ma'am, I apologize because I guess it's not really available for purchase. But... I mean... I guess you can... Just take it? It's not really ours to sell."

My heart fluttered as I gingerly took back the book. I cradled it in my arms and as I did, I felt a sense of security envelop me. I knew this was a message from my mother. It was a message of love, support, and understanding. It was her way of saying, "I will love you forever, no matter what." And I've never doubted that since.

~A.B. Chesler

Otherworldly Answers

When you open your mind to the impossible, sometimes you find the truth.
~From the television show Fringe

How does God, or Spirit or Jehovah or Krishna, depending on our personal belief system, decide when it's time for us to learn another lesson about life? Is it when we become too complacent, too sure we have all the answers? Answers not just to our own life's questions, but also to those of our family and friends?

The sign outside the large, old Victorian house read "Psychic Science Spiritualist Church." I had promised myself for years that someday I'd check it out. But if it hadn't been January, with little to look forward to until spring, if my friend Susanne hadn't been looking for diversion to take her mind off a failed romance, if I hadn't run into a couple at a Christmas party who had declared it fascinating, I probably wouldn't have been sitting in a wooden pew in the old house one Thursday evening.

The room was suggestive of the good parlor in grandmother's house, smelling not unpleasantly of furniture polish and old plaster dust. It had beamed ceilings and was lined with windows. Potted plants and ceramic figures of angels decorated the wide windowsills. A raised stage with a small piano, a lectern and several chairs took up one corner, and the empty fireplace under an ornate mantle attested to the house's domestic past. The entire house had that surface shabbiness generally indicative of limited resources, and there was definitely nothing otherwordly about it.

A dozen or so ordinary-looking people were scattered throughout the rows of pews. I glanced at one of the pamphlets I'd grabbed on the way in. "Serving the Indianapolis Community since 1923." I tried to dredge up any information I could remember about the Spiritualist movement, but pictured only séances and floating tables.

One of the pamphlets listed the nine principles of Spiritualism that had been established by the National Spiritualist Association of Churches. That information lent an aura of legitimacy to the group that I hadn't expected. The second surprise was that most of the principles sounded so normal, so similar to many slightly liberal Christian denominations. Excepting the one about spirits continuing to communicate with the living.

We sang several songs from the Spiritualist Hymnal, which looked a lot like the Methodist Hymnal of my youth. The realization that the Spiritualists had their own hymnal reminded me that this little group was part of a larger entity, a network that had been in existence for over a hundred years. Maybe not exactly flourishing, but still around.

The speaker, Bob Bianchi, led another Spiritualist church in Illinois. His talk, a pep talk for living our convictions, could have been given to many traditional church groups. Entertaining but hardly unique.

When he finished, his wife Sharon took the stage and started giving short readings to random members of the congregation, mentioning the name of a departed spirit as the source for each one. The messages sounded like the generic daily horoscopes in our local newspaper, and I could only concentrate for so long before my thoughts drifted to my own family problems.

My father, in his late eighties, needed round-the-clock care, and had recently entered a nursing home in his small Indiana town. He was not adjusting well, refusing all food and insisting that he was ready to die. But I couldn't just let him starve himself to death when he might live another few years with professional caretaking. He had a living will and a DNR order, but I knew that, as his healthcare proxy, I could override these documents. At a meeting with the doctor and nursing home administrator scheduled for the following day, I planned to ask for whatever it took to keep my father alive. Surely in time he would adjust to nursing home living.

As I was mulling over this problem, an image of an old photograph flashed through my mind—a photo of my maternal grandfather, William Franger, holding my three-year-old self in one arm and stroking the muzzle of a horse with the other. A rascal when he was younger, according to local legend, he'd been a bootlegger of regional renown back in the Prohibition era. Family history still includes tales about the prominent customers who drove down from Chicago to buy his "hooch." By the time I was born, though, he had become a prominent businessman whose opinion was respected in the community. He died when I was four years old and my memory of him is fuzzy, relying on old photos and stories more than actual recollection. But I've been told he called me his sweetheart child. Indeed, I'm sure I can remember sitting beside him on the porch swing while he sang "Let Me Call You Sweetheart" just for me.

Now, in the hushed atmosphere of this religious organization, I realized I'd only ever heard him referred to as "Dad" or "Grandpa," never by his given name. Had he been called William, I wondered, or was he called Bill? I felt a wave of sadness, not only for my father's situation, but also for all the time with my grandfather I had missed and the wisdom he could have shared.

My thoughts were interrupted at this point when Bob, the speaker, took over the readings. He was giving a message to a man behind me when he stopped.

"I'm sorry, I'll get right back to you. First, I have someone here who needs to talk to… you." He looked directly at me. "His name is Bill, and he says to tell you they call him Bill, not William." He paused, seemed to listen, then repeated, "Bill, not William. And he says to tell you, about that problem, the right decision has already been made."

I was stunned. It was unfathomable that Bob, or as he would

have insisted, a spirit named Bill, was aware of my silent question and had given me a direct answer. My belief system was rocked. And I knew, in that moment, that I had no right to decide life or death for my father. As painful as it was, I had to let his decision stand.

My father died two weeks later from a case of pneumonia that his body was too weak to fight off. He seemed at peace at the end.

Spiritualism did not alter my belief system. I can't say I truly believe that an individual's existence and personal identity continues after death or that communication with the so-called dead is a fact. I do, however, now admit its possibility.

~Sheila Sowder

I've Got Her

Death ends a life, not a relationship.
~Jack Lemmon

ngel was missing. Our six-year-old cats, Rusty and Angel, were mostly indoor cats. My husband Dave and I would treat them every day to some sunshine and fresh air in our backyard. We took them out only under our supervision. If they happened to get out on their own, we would both look and find them quickly.

Since Dave's unexpected death two months ago, I had become the kitties' only human chaperone. Most days Rusty and Angel were very cooperative, but on this morning Angel bounded out of the yard. When I turned around, she was gone. Usually she went into a neighbor's yard to eat their grass or catch some sunshine. This time she was nowhere in sight and I was scared—we live close to a busy road. I walked around our neighborhood calling her, but did not get an answer.

Then I remembered to take a breath to center myself. I heard Dave clearly say, "I've got her." In my mind's eye, I saw him holding Angel in his arms protectively and warmly, her tail swishing. Dave's energy seemed tall, bright and with a strong presence and vitality. With his words, a sense of calm and peace came over me.

"Where is she?" I asked.

"Turn left," he said, "then go straight."

I put Rusty in the house and got the container of Angel's favorite treats to entice her. I left the gate open in case she came back on her own.

Again I asked, "Where is she?"

Dave's reply came clearly: "I've got her." Again with the image of him cradling Angel, her tail calmly swishing.

As I approached the area that Dave indicated, I heard Angel's faint meow. I called to her. "Angel, I can hear you but I can't see you. Please show yourself to me so we can go home. I know you are safe with Dave, but it is time to go home now."

Dave told me to look left as I walked toward the meowing. There she was in the neighbor's yard, a bit excited but not hurt. In the past she had hissed, scratched and bitten when she was that far from home. This day, she casually came to me and rubbed against my legs. I spoke softly to her as I easily picked her up and carried her home, tail swishing. I sent a grateful thank you to Dave for keeping her safe.

I always thought that when someone died, they merged back into Spirit and God and were gone from us. I thought that though the love always remained, something important ended, and with rare exceptions, that was the end of our communication. What I didn't expect was to have an ongoing relationship with Dave since he passed. Dave has come to my dreams, spoken to me many times, offered guidance for decisions, and given wisdom and comfort in the midst of my deep grief. Our relationship continues, but the dynamic has changed. He is my spiritual guide now, and I treasure his company and love. He helps me in my healing work as a therapist, life coach and energy healer. Sometimes in the midst of my darkest moments of grief and transition, I hear him say, "I've got you."

~Mary P. Collins

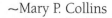

The Ten O'clock Chuckles

Bricks and mortar make a house, but the laughter of children makes a home.
~Irish Proverb

My son Joe is an identical twin. His brother John was still-born. On the days following their birth, many people told me that I would have an angel in Heaven.

For the first eighteen months of his life Joe cried. And cried. He was well fed, well taken care of, and no doctor could tell me why he cried so much. "He has colic," was the reason I heard most. But, in my heart, I knew why he was crying: he missed his brother. They shared a unique bond for nine months, and now they were separated. Joe on Earth. John in Heaven.

When Joe was only twelve hours old, the doctors discovered he had suffered a brain trauma during the pregnancy. One doctor told us he would be severely disabled. As the months of Joe's first year passed, he failed to reach any of the milestones a newborn should. Even though Joe has a sister who is two and a half years older, and I knew what he should be doing developmentally, I would still read and reread the *What to Expect the First Year* books. He never reached whatever milestone he was "supposed to" or even "might be able" to.

The one thing I wanted him to do more than anything else was to laugh. To giggle. To "squeal in delight," as the book described it. At ten o'clock one night, through the monitor, my husband and I heard something. Not knowing what it was, we went upstairs quietly and stood outside his door. He was laughing. He was giggling. He was squealing in delight. We stood there for a long time and just listened. He continued to do this for months, even years afterwards, and it was always the same time: ten o'clock. We called it the Ten O'clock Chuckles.

It was, and still remains, the sweetest sound I have ever heard.

A few years had passed, and one day my phone rang. It was my neighbor. She and several other women in the neighborhood were getting together for a ladies' night. One of the women has the ability to speak to people who have passed on, and would give private readings to anyone interested. I went, not knowing if I would have the courage to sit down and speak with her. Though I believed in it more than disbelieved it, I was still skeptical.

I sat across the table from her, paper and pen ready. Those who pass on, she explained, often remain with us. She asked if I would like to know who was there with me. I resisted the urge to tell her about John, and simply said "yes." As she started to tell me about the people who were present, she would occasionally ask me a question. I said very little. I didn't want to give her any information. The things she told me were things I had never mentioned to anyone, and the descriptions she gave were unbelievably accurate, so I knew she was honestly experiencing what she said she was.

She told me an infant was present, and the infant had a strong bond to my son. Was he a twin? I told her yes, and she repeated that the bond was very strong. It is possible she heard this information from one of my neighbors. It was what she said next that convinced me she could only know this if she was genuinely gifted.

She said his twin came to visit him at night. She described a big, brown bear leaning against a headboard, and a smaller bear that Joe cuddled with. She also mentioned that the music from a pull toy comforted Joe's brother. It is not easy to render me speechless, but I was. Not only did we place a brown bear by Joe's headboard, and give him a small Pooh bear to cuddle, but each night I would pull the string on a bunny toy so Joe could listen to "Twinkle Twinkle Little Star" before falling asleep.

She then looked at me and asked, "You want to know what time he comes to visit him, don't you?" I was shocked. I thought, though she didn't say it, maybe she could read minds too. I could only nod; I was crying too much to say anything intelligible. She told me he comes at night. Somewhere around ten o'clock.

For the second time, I briefly lost the power of speech. How could she know it was ten o'clock? I had never mentioned this to anyone.

Joe has never spoken, but he continued for several more years with his ten o'clock chuckles. Sometimes I would be in the room with him when it happened. I would ask if his brother was with him, and he would always laugh.

Joe is now sixteen years old. He still remains severely delayed in all areas, and relies on others to do everything for him. He is a very happy child and laughs a lot. He still has the ten o'clock chuckles, just not as often as he used to. Perhaps that was John's gift to his brother, to help move him past the grief of his loss and separation. I didn't realize at the time, but John also gave the rest of my family a gift, one that would last for long time—the gift of Joe's laughter.

~Laura M. Fabiani

A Visit with Mom

Hundreds of dewdrops to greet the dawn,
Hundreds of bees in the purple clover,
Hundreds of butterflies on the lawn,
But only one mother the wide world over.
~George Cooper

"Take her to the emergency room, Dad. I'm a half an hour away—I'll meet you there."

I met my ailing mother and worried father in the hospital waiting room. The next day, we received the grim news: Mom had stage IV ovarian cancer. The next four weeks, I rarely left her side. Dad was in a daze. Yet, with an incredible calm, Mom told me, "Jean, if this is my time, I'm ready. I know where I'm going and I'm okay with it."

In a weakened state from thirty-five years of rheumatoid arthritis, she was too frail for any treatment. After a reaction to pain medication, she slipped into a coma and passed from this world looking out the window, as if to another destination beyond.

The next day, our family circled around the desk of the funeral director. The choices that faced us—flowers, casket, and liner box—were easier than any in the last four weeks, but no less surreal. What would Mom like? What would she choose if she were here? But Mom was not here. How could that be?

We managed to make our decisions. The last choice was the

cemetery plot. We piled in our vehicles and drove to the cemetery that T-intersected the end of the street of my childhood home.

As we emerged from our cars, a small brown and orange butterfly flew close to my head and seemed intent on staying close by. My family spread out, walking the grounds in search of just the right place. My husband was fascinated with the older Civil War-era headstones in a more remote area. I followed my dad and brothers to the center of the grounds. It felt crowded and noisy, as it was closer to the street traffic. My husband joined us and I told him I just wasn't feeling good about the more "populated" area.

"What about over there, where I came from? It's quieter. Come on; come see it."

As he and I walked over to the area, the butterfly again found its way to us and landed on one of two tall arborvitae trees nearby. Beside the two sentinel towers of arborvitae, blocked from the noise of the street, was a quiet open place that exuded serenity. "It seems like a private outdoor room, doesn't it? Let's go get Dad."

I walked over to him. "I think we found the spot."

Everyone walked to the protected space and agreed, as my dad said, "You know, I can see this being the place I want to visit."

In the weeks after Mom's body was laid to rest, Dad and I designed a headstone with a bench extension for this space to be enjoyed. It couldn't be installed until spring, so in the meantime, next to her nameplate, we "planted" a fake arrangement of Mom's favorite flower — pink roses.

One late afternoon, I stopped by the cemetery as I drove home from an errand. Driving up the long driveway, hundreds of monarch butterflies launched en masse from the fir trees lining the driveway. This rush of butterfly wings created an unusual ambience. Yet, I yearned to see the smaller brown and orange butterfly among them. I sat down on the grass in front of the fake roses and looked up at the arborvitae. There on the same tree as before, landed my familiar brown and orange smaller butterfly, its wings a bit tattered. It flew around and I said, "Oh, please don't leave. Stay here a while with me."

A few minutes later, the butterfly landed right on the fake roses, only inches away from me. It slowly opened and closed its wings, as if it were listening. In a child-like wonder, I imagined that this weathered winged friend somehow represented my mother, if not embodied her. I said, "Okay, I will stay here as long as you do." I glanced at my watch—6:00 p.m.

I spilled out all the conversations I had longed to have with Mom after she died. I caught her up on the family news, how Dad was doing, how my daughter's pregnancy and my son's college days were going. All the while, the butterfly's wings kept their slow, steady pace—wide open, closed, wide open, closed—as if its body language was communicating that it was taking it all in. I suddenly realized I had been talking only about my life, and blurted out, "Enough about me, what about you? What's Heaven like?"

Suddenly, the butterfly's wings rapidly opened and closed like two hands clapping. Startled, I said, "Oh, I get it! You are praising and applauding. It must be so incredible! How exciting!"

Tears of joy for her filled my eyes, and peace settled in my heart, as I remembered Mom's favorite encouragement to me: "Keep your eyebrows up, honey!" I sensed her spirit buoying mine up again with her signature pep talk, as if to remind me, "don't cry for me—I'm happy. I can dance; I'm free."

Then the butterfly's wings flapped erratically, sometimes a rapid quiver, sometimes slow like drawing a slow breath. Time seemed to stand still. Before I knew it, fifty minutes had passed and I realized I needed to be somewhere else soon. I said, "Oh, it's ten till—I need to go or I'll be late." In a split second, the butterfly shot into the sky and left my sight. I instantly recalled a comment my mom had made about not ever wanting to make anyone late. That was the clincher: I knew I had just experienced my own personal moment with Mom.

~Jean Vaux

A Message for Mom

God blesses him who helps his brother.
~Abu Bakr

James, the youngest of my husband's three brothers, was twelve when a drunk driver sped around the corner and hit the bike James was riding. James died almost instantly.

The grief-stricken family pulled together tightly, but things changed. Vic, the youngest surviving brother, sixteen at the time James died, couldn't help wondering, what if there were no afterlife and James was just plain gone, snuffed out of existence? Vic's grades went down and he didn't sleep well for a long time after James died. He tried praying, but came away with an emptiness, wondering whether his prayers were heard. If there was no afterlife, then God didn't exist either. Eventually Vic quit going to church to put these questions out of his mind, but he hid his doubts and worries to make it easier on his parents.

My mother-in-law had a hard time, too. She faithfully went to church and kept telling herself James was in a better place. But five years later she still grieved for her baby and worried about where he was and whether she would see him again. She had a hard time recognizing the joys God gave her and took no pleasure in the fact that her three other boys had graduated from high school and found good jobs. Even when the oldest, Ken, married and presented her with a grandson, she couldn't take pleasure in her first grandchild, because her own baby was gone.

"I'm sure James is in a better place," she told her husband and sons one day, trying to reassure herself as much as the boys. "I just miss him so much still, every day."

"I miss him too," Ken agreed. "But I know he's happy where he is now."

"And he watches over us," Vic added, wondering why he had said that. After five years, he still kept his doubts to himself, carrying a burden that may have been too heavy for the twenty-one-year-old young man.

Dad, who never said much, nodded, and Mom smiled. Vic thought she put up a good front hiding her broken heart, just like he hid his own feelings of uncertainty so he could comfort her. It was important for his parents to believe that James was happy somewhere, but Vic just couldn't convince himself that the Biblical teachings about the afterlife were true. He glanced at Ken and wondered how Ken could be so sure that James was happy somewhere else.

That night, more troubled than usual, Vic woke in the middle of the night. His two-year-old English bulldog Smedley was whuffing softly, the way he did when someone he knew was about to enter the room. It sounded as if Smedley was asking a question. Vic sat up in bed and, by the glow of the streetlight coming through his bedroom window, looked at his dog, who sat expectantly on his red plaid blanket by Vic's bed. Smedley stared fixedly into the air. Wondering what the dog had seen, Vic followed his gaze.

Suddenly a tingling went through Vic's body, like a small electrical current, welling up from his toes to his head. At the same time the tingling started, the room became lighter. A football-sized spot of a gentle, golden light formed in the air in front of Vic and rapidly expanded. Vic glanced at Smedley. The dog's eyes were fixed on the light, he had quit whuffing and gently thumped his tail.

Somewhere in the back of his mind, Vic thought he should be scared, but he wasn't. As his eyes returned to the light, a figure appeared, the outline of a boy. With a shiver of amazement, but not of fear, Vic recognized his little brother. James looked just the way Vic remembered him, with his cowlick sticking up and his freckled grin still in place.

"I'm fine, Vic," the heavenly messenger said, still smiling. "Tell Mom not to worry. Tell her I'm okay."

Vic reached out to James. The questions that had tortured him for the last five years vanished, and peace entered his heart.

"I will," he said.

James, in his sphere of light, nodded. The light in the room shrank and faded away, taking him with it.

The peace that had entered Vic's heart didn't leave, however. He lay back in bed, and before he knew it, fell into a deep and dreamless sleep.

The next morning, Vic woke, instantly remembering the angelic vision of the night before. Suffused with happiness, he smiled to himself. All his doubts had disappeared, and he could hardly wait to deliver James's message. He rose and went to his job as the manager of a small store, but all through the work hours he thought about James's message to his mom.

Bit by bit, his joy was replaced by worry. Would Mom and Dad believe him? What if they thought he was crazy, and then Mom would worry about him too? Why hadn't James appeared to Mom instead of to him? Finally he decided that, whatever would happen, he needed to tell his mother as he had promised.

When he went to see his parents after work that day, Mom said, "It's good to see you, Vic. You look happy. What's going on?"

Vic followed Mom into the kitchen and sat down at the table, where Dad already sat, just home from work, drinking a cup of coffee.

Mom put another cup and a plate of cookies in front of Vic. "Eat," she said. "You must be starving after working all day." She sat down across from him.

Vic took a sip of coffee and said, "I have a message for you and Dad."

Dad looked up, a question in his quiet face.

Mom frowned. "From whom?"

"I don't know how to tell you, but…"

"Did something happen to one of your brothers?" Mom interrupted, eyes wide in alarm.

Vic shook his head. "Nothing bad happened. I had a strange experience last night." He told them about his nightly visitor.

Mom stared at him, a mixture of doubt and belief in her eyes.

"Are you sure you didn't dream it all?" Dad asked.

Vic patted his mom's hand on the table. "I'm positive I was awake. If Smedley could talk, he'd tell you the same. James is all right, and he doesn't want you to worry. I'm not worried anymore, either."

"Why didn't he appear to your mother then, and let her know directly, instead of sending you to tell her?" Dad challenged him.

"Ever since James died, Dad, I've had serious doubts about God and the afterlife," Vic answered. "I think God has sent him to me with his message so I would know for sure." He squeezed his mom's hand. "I'm so glad this happened. My doubts are gone now. I know James is happy and is somewhere, watching over us. Maybe God knows you have the faith to believe me, when I may not have believed you."

Eyes bright with relief, Mom smiled, took Vic's hand into her own and patted it with hers. "I do, son. I believe you." She took a deep breath and glanced at Dad.

Dad shook his head. "I have always felt James was all right where he is now," he said. "God's ways are mysterious, and sending James might just be how He wanted to reassure you and your mom."

In the days that followed, the other brothers too heard the message, and they believed Vic. The family pulled closer together, united through their faith in what had happened. Soon after, Mom put aside her grieving and started taking joy in the children she had left and the grandchildren. And Vic felt as if a new life had been given to him, through the grace of God who had sent the perfect heavenly messenger to the right person.

~Sonja Herbert

Voice of an Angel

Mother, the ribbons of your love are woven around my heart.
~Author Unknown

made it through Thanksgiving. I was relieved it was over. It wasn't easy, but I was so busy with food preparation and getting the house ready, I had little time to lament Mom's not being with us.

Now, I was going to have to face Christmas. It was going to be harder than anything I have ever faced before.

Mom had succumbed to colon cancer the previous January. I had lived through the first Thanksgiving without her and now I faced the first Christmas.

It was the first weekend of December. I tried to muster up the courage to visit Mom's grave to decorate. I had visited her grave on her birthday, Easter, Mother's Day, Memorial Day, during the summer, and earlier in the fall. I had only missed two months all year. Somehow, my heart wasn't in it now. I couldn't bear the thought of standing there mouthing the words, "Merry Christmas, Mom," to a stone. I began to cry every time I thought about it.

I let the first weekend of December pass without making myself go there. The cemetery was over an hour's drive. This provided a ready excuse. I was just too busy shopping and getting the house ready.

Back at work Monday morning, I knew I was dragging my feet. I would, eventually, have to face the music and go. Mom deserved it.

That next Saturday, we had unexpected company. Some friends from out of town were visiting their parents and stopped by for an early lunch. The day was shot by the time they left and we cleaned up.

Sunday, I went to late mass and wasn't quite feeling up to par. I told myself I didn't feel like driving all that distance. Another weekend had passed. I was feeling guilty about not having any decorations on Mom's grave but I knew she wouldn't expect me to go out when I wasn't feeling well.

Only one weekend left. I had so much wrapping and food preparation still to do. Our children, their spouses, and our three grandchildren would be with us Christmas Eve. They always spent Christmas Eve with us and went to their in-laws' homes on Christmas Day.

I had always spent Christmas Day with Mom, and it transported me back to my childhood. With Mom, I was the child, not the wife, the mother, or the fifty-year-old grandmother. Now all that was gone. There was no going back to my childhood. There was no Mom.

The last weekend and the last chance to decorate arrived. How would I be able to get through this? I was depressed. I cried at the drop of a hat. Again, I let the weekend slip by and made up more flimsy excuses. Since it had snowed a flake or two, I thought "inclement weather"—yet another reason not to go. The streets were barely wet.

It was Monday morning. I took Monday and Tuesday off from work to try to get caught up with the wrapping, cleaning, decorating, and baking Christmas cookies. This year I felt more overwhelmed than ever. I slept fitfully at night. I was more fatigued every day. I couldn't shake that sorrow deep inside.

I hadn't finished our laundry over the weekend. I had one more load of clothes. I began filling the washer around 7:45 a.m. My husband left for work and I was alone. Gloom wrapped around me like a shroud. My eyes began to fill with tears. As I was starting to load the washer, suddenly, I felt weak.

All at once, my head began filling with the words of a poem. I dropped the clothing I had in my hands and they fell to the floor. I frantically reached for the pencil and paper we kept by the telephone. I began to write the words down as fast as they came. It was like I was possessed. When I finished, I had filled two sheets of paper. The poem rhymed and flowed nicely, as if I had deliberately composed it. Well, I hadn't. I read over what I had scribbled down.

It was at that moment I was certain where the poem had come from. Straight from heaven. I had no doubt that my mom was comforting me as she had so many times since I was a child. Here are the words that came in that sudden rush:

FROM MOTHER
The somber figure stood before,
The marker of cold stone,
She felt such pain, her loved one lost,
She stood crying, all alone.

Then, a voice spoke softly to her,
Like the voice of an angel in prayer,
"Do not weep for me, not ever my child,
For you see, I'm not really there.

My soul is at rest, peace and joy are mine,
So wipe those tears from your face,
Go on with the living, who share your life,
Take them in your loving embrace.

I will never truly be lost to you,
Because of the love we hold dear,
Dear child, love never, ever dies,
Isn't love what has brought you here?

The light of God's love, shines on us,
And with Him, we're never alone."
The voice was fading, just like it began,
To a low and whispering tone.

The somber figure lifted her eyes,
The sun had come out from above,
Slowly she walked away from the grave,
Her heart filled with lasting love.

I quickly finished the laundry, and got ready for my journey. I felt renewed and eager to do what I had put off for so long.

I had a beautiful bouquet of poinsettias, edged in gold, with holly leaves and berries. I couldn't wait to place it in Mom's vase.

On the drive to the cemetery, a panorama of fifty wonderful years I had with Mom flashed through my mind. I was no longer daunted by prospects of another encounter with her grave. I felt gratitude, instead of sorrow, knowing that God had richly blessed me with a loving, kind, and caring mother. A mother who was still comforting me from beyond the grave.

That Christmas was quite different for us, but a good Christmas overall. It wasn't sad or overshadowed by gloom and regret. Yes, we remembered Mom—only in a completely different way than I had anticipated.

At dinner Christmas Eve, the family sat and recalled all the good times we had shared with that wonderful lady who filled our lives with love and all those happy memories.

Thanks, Mom, you've always been there for me.

~Joyce Sudbeck

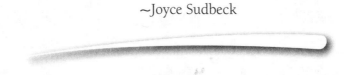

Hourglass of Love

Love is a symbol of eternity. It wipes out all sense of time, destroying all memory of a beginning and all fear of an end.
~Author Unknown

I am a counselor and a professor of counseling. A few years ago, I decided to learn Induced After-Death Communication (IADC) — a professional counseling technique designed to help clients directly communicate with a deceased loved one. I brought three graduate students with me to the training in Chicago. After we got back home, we spent a few months meeting weekly and practicing on each other to develop our skills before we employed the technique with clients in our counseling practices.

During a practice session one day, my student Jenny was practicing as an IADC guide with me as her guinea pig. I decided to try to contact my beloved cousin David who had died many years before, shortly after his return from military service in Vietnam. As we proceeded, I closed my eyes and in my mind's eye did indeed see David — but only long enough to be reassured about his well-being and our mutual love. Within seconds of his appearance, his father, my uncle Ray, literally elbowed his way in front of David! Uncle Ray had died just a few years earlier from cancer. He stood before me healthy and whole, and he immediately held out his hand and showed me what looked like an hourglass, but with no sand inside. I didn't understand what the hourglass meant. When I tried to zoom in on it, it disappeared. When I backed away, it reappeared.

Apparently, the hourglass—just as it was—was all he intended for me to see. Without him communicating anything else, I knew he meant for me to contact his wife, my still-living aunt Norma, to tell her about seeing her husband and the hourglass.

When I opened my eyes, I described to Jenny what I'd seen, and expressed my reluctance to contact my aunt Norma. I had never been close with her. Except for a condolence card when Uncle Ray had died, I hadn't communicated with her for probably more than twenty years. I had no idea what she thought of things like ADC, and I didn't want to upset her with unwanted information that might reactivate painful grief. I said to Jenny, "Rather than call her, maybe I'll write her a letter. I can even start the letter with, 'If you don't like what you're reading, you can stop and throw the letter away.'" Jenny said, "Why don't you check with your uncle?" I agreed, and as we proceeded with IADC, I closed my eyes and immediately saw Uncle Ray again—this time insistently holding out a telephone receiver. I opened my eyes. "He wants me to *call* her!"

Over the subsequent months, I repeatedly thought about my experience with Uncle Ray but just could not screw up the courage to call Aunt Norma. One day, I told my aunt Nancy, Uncle Ray's sister, about the experience. I felt safe telling her because, years before, Nancy had had a near-death experience in which she had seen her brother, my uncle Leonard, who had died shortly after returning from military service in World War II. Nancy surprised me by saying she was good friends with Norma and would be visiting her in a few weeks. Nancy offered to tell her in general—no details—about my experience, inquire whether she wanted to talk with me about it, and report back to me. I agreed eagerly. When Nancy got back to me a few weeks later, she reported Aunt Norma was receptive and interested.

Still it took me a few more months to build up the courage to contact Aunt Norma. Finally, while driving alone one day on a long-distance trip and on a long, straight stretch of interstate highway, I felt brave and called her on my cell phone. She answered, and after she got over her surprise to hear from me and we caught up a bit on each other's lives, I reminded her of Nancy's visit and her mention of my IADC experience. I asked Aunt Norma if she would like to hear about it, and she said yes. I proceeded to recount my experience to her in careful detail. I ended by saying, "I have no idea what the hourglass means; I'm just telling you that Uncle Ray seemed very purposeful and insistent when he showed it to me."

She replied with confidence that she knew *exactly* what it meant. "When I was a little girl, I loved my grandmother dearly. When we used to visit her house, she had a pair of cut crystal vases that she kept on an end table with a glass top. I used to lie for hours under that table looking up through the glass shelf at how the sunlight glinted through the facets of the cut crystal. When my grandmother died, I wanted only one memento: that pair of vases. In fact, as I sit here right now talking with you, I'm looking at them. Ray knew that if we were to awaken in the middle of the night with the house on fire, and could quickly grab only a few things as we escaped, those vases are what I would grab. Although each is uniquely shaped, they are both clear glass: wide at the top, then narrow, then wide at the bottom. They are among the very most precious things I possess."

I was amazed. Uncle Ray apparently had known exactly what he was doing by choosing the one object that, though I had no knowledge of it, Aunt Norma would recognize unmistakably. Upon reflection, I was touched and awed to realize that, probably more than any other objects, those hourglass-like vases represented ongoing and eternal love—between Norma and her grandmother, and between Norma and Ray.

From this and other experiences, I look forward, when I have transitioned beyond physical form, to reuniting with those with whom I have a love connection. From my study of transpersonal experiences—those that transcend the usual personal limits of space and/or time—I believe we are on earth for a reason, so the transition should not be hastened. But that joyful reunion with our loved ones awaits us when the time comes.

~Janice Miner Holden

Not All Alone

Love is not singular except in syllable.
~Marvin Taylor

"How many?" The perky young restaurant hostess asked with a professional smile. She picked up a stack of menus and peered over my shoulder.

"One," I murmured, looking at the floor.

"Oh, you're all alone." Her smile faded to sympathy. She led me to a small table in the corner and quietly removed the second place setting.

It's true—I live alone, eat alone, go places alone. I am a widow, a word I still can't believe is used to describe me. When my husband Jim died, I thought the days of the two of us against the world were over. I would have to manage by myself. That was before I experienced the miracles. Not parting-the-seas, raising-the-dead miracles, just everyday small-m miracles that showed he was still with me.

While making arrangements at the funeral home, my husband's gray suit hanging on a rack in the next room, I spotted a $1,000 error in the itemized statement. It was merely a typo, easily corrected, but I had never found a mistake involving figures in my life. My husband used to nag me about it. "Look the bill over before you pay it. It might be wrong." Maybe other people routinely notice incorrect numbers. For me it was a miracle. I could almost see Jim's finger pointing at the offending number.

That was the first.

In April, six weeks later, I attended a family funeral in another state with my grown children: Julie, Veronica, Kathy, and Jean. We were all hovering by the door of our motel room waiting for Veronica when she asked, "Has anyone seen my little black dress purse? The car keys and my driver's license are in it."

We quit leaning against the wall and began looking around the room. As time passed, our alarm increased and the search intensified. We stripped bedding, shook shoes, crawled around the floor peering under furniture. No luck.

One by one, we admitted failure. "It's not here," Veronica said. "I know I had it last night. Maybe it fell into the car trunk when we got the luggage and we missed it in the dark." She reached for the phone book. "I'll call the rental place and see about getting another key. Why don't you guys go ahead with Jean?"

We said we'd stay with her even though we would miss the funeral. With sighs and slumping shoulders we plopped down to wait while she looked up the number. I had a conversation with my husband and reminded him of the times we'd searched for missing items—glasses, gloves, especially keys. "We could use some help here," I told him.

Before Veronica could pick up the phone, Kathy looked down at the floor between the beds. "Is this it?" She held up a small black purse. Hard to believe none of us had seen it lying there in plain sight.

Jim always found his keys eventually.

That was the second.

The next month Kathy had surgery. I stayed in the hospital with her the first night and Julie took the second. From birth, one of Julie's best talents has been sleeping. Not much interrupts it, but that night she was roused by a voice saying, "Julie, wake up. Kathy needs you." And sure enough, she found Kathy struggling to breathe and unable to reach the call button for the nurse.

In June I attended my grandson's high school play fifty miles away. By the time I started home, we were in the middle of a down-pour. Rain beat against the car so hard my windshield wipers could not keep up. Since on previous trips I had napped in the passenger seat while my husband drove, I wasn't totally familiar with the road. However, I did know I would have to negotiate two hard-to-see exits. The first one was a cloverleaf off an overpass. If I turned too soon, I could plummet forty feet down an embankment. If I missed it, the next exit was eleven miles away. I could barely make out the center line on the highway and reading traffic signs was impossible. "Honey, I can't see," I said, and the rain lifted long enough for me to make the turn. At the next exit, the rain let up again.

Shortly after Jim died, just as I was adjusting to the quiet house and his car never leaving the garage, I started having dreams that he was back, sitting at the dining room table waiting for bacon and eggs, the TV remote in his hand. A few weeks later I dreamt he was reviewing the bank statement. With the stern expression I remembered so well, he told me I had money, but not a lot. I could live comfortably but did not need another pair of black shoes. Another time he stood looking out the window at the garden. "Better pick the tomatoes before they freeze," he said. I argued that the temperature never got that low in early September. The next night we had a record-breaking early frost.

Similar dreams came periodically for almost a year. Then one night he said, "I have to go now." I asked what to do about a funeral. Most people had only one. How was I going to explain a second? He shook his head. "No funeral. You're the only person who could see me." And he left. That was the last time I had one of those dreams.

Before my husband's death I would have scoffed at such tales. But not anymore.

~Sally O'Brien

17

Channeling Dad

Death is not extinguishing the light; it is putting out the lamp because dawn has come.
~Rabindranath Tagore

ather and I agreed on many things in life but strongly disagreed about some issues, including what happened after death. He believed that when a person died, that was it—no heaven, no hell, no bells tolling, and no continuation of the soul.

I believed that when a person's body died, the soul crossed over to somewhere. I didn't necessarily imagine that "somewhere" as heaven, but rather that the soul returned to God, Spirit, Source, or whatever anyone else called that sense of the Divine. Then, after resting and reviewing the life just left, the soul could choose to return to earth—reincarnated.

Mom and Dad lived several provinces away from me for the last twenty years of their lives. Every three months I would fly out to visit for a week or so and I did that consistently until they died. Mom left first. Dad and I were there in the end and he dispassionately described the physical dying process to me (being a retired nurse) as Mom lay slowly leaving. Although it was a lesson in the physicality of dying, it was a hard one emotionally for me, as she and I had been extremely close.

They had been together almost sixty years by that time and her passing left a huge hole in Dad's life for a time. He lived in a retirement community in the beautiful Okanagan Valley in British

Columbia and over the years they had lived there he had made many friends, who all rallied round him. For the next five years he stayed actively involved in the community in a variety of ways. I continued to visit regularly.

We talked about death and dying from time to time. Dad researched the funeral costs and picked the provider he wanted us to use. He posted his wishes on the fridge door so my two brothers and I would know what to do when his time came. He was very pragmatic about it all. And he and I talked. Our different views about death were very apparent and rather then get into any argument about it I started to use humor with him. As I spoke of the soul journeying onward and not dying Dad would tell me that I was just plain crazy! In turn I would tease him and say that when he crossed over I expected to hear from him. Further I gave him the words I expected him to say to me — "You were right, daughter!"

When it was Dad's turn, I was there along with one of my brothers. Dad passed in the early summer. About six weeks later, a friend and I travelled into a neighbouring province to visit another friend at her camp at a lake for a weekend. On our way home, we happened to be driving by a retreat centre that we both visited from time to time. We decided on the spur of the moment to pop into the retreat and see if anyone was home and have some tea.

Sun Carrier, one of the partners at the retreat centre, was a person who channelled three different sources of Enlightened Beings. She and her partner were home, and as we sat with our tea and caught up with events, she offered to channel for us. My friend Priscilla and I were delighted to have that opportunity and quickly agreed.

After we all meditated Sun Carrier began to channel. The guidance offered through the channel was loving and expansive — which had always been my experience. The message was flowing along when all of a sudden there was a switch from that channel and my father came into the channel with a message to me.

Father's message to me was not, "You were right, daughter!" He did not use those words. What he did say was that he was sorry for being such a stubborn old codger (words that were common for him to use), and that I had more knowledge about dying than I even knew. He continued on by saying that my use of humour when talking to those who were getting close to dying was a gift, as it eased the fear in the individual, and I should continue to do so. His closing words had me laughing and crying at the same time. He touched on his stubbornness again and said that I had a bit of the same — something that I had been struggling with for a number of years. Then he was gone and the other channel continued.

As we sat around at the end of the channel and talked, Sun Carrier expressed her surprise about Father coming into the channel. I was astonished, and emotionally elated and grieving at the same time. Although Sun Carrier had known that my father had passed, she had no prior knowledge of how he and I used to talk about death. When I explained the conversations he and I had about death, about my expectations that he would contact me and say "You were right, daughter," we laughed about his message to me. Even then, he was not willing to say the actual words, but the message was clear — my view of death was "more right" than his view. An argument I was happy to win!

~Camille Hill

Chapter
3

Messages from Heaven

Signs from Beyond

18

Happy Birthday, My Sunshine

Coincidence is God's way of remaining anonymous.
~Albert Einstein

It was my fiftieth birthday. Fifty! And no one seemed to think it was a big deal, except for me. Well, Mom would have thought it was a big deal, I told myself. And she would have made a big deal out of it, too, that's for sure.

Where birthdays were concerned, my mother's motto was always "bigger is better." The first time my brother requested a birthday party, she insisted on inviting each of his classmates, accompanied by a parent, for a birthday bash that has become part of our neighborhood history. When I turned fifteen, a very special age in the Latin culture, a party at home wouldn't suffice according to Mom. We celebrated by visiting family in my mother's South American hometown so that I could have an authentic experience. Even when times were lean, as they often were, I was guaranteed whatever small gift my parents could afford, my favorite cake, a special card, and the largest bouquet of wildflowers Mom could pluck from her garden.

It was no surprise to my family then, that after Mom's passing several years ago, I continued her tradition of celebrating big. I began hosting birthdays for my father and brother while also extending the tradition to my own family. I must admit, though, that at first these get-togethers were not the fun times they once were. These occasions just felt so empty without Mom — the driving force in our family, the cheerleader always at the ready with her round-faced smile, corny jokes, and off-key rendition of "The Birthday Song." It took a while for the rest of us to recapture our spirit after her passing but eventually, with the help of time and determination, we did. So why, now, did I feel the emptiness of her loss so deeply once again?

I sat down at my piano in search of a distraction. Perhaps I was feeling so melancholy because I was experiencing what I thought of as a milestone. Mom had been with me for all my other milestones, big steps, little steps, tears, and triumphs, and this was the first such event I was not sharing with her. I lifted my hands from the keyboard, then reached into the wicker basket full of sheet music in search of an uplifting selection. There, between my collection of classics and show tunes, I found an old manila file folder. Odd, I thought, what is this doing here? I opened it and found nothing much of interest — a few yellowed newspaper clippings, old recipes, and long-expired grocery coupons. I stood, folder in hand, then walked to my kitchen trashcan. Just as I was about to drop it into the pail, a card slid out. There on the front of the card was a painting of a wildflower bouquet similar to those Mom often presented to me from her garden. Inside, written in my mother's familiar scrawl, were greetings in honor of my fortieth birthday.

That night, after my husband Bill and I were seated at my favorite restaurant for a special birthday dinner, conversation inevitably turned to the long-lost card. I so wanted to believe that somehow the card was more than mere coincidence and turned to Bill for confirmation. "I mean, what are the chances of finding that card today of all days?" I asked him.

Bill just shrugged his shoulders, noncommittally.

Still, the question haunted me.

Later that evening, after Bill and I got home, I sat down at my computer to check the last of my e-mails. There were several birthday greetings among the advertisements and other junk mail. I opened them and read each one, finally scrolling down to the daily newsletter I receive from Chicken Soup for the Soul. The featured story of the day was "What is Your Feather?"—my contribution to one of their books, *Chicken Soup for the Soul: A Book of Miracles*. It was a story I had written about dealing with the initial grief of my mother's loss. A story I wrote about my mom, included in that newsletter on my actual birthday? Now that was eerie.

Surely, Bill would have to admit this was more than coincidence. My heart racing, I printed the newsletter and sprinted down the stairs to the first floor where Bill readied for bed. "Look at this," I said as I thrust the papers toward him. "Now this can not be a coincidence," I insisted. I watched as Bill remained cool. Hmph! Now I knew for certain my mom was contacting me. What would it take to convince my husband?

Frustrated, I went into my bedroom and flipped on my radio to listen for the weather report as I did each evening. Static. I ran the tuner up and down the band. Nothing but static. Finally, I tuned in to the only station that came in loud and clear to hear Willie Nelson warbling a country tune in his inimitable style. Now, I'm not necessarily the biggest fan of country music. But my mind was so distracted by the events of the day, I sat on my bed, closed my eyes, listened, and tried to make sense of it all. Still with a glimmer of doubt in my mind, I asked myself: Could the card I found and my story posted on the Internet really be signs from my mother? Could those passed on to the next realm of existence really communicate with those of us left behind on Earth? No matter how much I wanted to believe that my mother could still send me greetings from beyond, really, was something like that possible?

Then I got my answer.

Strains of Johnny Cash's rich baritone came through the airwaves singing the old folk song, "You are My Sunshine," the very same song that was my mother's childhood lullaby to me. Right there, I broke down. I started to sob deep and hard, but not in sadness, in gratitude for my mother and for the love we shared that was so powerful it could travel across the realms. When I opened my eyes, I found my husband hunched over me, his hand covering mine. "It looks like your mom did remember your birthday," he said.

Yes, my mother did remember my birthday. And she did it in the same grand style she always did. After all, she sent me not one but three signs that day. Of course. My mother always did do birthdays in a big way.

~Monica A. Andermann

An Inexplicable Gift

Reason is our soul's left hand, Faith her right.
~John Donne

As the minister talked about my sister Laura, she wove images of one of Laura's favorite flowers, the blue iris, through her comments. She described how Laura brought iris flowers to her when she was in the hospital, of how Laura spoke at her ordination service overlooking an arrangement of blue irises, and how she wore an iris-blue bridesmaid's dress in Laura's wedding. I had to smile even in this most solemn service — the memorial service for my sister's life. The minister eulogizing Laura so eloquently had been one of her best friends since childhood.

I was caught off-guard by the pleasant, yet unexpected, memory of that lovely blue flower. It brought back memories of the border gardens filled with irises at our Aunt Margarete and Uncle Cliff's home — a place where my sisters and I spent many happy hours. My daughter Lila and I had even enthusiastically planted iris bulbs in our own border garden a few years ago in the fall, eagerly awaiting the reward of beautiful blue blooms in May... to no avail. We chalked it up to a lack of gardening experience and promptly forgot about our lost flowers. Now I made a mental note to try again. A bed of blue irises would be a happy reminder of Laura's life.

The days that passed after Laura's memorial service were difficult and we all coped as best as we could. It truly seemed unjust when exactly three weeks later Aunt Margarete also went to heaven. Knowing that she was in her last hours on earth, I told her that I loved her, and asked that she please hold onto our beloved Laura and Uncle Cliff for us when she got to heaven.

Even in her uncommunicative state, her eyebrows raised and she smiled.

When I came home from my final visit with Aunt Margarete, I was saddened and overwhelmed by the loss of two family members in three weeks. I could not make sense of the trials my family and I were experiencing. Reality continues whether we are ready to face the day or not though, so I was up early the next morning to get my daughters off to school.

As we rushed out in the dawn to go to the bus stop, Lila noticed something strange in our yard. Among the fallen brown leaves, and the yellowing fall foliage of our border plants in November, stood one lone beautiful blue iris bud, inexplicably ready to bloom out of season. I have already confessed to my lack of gardening expertise, but I do know that irises are not supposed to bloom in North Georgia in late November! Reverend Teresa's words came back to me, and I just couldn't stop smiling over the coincidence of this single, seemingly mixed-up flower. We watched it every day that week, and on the day of Aunt Margarete's memorial service the blue iris bloomed fully, perfectly, amazingly!

I wrote this story quickly and sent it by e-mail to friends and family as a message of faith and encouragement, accompanied by a photo of the iris. I truly believe the iris was a message from heaven that my loved ones are happy in their eternal home and that I was going to be just fine as well. It was as if God was holding me tight, just as I do my girls, patting my back, comfortingly saying, "Everything is going to be all right. I love you." I felt an indescribable peace and joy in the faith that God had reached out to me with such a personal, caring and miraculous sign, so meaningful to me.

When my friend Dawn responded to my e-mail with the message to "Hold onto your hat, Susan, this is amazing," the message became even clearer. Dawn's research of the iris flower symbolism revealed that it was named for Iris the Greek goddess of the rainbow. In Greek mythology, Iris was the messenger of the gods, acting as the link between heaven and earth!

Purple irises were planted over the graves of women to summon the goddess to guide the dead to heaven. Now my message from heaven was undeniable and even more significant to me!

I do not ascribe to the ancient Greek beliefs of goddesses and gods, but I do believe that God uses everyday events and symbolism for eternal significance! Some may see my single iris bloom in November as a fluke, a rogue botanical specimen, noting that the weather has been strange, explaining it away in many logical ways, a stretch of faith. All I know is that at the time I was slogging through grief, and that I felt joyful comfort in that iris bloom. I am calling it a gift, a message from Heaven. I am so thankful that I was aware enough to hear it.

As a postscript to satisfy the curious, yes, that one iris bloomed again this year, but earlier than the year before. This year, the lone iris bloomed the week of September 27—what would have been my sister Laura's fifty-first birthday. Not a coincidence—my message from heaven continues, and so does my joy in having received it!

~Susan L. Ellis

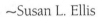

Just When She Needed Him

Even hundredfold grief is divisible by love.
~Terri Guillemets

Could it be true? That was all I could ask myself as I listened to my daughter share her experience at school that day.

Five months earlier our thirteen-year-old son had lost his fight with brain cancer and gone Home to be with the Lord. We had watched Nick fight a brave and faith-filled fight for over six years. Olivia, who was nine at the time of his death, struggled deeply with the loss of her older brother. On top of the grief, Olivia was dealing with some complicated and hurtful friend issues at school as well as having difficulty concentrating in many of her classes.

At the same time, several members of our family were finding pennies in unusual places just when they needed a little reason to smile. These pennies were like gifts from Nick. I'll never forget taking down our Christmas tree and finding a single penny immediately underneath the tree stand. Nick had been alive when we put up our tree, so taking it down was painfully symbolic of how much our family had changed over one short holiday. When I saw the penny, I felt as if Nick was saying, "You're doing good, Mom, keep pressing on!"

On the day of Olivia's unbelievable experience, I had picked her up from school as usual. Olivia seemed to be in a somber mood all evening. I assumed it was due to the stress she had been under recently, so I did not question her quiet, reflective spirit. As I tucked her into bed later that evening, she began to cry as she shared some of the details about the tough situations she faced each day at school involving a few of her closest friends.

Suddenly Olivia blurted out through her tears, "And Nick was at school today!"

I thought I had not heard her correctly.

She said it again with even more passion. "I saw Nick today at school. He wasn't all the way there, Mom, but he was there!"

I sat in disbelief for a few minutes. Then, trying to be calm because she was very serious and passionate about this, I asked her to tell me exactly what had happened. She told me that as she was walking back to her classroom after lunch, she saw a penny lying on the floor. She picked it up and glanced down the hall to see if someone nearby had dropped it. When she looked back, she said that Nick was standing next to the water fountain.

"What was he doing?" I asked.

She replied very calmly, "Smiling."

I sat again for a few minutes, soaking in the experience Olivia had just described. Then I asked the only thing I could think to ask. "What was he wearing?"

She confidently said, "Jeans and a jacket."

I thought of how Nick had gone through difficult times at school when he was a young boy and how he had fretted about friendships from time to time. I then thought of how much he loved Olivia and how the Bible says we are surrounded by a cloud of witnesses as we walk the road of faith. Suddenly, I knew without a shadow of a doubt that God had allowed Nick to step through the thin veil between life and death so he could let his sister know that even at school, where she felt all alone at times, he was there, cheering her on with his precious, unforgettable smile.

When my husband arrived home from night class that evening, I shared the entire story with him. He took Olivia's hand and said, "Olivia, you are a lucky little girl. I wish I could see Nick too."

Since that day, we have found many more pennies in strange

locations and at special times when we need to be reminded that this world is not our home forever. I believe that God has given Nick the fun task of keeping us all alert, looking up, and longing for the day when our faith becomes sight!

I'm so thankful that Olivia, with her childlike faith, was allowed to see more than an adult mind could ever comprehend.

Thanks to a Father who longs to give good gifts to His children, Olivia was able to see her brother Nick just when she needed him.

~Tammy A. Nischan

My Gardening Angel

*In the garden I tend to drop my thoughts here and there. To the flowers I
whisper the secrets I keep and the hopes I breathe. I know they are there to
eavesdrop for the angels.*
~Dodinsky

There I stood at my local nursery's annual flower show between
displays of fragrant roses and delicate lilacs, taking in their
sweet scents. The flower show had always been one of the
highlights of my year. Mom and I would attend together, looking to
the various displays for inspiration for our own summertime gardens.
Afterward, we would stroll through the amply filled greenhouse,
making plans for the upcoming season and purchasing our supplies.

Now, though, everything was different. Mom had passed away
the year before and this year, only a few weeks earlier in fact, I had
unexpectedly lost my longtime job. I was barely over Mom's passing
and now I was at another difficult juncture. As I walked through the
aisles of blooming flowers and potted vegetable plants, I felt dazed.
My brief job search had proven fruitless. It hadn't taken long to discover that I would not be able to find the same type of position I had
enjoyed for the same amount of pay without finishing my college
degree. I had two years of schooling behind me and longed to earn
my degree. Yet, with all my other responsibilities that proved a difficult undertaking. In the past, I had made several failed attempts to

return to college. Now, I asked myself what I should do: take a lower paying position, or return to college for the next two years.

Mom would have helped me think this through, just like she always helped guide me toward the healthiest plants for my garden. My mother had a special way of picking up on signals that certain plants showed. The turn of a leaf, the thickness of a stem, or the color of a bud were all signs to Mom. Now I wished she could send me a sign about which option was best for me. Well, I decided, I'll have to figure this out on my own.

Still pondering my decision, I pulled a rosebud toward me and sniffed. Instead of the usual sweet scent I expected, there was an acrid but familiar odor. I walked a few feet and stuck my nose into a patch of usually fragrant wildflowers only to inhale the same very unpleasant odor. Suddenly, I placed the scent: my mother's hairspray. She always used a large amount to keep her fine hair in place. I often joked that I knew when she had been in a room, because the smell of that product lingered long after she had left.

I looked around. "Mom, are you here?" I asked. The scent became overwhelming and then just as suddenly subsided. Immediately, I felt as if I were directed to go straight home and fill out my college application.

As I drove home, I questioned the possibility of receiving a sign. Probably, I knew deep down that college was the right track for me, and my sudden leaning in that direction had nothing to do with Mom at all. Yet, when I sat down later that evening and filled out the college application, I received undeniable proof that Mom had guided me. The day of orientation was to be held on May 18th—the anniversary of Mom's passing. I went on to earn my degree with a 4.0 average and I have no doubt that Mom's encouragement was with me every step of the way.

~Monica A. Andermann

My Son's Sign

You are my sonshine.
~Author Unknown

I firmly believe our loved ones who have passed on give us signs they are around us. They are such simple things that happen we attribute it to coincidence. I think if we are aware and watch closely, those we love give us a nudge here and there.

Almost seven years ago I lost my precious son, Dominic, in a car accident. He was nineteen years old. It took me a long time to go to the cemetery after losing Dom because I didn't want to deal with the cold, hard reality of it all by seeing his name on a headstone. Now my husband Manny and I go almost every weekend, and no matter how many times I look at our son's headstone I still stand there in disbelief.

One day I went to visit Dominic alone. I wanted to sit on the bench near his grave and talk to him. It's a strange thing to sit and talk out loud to someone no longer physically there. After I finished my talk with Dom, I sat there and looked around. It's sad having a one-way conversation. So I said out loud: "Dom, I sure wish you'd give me more signs you're around me." Did I mention the bench I was sitting on was under a tree? Just as I finished speaking I felt bird droppings on my head! I started to laugh. "Okay, Dom, not exactly the sign I wanted," I said. When I looked up to find the bird, a beautiful butterfly flew overhead. I guess Dom wanted to make up for the bird droppings.

My husband and I experienced another butterfly incident together at the cemetery that I will never forget. Each time we go, Manny takes an empty water bottle and fills it from a water spigot close to Dom's grave. I get the fresh flowers ready to put in the vase and Manny fills it with water from the bottle. This time as I waited for Manny, I noticed a butterfly perched on the edge of Dom's vase. I got right up next to it and it didn't move. I pointed it out to Manny and he put his finger next to the vase. The butterfly calmly took its place on Manny's finger and slowly batted its wings. He stood next to me and we both watched intently. I put my finger next to Manny's and as if on cue, the butterfly slowly climbed onto my finger. For several incredible minutes we passed this butterfly back and forth. We couldn't believe this was happening.

When the butterfly finally flew off, it kept coming back to land on Manny or me as if it were playing a game. We decided to see if this special butterfly would follow us. We walked over to a bench nearby and sat down. It did not follow. Then we went back to Dom's grave to say goodbye, and there was the butterfly. Up and back it flew, coming back quickly to land on us over and over. As we walked to the car, I said to Manny, "You know that had to be Dominic." We couldn't get over it.

Several days later as I opened the family room shades, outside of the window was a butterfly. I moved right up to it and noticed it was the same size and color as the butterfly from the cemetery. It did not fly away, but stayed for a while. When it finally flew off, I had a peaceful feeling.

I get it, Dominic. You're watching.

~Cathy Pendola

23

Honk If You're Home

*No one ever really dies as long as they took the time to
leave us with fond memories.*
~Chris Sorensen

The phone call came at midnight. "Jackie was in a car accident," my father-in-law said. "It was a head-on collision with a drunk driver." He spoke the words we dreaded. "She died instantly."

I felt numb. Jackie was my husband's only sibling. We had just celebrated her fortieth birthday seven days before. She loved her new job, which involved a lot of driving through small towns in the rural part of the state. She enjoyed meeting new people and selling a product she believed in.

Now her life had been cut short by a man who had several previous DUIs and was driving without a license.

Jim and I packed a few things and drove five hours to Mom and Dad's house.

We arrived just before sunrise. For the next several hours, as we answered the phone and neighbors rang the doorbell with food and condolences, we asked ourselves over and over why Jackie's life had to end in such a shocking way. No answers came.

Three days later, the funeral service was everything it could be. A recent photograph of her, vibrant and smiling in her favorite red dress, sat atop the closed casket, along with a blanket of roses, her favorite flower. In the foyer a table held other photos, along with a letter she had received a week before her death, congratulating her for being "Top Salesperson of the Month." The chapel overflowed with relatives and friends.

Jim gave the eulogy. He spoke of Jackie's generosity, her love of animals and her generous spirit. He worked hard to make his words uplifting and inspiring, while giving a true portrait of his sister's unique personality and quirky sense of humor.

"Sometimes she could be a bit demanding," he recalled. "In college, when she came home on weekends, she always laid on the horn when she drove into the driveway. That was the signal to come out and help her unload her laundry."

Jim also spoke of her deep faith. In her view, death was a "graduation" to something better: eternal life.

"There's a temptation to think of her life being cut off at a young age," he said, "but my sister might disagree. She always thought that the time to leave was 'while the band's still playing.'"

When the service concluded, we walked out to our car for the drive to the cemetery. Our sedan, only a few weeks old, was parked directly behind the hearse. As we came down the steps in dignified silence, the car horn suddenly began honking.

Embarrassed, we hurried toward the car. Just as we got there, the honking stopped. Jim chuckled and said, "I think that's Jackie."

We got in the car and sat waiting for the others.

"Do you really think that was Jackie?" I asked.

Jim put his hands on the steering wheel and said, "I'm sure of it. This wheel is still quivering. I guess she approves of what I said about her."

Just then, the horn gave a couple of short little honks, as if to confirm what he said. Jim laughed.

"Now I know it's Jackie. She always did have to have the last word!"

We proceeded to the cemetery. Though we said nothing more about the honking, I realized the dull ache in my heart had lifted.

Later that evening, my mother-in-law revealed that she, too, was convinced that Jackie's spirit had "come through" and caused the honks.

"Every time she came for a visit, she let us know she had arrived by honking the horn. When I heard the horn honking at the funeral," she said, smiling through her tears, "I knew it was Jackie saying 'Don't worry, folks—I'm home.'"

~Maril Crabtree

24

On Scarlet Wing

The union of heaven and earth is the origin of the whole of nature.
~I Ching

The restored 1883 brick carriage house boasts high ceilings, a huge natural stone fireplace, and four large windows in the living room. Peering out the wavy glass of the side windows, I sighed in despair. In the country home I had just sold after my husband's death, the windows looked out on a bird feeder with a pair of cardinals flitting about. Here I looked out at a junk heap of city litter—bottles, cans, rags, papers, plastic bags, and foam cartons.

I appreciated the urban conveniences of this restored carriage house in the city, but I missed my birds. I planned to install bird feeders, and I sure hadn't expected the side yard to harbor a city dump! After a day of filling recycling bins and trash barrels with the many years of debris, I unearthed a little square of earth.

I hung large, squirrel-proof feeders and a suet cage from an old shade tree that crowned my new patch of yard. Sparrows and pigeons explored first, but soon black-capped chickadees, a pair of downy woodpeckers and a pair of mourning doves arrived. On occasion a blue jay wandered by to see what was happening and then one day I saw a spot of red in the bushes. And a pair of cardinals thrilled my heart.

The male cardinal became a persistent visitor to the black oil sunflower seeds. His boldness amazed me! When I checked my mailbox outside, he appeared. Wherever I walked, he was there. Was he following me? One day my son was helping at a neighbor's house. How I wished his father could see him now. A flash of scarlet caught my eye and there was the cardinal clinging precariously to a string of ivy that adorned the adjacent brick wall. My heart fluttered. Could it be my husband letting me know he was still nearby?

The following day my husband's sister visited, and as we crossed the patch of lawn between buildings I started to tell her about the cardinal's strange presence. I halted. "Shhh!" There, on the grass near our path, sat—the cardinal! Furthermore, he made no attempt to leave.

Different birds came and went; a pair of red polls one season, black grackles another, but for some reason the cardinals never returned. Then one day as I was going through a trying period, I wept as I begged my husband, "If you are still around, please show me a sign—a rose or a cardinal." Dawn slithered in with cold, wet rainy snow and I sighed, as my feeder was empty. Staring out with sleepy eyes I saw it. A cardinal just sitting on the wet ground outside my window. I rubbed my eyes in disbelief—looked again, it was still there—definitely a cardinal. The bird flew off but now I am content. My husband's spirit remains, still looking after me!

~Esther Griffin

Dancing with the Angels

Angels have no philosophy but love.
~Terri Guillemets

Every year for my birthday my sister Gale, the artist of the family, would send me a one of a kind masterpiece she'd painted. A cabin resting on a lake, an ocean wave crashing against the beach, three palm trees bending in a breeze... The painting, carefully wrapped in brown paper, faithfully arrived in September, the month both Gale and I were born.

As summer approached, I already wondered what subject my sister would choose to paint for this year's birthday gift. Would it be another ocean picture? Would she choose a mountain scene this time?

Then we received the devastating news. Gale had cancer. Unfortunately, it had already metastasized. There was nothing the doctors could do to prolong my sister's life.

By the time July arrived, with all its fanfare, waving flags, and fireworks, Sissy was already being visited by hospice. By August, she was planning her funeral, with loved ones surrounding her bedside. We released butterflies heavenward, shared childhood memories, and wiped away each other's tears.

Soon Sissy headed for heaven as well, and as I sat in front of her coffin while the pastor delivered her eulogy I wondered if my heart would ever be whole again. I'd been my sister's shadow growing up. She had been my hero.

Days earlier she'd asked a favor of me.

"Promise me you will be a happy camper now, Sissy. Life is short. Promise me right now! I am going to check in with you on my way to heaven you know. I'll be sending you a sign that I am dancing with the angels like I promised."

Too teary-eyed to see my sweet sister's face in front of me I blindly reached for her arms, nodding my promise.

Sis knew I'd been making major changes in my own life for months. After a thirty-four-year marriage that had seemingly died, as well as having raised four beautiful kids, I'd moved out of our home in Virginia and returned to my roots in a small town in Ohio. I rented a one-bedroom apartment, already feeling more at peace than I had in years. My niece, however, offered to deliver any keepsakes I might want from the Virginia homestead when she returned from a visit to my brother's.

It was then I remembered my sister's paintings, suddenly wanting them around me more than the air I breathed.

That weekend Amy and her husband and boys arrived with the cherished items.

"Here they are, Aunt Mary... there's something we have to ask you though. We couldn't help taking a peek at the paintings. We're curious people you know. When we pulled out the painting of the palm trees bending in the wind it was the back of the canvas that captured our interest most. Have you looked at it before?"

I couldn't help scratching my head in bafflement.

"I'm sure I have, but there wasn't anything on the back of the canvas that I can remember."

"Well there is now," Amy murmured solemnly as she flipped the canvas over.

I heard myself gasp as I spotted the pencil-sketched angel, her outstretched hands joyfully praising God as she danced amongst the clouds. Next to her, a banner in bold letters trailed across the sky. It read: 4 My Sissy.

My sister had kept her promise. She'd made sure I knew she was dancing with the angels at last.

I knew what I needed to do. Making my way to an open window of the apartment I slowly blew a kiss on its way.

"Here's to you Sissy…."

"What was that, Aunt Mary?" my nephew asked.

I gathered Nathan into my lap.

"That my dear, was a kiss from a very happy camper."

~Mary Z. Smith

The Unforgotten

The most beautiful thing we can experience is the mysterious.
~Albert Einstein

I've never been much of a believer in the supernatural, but my late husband, Ken Wilson, definitely was. Though he disdained stories about zombies and mummies, or werewolves and vampires, tales of psychic phenomena thoroughly mesmerized him.

For years he'd collected books on astral projection, parapsychology, telepathy, hauntings and possessions. He subscribed to *Fate Magazine*, and read it from cover to cover. And aside from Westerns, his favorite movie was *Ghost*, with *The Sixth Sense* running a close second. Ken didn't espouse any particular religion, but I've always felt that if there had been a Spiritualist church nearby, he would have been a regular.

A few years ago, Ken was diagnosed with pancreatic cancer and he took the news with astonishingly good humor.

"I'm ready to visit the other side," he said, and then proceeded to regale me with yarns about how he'd come back to haunt me and both of his beloved dogs.

"There's no good reason not to believe in an afterlife," he explained. "Harry Houdini did, Arthur Conan Doyle did, and I do, too. I'll find a way. I may not communicate directly, but I'm certain I'll be able to let you know I'm still around and thinking of you."

"Just don't do anything too spooky," I pleaded. "I don't want howls and squeaks coming off the walls of the bedroom. You know what a scaredy cat I am. I didn't sleep for a week after we watched *The Blair Witch Project*."

"I wouldn't want to frighten you, baby, but I do want you to remember me and that I'm not completely gone. My body might not be there, but my spirit will be."

The morning he died, I thought about what he'd promised. I'd heard that recent widows often feel the presence of their departed spouses in the corridors. But all morning our house felt completely empty as I wandered its rooms and hallways, wondering if I'd ever find the time and energy to clear Ken's clothes from the closets.

Then that afternoon, the dogs escaped. The young man who had come to mow our lawn absentmindedly had left a gate open. Ordinarily when the pair broke loose they'd be gone for hours, but this time the dogs dragged themselves home in less than thirty minutes. And though they usually head for the river and a swim, this time their fur remained completely dry. Nonetheless, they both plopped down on the tiled entryway, acting as exhausted as if they'd swum the English Channel. They stared at me with the most sheepish expression that a pair of canine faces can assume. I suddenly believed Ken had tracked them down, scolded them and sent them home. Moreover, the house no longer felt so empty. Ken's spirit had returned.

Not long after, a writer and editor acquaintance launched a new career as a psychic. He knew I'd been recently widowed, and offered me a telephone consultation. He told me that Ken's spirit indeed was present on my property, and that it frequently walked around the backyard with the dogs. I believe that's why Natty, who was particularly attached to Ken, lies out there for hours looking blissfully zoned out. He especially demands to go out at twilight and comes in only reluctantly when I'm ready for bed.

Ken had reminded me of Houdini's avowal to contact people from beyond. I don't think I've ever heard that the magician managed to succeed. But twice in the couple of years since Ken's death, I've found books overturned from the case that's adjacent to my writing desk in the family room.

The first incident, about a month after Ken's death, involved

Over Tumbled Graves by Jess Walter. Ken and I met this Northeast Washington writer when he came to our local Colville library to give a talk. Ken had accompanied me when my book group dined with Walter before his presentation. This was a book Ken had read and an author he had met. I shivered as I set the book back in place.

Then about a year later I spied a second book on the floor, apparently knocked loose from the same bookcase. This time it was Faye Kellerman's *The Forgotten*. Both of us had been fans of this novelist, and had frequently discussed her mysteries. I couldn't help but reflect on the title of this particular book as I tucked it back into place. Some time had elapsed since my husband's death. Could he be sending me a message from beyond that he worried I'd begun to forget him?

I'm not certain I'm ready yet to declare myself a believer in psychic phenomena, but this is the kind of spooky coincidence that Ken adored. I've always doubted there's any literal heaven populated by angels and filled with harps and fluffy clouds. But Ken was convinced that some aspect of the human personality or mind survives death and continues to exist on a spirit plane. As for me, I've always believed in the power of prayer. So that night I said a special prayer for my very special late husband.

I asked that he be guaranteed that he's not forgotten. Not now. Not ever. I prayed he'd be reassured that his portrait still hangs in our bedroom, and informed that I've also put up the framed maps of ancient Briton that he never got around to displaying.

I added that I'd weed around his Asian lilies the next afternoon and sprinkle them with deer repellent. I vowed that on his birthday I'd haul down his special ceramic cup and pour him a brandy Manhattan and place it by the lilies. I wanted him to know that I'd think of something special to commemorate him on what would have been our tenth anniversary.

Finally, I conveyed that I'd continue to write about him and our life together. Ken Wilson wouldn't be forgotten at all. He'd live on in my stories, just as his spirit continues to inhabit our home. He'd be eternally "The Unforgotten."

Every morning I still cast a hopeful glance at the floor in front of the bookcase. I would be neither surprised nor frightened if I received yet another message from heaven, wherever and whatever it may be.

~Terri Elders

Fly on the Wall

Angels are not merely forms of extraterrestrial intelligence.
They are forms of extra-cosmic intelligence.
~Mortimer J. Adler

My friend and co-author Harriet May Savitz passed away in 2008. We had been involved in many projects together and although we specialized in different children's genres, we worked well together. Harriet wrote more for the young adult market while I preferred writing picture books. She had lots of ideas for early stories, however, but said that she couldn't write for that young age. I would often get an excited call detailing a story idea, which I would then put into picture book format. We'd revise until we both were satisfied and then send the manuscript out. We had two picture books published together and were working on several more.

One day Harriet told me that she had sent away a manuscript that had four points of view in it but no protagonist. The editor suggested that she put it into a more traditional story form. She asked if I could help her create a storyline. I had read the manuscript and knew it would be great for a middle grade book. I agreed to work on it with her.

I introduced some main characters and a more connective plotline. She tweaked the story as it went along. But when we got to the middle of the book it seemed to stop. Harriet and I each had some ideas about how to fix it but somehow the enthusiasm for the project waned. We were not agreeing on its direction. We let the project drop. She decided to keep her original format.

A year after she died I joined her daughter for lunch at a restaurant near Harriet's house. We reminisced, laughing at the delightful quirks of our friend/mother. But this was not just a compassionate social call. I needed to know what to do with our joint work on many projects which still occupied space in my files as well as in my head and heart.

As we talked I shooed away a fly that seemed to discover our table. We came to an understanding about most of the work. Some of the projects Harriet had told me, well before she became ill, to take on my own. Some were so integral to us both that I would have to include her as co-author, regardless.

Then we came to the middle grade book. I brushed at the fly again. I made some suggestions about how to fix the story, and explained that I always liked it and would love to continue working it out. The fly was batting itself against my head as I spoke! I felt like an octopus with eight arms flapping away at that annoying fly.

I finally said that much as I would really like to bring the book to publication, I probably should leave it alone because I thought Harriet wanted it that way. Her daughter agreed. The fly suddenly left and her daughter laughed. Nothing I said had seemed funny. What had I missed?

"When Mom was in the hospital," she said, "she told me she knew that one day we would get together and talk about the work and she wished she could be a fly on the wall for the conversation."

For the first time I had no words. The fly was gone. The subject was closed. I imagined her grin. It matched mine. We always had been connected and it seemed that we still were.

~Ferida Wolff

Well Manicured

Taking joy in living is a woman's best cosmetic.
~Rosalind Russell

My twin sister and I have been using nail polish and make-up since we were seven years old, when our mom became an Avon Lady. Mom was the quintessential saleswoman, a charming conversationalist with impeccable style who loved the luster of cosmetics. I still remember the matte black Avon cosmetic sample case filled with fabulous colors and scents: nail polishes, perfumes, lipsticks, eye shadows, hand and face creams. These tiny samples were just enough to capture your attention.

Mom taught us her cosmetics tips beginning with the "less is more" philosophy, as she believed that make-up should look natural. Her number one rule was that nail polish should never be chipped, for soft, manicured hands create a wonderful impression. We'd smooth on hand creams and manicure each other's nails every week with colors that got bolder as we matured.

She allowed us to dye our hair when we were sixteen, because it was fun. Our mom was progressive like that. Instead of continual arguments with her teenage girls about beauty products, she showed us how to use them properly. She taught us that, in a pinch, a bit of lipstick could be dabbed on your cheeks as a substitute for rouge. Nail polish was her emergency repair product for ripped nylon stockings. Just dab the polish around the rip and the "stocking run" was stopped in its tracks.

When we got older we'd shop together for department store make-up bonus packages that were offered with a purchase. The alluring parcel would contain sample-sized products of rouge, lipstick, face cream and mascara in a dazzling carrying case. It was delightfully reminiscent of her Avon days. We loved to sit and trade our make-up jewels like kids with Halloween candy.

She was an adoring grandmother and great-grandmother. Even when she and our dad moved to Florida she'd buy and ship stylish clothing to her great-granddaughters (with instructions for me to purchase matching nail polish). When she became too ill to shop, my sister and I would buy the gifts, take digital pictures of the bounty and mail them to Mom for review and discussion. That was our version of virtual shopping.

Because our folks worried so much about air travel during the wicked winter weather, my sister and I surprised them with an unannounced visit one weekend in March. We both felt the need for an extra visit as our mom's health was deteriorating rapidly. It was a comforting and well-timed trip, and before we left for home I gave our mother a manicure. I filed and smoothed her nails, massaged lotion into her hands and polished her nails a regal violet.

Two weeks later Mom was in hospice and we were on the way to see her. Regrettably, we were trapped at the airport in the aftermath of a severe snowstorm that delayed our flight for hours. We did, however, speak with our mother just before we boarded and in a whisper she wished us "travels with milk and honey." This was a traditional family saying to ensure us a sweet and safe trip.

Unfortunately she lapsed into a coma an hour before we landed. Yet I firmly believe that she waited for us to arrive at the hospice and hold her smooth, manicured hands for an hour before she took her last breath. We opened the patio doors to let her spirit soar and wished her travels with milk and honey.

Months later my sister and I were walking through our local mall when we came upon a chic store dedicated exclusively to cosmetics, skin care, fragrance and accessories. We both looked at each other and said in unison (as is usual for us as twins) "Mom would love this place!" We walked in and were delighted with the colors, scents and energy that seemed to give the store a pulse.

Our eyes centered on an enormous carousel of nail polishes, which contained hundreds of bottles in every color one could imagine. We were both drawn to and reached for one particular glitzy purple among a dozen variations in that shade. Looking at the bottom of the bottle for the name of the color we were stunned to see it — "Call Your Mother."

We hugged each other and knew it was her spirit sending us a sign. We smiled knowingly. "Of course," we said, "a cosmetics shop."

~Lee Rothberg

A Promise in the Rainbow

May God give you… For every storm a rainbow, for every tear a smile,
for every care a promise and a blessing in each trial.
~Irish Blessing

"Please God, don't let me cry. Please God, don't let me cry." I prayed urgently before my wedding because I knew it would be hard not to have my father walk me down the aisle. His wedding ring was attached to the ribbons flowing from my bouquet. Alongside the ring was a tiny golden angel pin that I wore every day while he was fighting cancer.

I had considered an outdoor wedding, but I knew that would be impossible. I was certain it would rain on my wedding day. How else would a rainbow appear in the sky?

Rainbows had come to mean something very different to our family ever since the funeral. At the graveside services, there had been a huge clap of thunder, but the rain didn't pour. When we returned home, my brother said, "Come look outside!" There was a gigantic double rainbow over the house. We knew it was Daddy's smile, covering our house in a veil of security.

On my parents' anniversary, the double rainbow returned in the same place. We rushed outside to take a picture of it, with happy tears falling. It was like a little note from Daddy letting us know that he was okay and smiling even brighter.

The following August, I could hardly wait to show my mother my Sunday School lesson page for the day, Daddy's birthday. The illustration was a photo of a rainbow and above it August 27th.

As I clutched my wedding bouquet, I was certain there would be a rainbow in the sky that day. He wouldn't miss my wedding. As I took my grandpa's arm, I figured the flood of tears would shock even Noah. My prayers seemed to be working though. I just smiled as I walked and was grateful to have my grandpa next to me.

When the preacher asked, "Who gives this woman?" I thought that would do me in, but it didn't. I joined my soon-to-be husband at the front and then realized my prayer should have been much more specific—a prayer to be in control of my emotions completely. I felt a little giggle trying to escape. Then, the more I tried, the less it worked until I couldn't stop laughing at all! My shoulders shook like I was having convulsions. Then, my sister started laughing. Then, it caught my soon-to-be husband and his brother. We were all falling completely apart!

We planned to leave the church in a 1957 Bel Air convertible. Balloons were attached to the back, and we set off down the road with gray skies and the top down. Light sprinkles hit my face as I searched the sky for a rainbow but saw nothing.

When we returned from our honeymoon, my mother handed me the front page of the paper for the day after our wedding. The caption underneath the giant rainbow said, "A rainbow appears over downtown Lubbock after a thunderstorm Saturday evening." It looks like Daddy not only showed up for the wedding but managed to be in the pictures as well.

~Heather King McGee

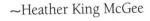

Chapter 4

Messages from Heaven

Dreams and Premonitions

The Message

We cannot banish dangers, but we can banish fears.
We must not demean life by standing in awe of death.
~David Sarnoff

woke up with an uneasy feeling. Something was niggling at me—a thought swirling in my mind that I couldn't quite grasp. I looked at the clock on my night table, remembering that I was due at the office for an early meeting. I jumped up and went into the shower. My throat began to constrict and my stomach cramped and churned. A sure sign of an impending anxiety attack. Why? What was bothering me? I didn't know, but I was definitely experiencing discomfort.

Snatches of a dream surfaced as I headed towards the subway station. Parts of the dream came to me as I sat on the train. In the dream I was walking on a street in Brooklyn and I saw two of my mom's dearest friends heading towards me. We greeted one another, and her friend Tillie said, "We're looking for your mom, but she isn't home."

"Oh, she's probably at the grocery store. Why not wait in the lobby? I'm sure she'll be home any minute. It's getting dark."

"Okay," Tillie and Ann answered in unison.

As I left them, I thought how strange it was to see them. I couldn't recall for the moment whether they were still living or had passed away.

I woke up.

Instinctively, I knew this dream was symbolic. A sense of fore-boding engulfed me. I felt chilled and my hands were cold. I was having trouble breathing. My windpipe was closing. I concentrated on calming myself, visualizing my throat relaxing and attempting to take deep cleansing breaths, as in yoga.

My brain kept telling me this was important. That it was one of those dreams I needed to pay attention to and understand. I felt anxious and pressured, my body's way of signaling this was significant.

I exited the train and slowly climbed the stairs to the street, conscious of my ragged breathing. At the top of the staircase, I was seriously gasping for air. My shoulders felt heavy, as if I was carrying a heavy backpack.

I hailed a taxi to go the three blocks to my office. Think! Think! Think! What was the message? It was urgent I understood the meaning.

No sooner had I sat down at my desk, my assistant said, "Wendy's on the phone." Wendy was my mom's aide and companion. She was with my mom from early morning to after dinner.

"Wendy, hello..."

"Mrs. L., something's terribly wrong with your mom. She's sitting up in bed, wild-eyed and scrunched up by the headboard, but she can't see me or hear me. She's talking, like foreign. I can't understand anything she's saying. I don't know what to do. It's scary seeing her like this. What should I do?"

Oh my God. I was an idiot. How much more crystal clear could the message have been? Tillie and Ann were letting me know they'd come to escort Mom to the other side.

"Wendy, I want you to hang up and call 911, immediately. I think she's having a stroke. She's speaking Hungarian. Make sure you have them take her to Lutheran Medical Center. If they give you any prob-lems, call my sister and let her speak to them. I'll call Dorothy and let her know what's going on. I'll meet you at the hospital. Call them now!"

I dialed my sister, Dorothy, who was a nurse at Lutheran, and only fifteen minutes away from Mom's apartment. After I hung up with her, I called my husband Alan. His office was on the same floor as mine. I told Francine, my assistant, to cancel everything on my schedule.

By the time we reached the hospital, Dorothy was standing by the bed as Mom lay there with her eyes closed. She remained unresponsive to our voices or touch.

"The doctor believes she's had a massive stroke. If she survives, she'll be in a vegetative state," Dorothy whispered to us.

I continued to hold her hand, stroking her forehead as I talked quietly to her, trying to will her to respond.

We had her moved to a private room and we took turns being with her for the first week. When we weren't with her, Wendy and her mom stayed with her. We wanted someone who loved her to be there as much as possible.

Both Dorothy and I agreed that it would be far better for her to leave us than survive in a vegetative state. Mom was fiercely independent and never would have wanted to live in a suspended state.

On Friday, the end of the second week, I woke up crying. I called my sister and told her we were going straight to the hospital. "If you have anything to say to Mom, do it now. She's leaving us at sunset tonight."

"Did you have another dream? Or are you feeling something?" Dorothy asked.

Over the years my sister had become accustomed to hearing about my dreams and premonitions.

"Both Dad and Aunt Belle died on a Friday night at the start of the Sabbath. Mom's going to join them tonight. Call your girls and tell them to be there by the afternoon. I didn't have another dream. It was more an awareness and sensing. I was crying when I woke up."

"Okay, I'm not going to argue with you, you're always right when you get like this. See you later."

As the sun began to set, we gathered around her bed, each saying our final farewells. We told her she could let go. "Everybody's there waiting, Dad, Belle, your mom and poppa, your brothers and friends. Tillie and Ann are waiting to greet you and guide you across."

I bent down, whispering in her ear, "Mom, we love you and if you are ready to go, we are ready. It's okay. Go with our blessings and love." I kissed her cheek as I squeezed her hand.

We formed a circle around her. We held hands with each other. We held her hands. Wendy led us in reciting the twenty-third Psalm.

We watched her, heard her breathing grow slower and shallower. We hardly moved. Calmness permeated.

As the sun set and the Sabbath began, she quietly and peacefully left us.

~Margo Berk-Levine

31

A Message from My Mother

We cannot destroy kindred: our chains stretch a little sometimes,
but they never break.
~Marquise de Sévigné

I don't know much about my mother, only that she died at the age of nineteen, a few weeks after I was born. Her mother rarely talked about her to me because it hurt too much. She never got over losing her only child. But I do know one thing for certain about my mother. She loved my father deeply.

When I was a child, my father was the stranger who occasionally visited me at my grandparents' home where I lived. Of course, I knew he was my father, but he seemed so awkward and shy in my presence that he made me feel uncomfortable.

It was during the spring of 1944 when I last saw my father. He brought me a shiny, new red bike, and he took me for a ride on it. I was seven years old and loved the bike. But when my father asked me for a hug after our ride, I offered him a handshake instead.

"I know I'm almost a stranger to you, but you are my only child and I love you," my father told me that day. "I loved your mama, too, more than I can ever say. When the war ends, you and I will get to know each other better, I promise you that."

Of course, so much happened in the next three years, among them the Soviet occupation of Hungary. When we finally managed to escape our war-torn country in 1947, we landed in a refugee camp in neighboring Austria. Finally, in 1951, our hopes for a better life became a reality when we were allowed to emigrate to the United States of America.

After we boarded the old Navy ship, the USS General M.B. Stewart, in September of 1951, on our way to America, we watched from the deck as the ship pulled out of the harbor in Bremenhaven, Germany.

"We will never see our old homeland again," my grandfather lamented.

"But we're on our way to America, the land of new opportunity!" my grandma said.

It was at that moment that I thought of my father and the promise he made the last time I had seen him. Perhaps he hadn't even survived the war, and if he had, we had no idea where he was.

In the United States, life was busy and good. My grandparents both had new jobs and I went to school. We never talked about my father, and I can't recall ever thinking about him. It was as if he never existed.

In June of 1954, after I had not seen my father for ten years, something intervened on his behalf. I had gone to bed, as usual, my mind filled with plans for the coming weekend. I was going to a dance and a special boy would also be at that dance. Sweet promise was in the air.

Suddenly, a vision appeared at the foot of my bed. It was a beautiful young woman with long, flowing blond hair, wearing a sad expression on her strangely familiar, lovely face. I sat up and gazed at her, not at all frightened. For though I had been an infant when she died and didn't even have a picture of her, I knew who she was. She was my mother.

She spoke to me in a voice just above a whisper, "You must get in touch with your father. He is very worried about you because he doesn't know what happened to you, or where you are. He needs to know that you are alive and well so he can go on with his life, so he can have peace of mind. You must do this very soon." Then, she was gone, vanished into the thin air she had come from.

I sat there on the bed and began to cry. I cried for never having known her, and I cried for my father and all the sadness and worry I had caused him. My grandmother must have heard me because she came into my bedroom to ask what was wrong. I told her about the vision. Or had it been a dream? I wasn't quite sure. Grandma began to cry, too, as I described the young woman who had come to me with a message.

The following morning, my grandfather wrote a letter to relatives who still lived in the old country, inquiring about my father's whereabouts. Three weeks later, I received a jubilant letter from him.

"Though we're separated by a great ocean now, I'm happy and relieved to know that you are alive and well, my dear daughter. Never forget that I will always love you. And I will always love your dear mother, too," my father wrote in that first letter. And when I answered his letter, I told him about the vision from my mother, and how she still loved him, too, even beyond the grave.

"I cried when I read your letter, my dear daughter. And oh how I wanted to visit the cemetery where your mother was laid to rest," my father wrote. "Sadly, the cemetery is long gone, having been plowed under by the communist regime. But I know that my darling Irenke knows that I will always love her and one day she and I will be reunited in Heaven."

My father and I kept in touch over the years and even spoke by telephone many times, but unfortunately we never had the chance to see each other again in person. And to this day, I regret not having given my father a hug the last time I saw him. When he finally went to his heavenly reward in 1987, my only consolation was that he and my mother were together again at last. For I saw them in a dream, walking together while holding hands, young and beautiful and smiling at each other, and that dream brought peace to my heart.

And one day, I will join them, and we'll all be together at last.

~Renie Burghardt

32

Heart Attack

Dreams are today's answers to tomorrow's questions.
~Edgar Cayce

"Get up, Jeanne. Get dressed!"

I try to open my eyes, but my lids are stuck closed, as if glued.

"What is it, Pop? What's wrong?"

"Hurry, get dressed. We have to leave now." I rise from the daybed, quickly pull my pants over my pajamas and throw a sweatshirt over my eighteen-year-old frame. My eyes try to adjust to the darkness as I maneuver down the thin hallway in my grandparent's one-bedroom apartment in Flushing, Queens.

"Don't turn on the light," my grandfather says. "Take Grandma's hand and follow me."

"Ed, where are we going? What's wrong?" Grandma asks.

"Just follow me. Don't say a word," he whispers.

I run my hand along the bumpy stucco walls as we pass by the kitchen, into the living room and out the front door. I'm not sure of the time. We quickly leave the apartment and descend the short staircase to the street and then turn right. We pass the well-manicured shrubs that Pop has tended to as property manager since he and Grandma moved there nearly thirty years ago. Walking a little further, we make another right up the narrow path that leads us toward the basement door. I can smell the fresh mint that comes up every year for my grandmother's tea. Clutching the cool, damp, wrought-iron railing, we descend the narrow staircase.

Pop gently grabs Grandma's elbow, guiding her to the basement door. He picks one key from a ring of many, and inserts it. As he opens the outside door to the basement, a hard, stale smell smacks me in the face, waking me to the reality that something is desperately wrong.

As a child, I often played in this basement. Grandma would hang her fresh laundry on what seemed like rows and rows of laundry line. I would go downstairs and play hide-and-seek with her, running in-between Pop's shirts and Grandma's nightgowns, interspersed doilies occasionally falling to the ground.

Pop's workshop is adjacent to the laundry room. It is where he stores his tools and an occasional bottle of schnapps. When I dared to venture off course from the laundry path, I would go to Pop's room. Occasionally I would find the door slightly ajar and I would squeeze my way into his world. Pop spent a lot of time down there, fixing things that needed to be fixed and, I suspect, fixing things that did not need to be fixed. It was his private space where he found refuge.

Once inside the basement, the three of us travel in and out of Grandma's hanging laundry. Each touch of clothing brings a clean, light smell and then we are back to the heavy, stale darkness. We approach Pop's workroom, which is locked. He takes out his ring of keys, and once again, immediately picks the right one.

The door creaks as he slowly opens it. He turns on a small flash-light, the tiny light illuminating our way. I look at Pop and see a look of terror on his face. I have never known my grandfather to be afraid. Indifferent, mad, loving, intoxicated, proud, but never afraid.

He guides us in and starts up a dark stairway. A crackling sound follows behind us. I look at Grandma. She cannot keep up the pace.

Pop looks up and spots a narrow space hidden under the stair-case. "Help Grandma in there," he says to me.

Somehow, I am able to pick her up and slide her into the small space. "Grams, stay here and don't make a sound. You must be quiet."

She looks so tiny, so frightened. I hate to leave her, but I trust this to be the best course.

"We'll be back for you. You'll be safe here," I promise.

Pop stretches up to touch her hand. "Stay here, Anna. Jeanne will be back for you soon. She will take care of you." We leave my grandmother there, hidden from something or someone that I don't know.

Pop and I continue on. Out of nowhere, a huge shadow appears behind us. Pop pushes me aside and tells me to run. "Run, Jeanne. Don't look back. Take care of Grandma. Run." Despite his warning, I can't help but look behind me, only to see a massive silhouette lift my grandfather and then stab him through the heart.

I spring up in bed, shaking uncontrollable, crying, and realize I have woken from a nightmare.

I go back to sleep, managing to get in an hour or so before going to work and then an afternoon lecture at the local college I am attending as a freshman. By the time I get to class, last night's dream has left my immediate thoughts and my mind is focused on Psychology 101. I find my seat among 200-plus students and settle in to hear about abnormal behavior. Midway through the lecture, I stand up abruptly. My friend sitting next to me grabs my arm and asks what's wrong. She tugs at me to sit down.

"My grandfather just died," I say almost matter-of-factly and storm out, leaving abnormal behavior behind.

Tears flow as I drive home. I park the car, knowing in my heart that Pop is gone.

Later that night I learn that Pop had died from a heart attack at the same moment I stood up during class. That day, he had worked outside raking leaves and was feeling tired, Grandma said. He had given her a big kiss and laid down on the daybed, arms crossed, with a content look on his face as if he knew. Pop was ready.

After his death, I visited my grandmother as often as I could. She was exhibiting signs of dementia, although back then, it was simply labeled old age. I would visit weekly and we would do her shopping, watch her soaps and play *Scrabble*. I worried about her living alone, so I called daily.

That spring, Grandma had a slight heart attack. I went to visit her in the hospital. It was a dreary place. She was in a large dim room with rows of patients separated mostly by visitors sitting in short, narrow aisles. I saw her lying in her bed at the far end. Trying to maintain a brave front, I called to her, "Grandma, I'm here." As I approached her bed, I could see she looked anxious.

"What's the matter?" I asked, as she pulled me down next to her on the hospital bed.

"Thank goodness you're okay," she said desperately.

"Grandma, what's the matter? What are you taking about?"

"I thought you were dead. I thought he got you," she whispered loudly.

Figuring that she was hallucinating because of the heart attack, I asked again, "Who got me?"

"That man."

"What man?"

"The man that killed Pop in the basement."

I froze.

"You saved me, Jeanne. You hid me under the staircase. I was so afraid but Pop said you would come back and you did. He said you would come back and take care of me and you have."

I had thought that my dream wasn't real. I had never told my grandmother about it, knowing it would just confuse and upset her, as it had me. It wasn't until I heard her recite the same events, months after my grandfather's death, that I realized that just maybe it had been more than a dream. Just maybe it was Pop's final message asking me to watch over my grandmother and keep her safe.

~Jeanne Blandford

Papaw's Visit

There is a wisdom of the head, and... a wisdom of the heart.
~Charles Dickens

eep under the covers, sound asleep, I felt someone shaking my shoulder and heard my name whispered: "Linda." I sat up, rubbed my eyes. Mom sat on the side of the bed. "Honey, get up. We are leaving for Mississippi to visit your grandmother and father." Outside the window was pitch black. Still in my nightgown, I followed Mom to the car where my stepdad waited.

This midnight adventure thrilled me. It never occurred to my eleven-year-old mind to wonder why we were leaving in the middle of the night on a school day. I fell asleep soon and began dreaming. I saw myself walking toward a coffin. I peered into it to find my father lying inside. This shocking vision woke me, but I didn't say anything. Instead, I stared out the back window and watched the stars slide by. It wasn't long until the hum of the motor and movement of the car lulled me back to sleep.

At daybreak we arrived at my grandmother's home. It was then I learned that my father was very ill and the family had been called in. A few days later he died.

He was only thirty-six years old.

A week after we returned, I was awakened a second time in the middle of the night. I felt the mattress move as if someone were sitting at the foot of the bed. I opened my eyes and sat up to see Papaw. The odd thing about this was that Papaw had died when I was a baby.

The only way I recognized him was from the pictures I had seen in my grandmother's home.

"Papaw?"

He smiled and asked, "Are you still my little red rooster?"

I had no idea what he meant by that but I said, "Yes."

Then he said, "I want you to know that your daddy is fine."

His message went over my head. What I really wanted was for him to hug me and I leaned toward him. He held his hand out and said, "No, I can't hug you. I have to go. I love you." And then he disappeared.

In the darkness I whispered, "I love you too." I have to admit, my feelings were hurt. Why couldn't he hug me? I got out of bed, turned on the light and looked for some kind of evidence that he'd been there—a wrinkle in the bedspread? A warm spot where he sat? Nothing.

I went to Mom's room and woke her. She slipped from bed and followed me to my room. Feeling my forehead she said, "Are you feeling all right? You are as white as a sheet."

"Did Papaw call me his little red rooster?"

She frowned and said, "Yes, I'd forgotten that. How did you know?" Then I explained what had happened. We both were filled with wonder. However, as time passed, I rarely thought back to that night.

Until the day I turned thirty-six.

On that birthday, it hit me how young my father had been. Sorrow filled me for my poor daddy, struck down in the prime of his life. I realized how little I knew about him. He and my mom divorced when I was four years old and I only got to spend a couple of weeks each summer with him and my grandmother. My clearest memories of times spent with him were between the ages of six and eleven. Five short summers.

For the first time since his death, I truly grieved. I spent the day crying for both of us and all the things we'd missed together—my wedding, knowing each other as adults, and of course the birth of his grandchildren. Oh, how he would have loved them.

But knowing what he missed wasn't my biggest heartache. When I became an adult, I began to wonder about something that didn't concern me as a child. Did he ever make peace with his God? This, I felt, was something I'd never know.

Or would I?

The recollection of Papaw's visit suddenly came to me. "I want you to know that your daddy is fine." The memory of his words enveloped me with peace.

Since then I've often wondered why Papaw came to me as a child instead of my crisis moment when I turned thirty-six. Maybe he knew a child wouldn't question such a visit. Perhaps he was there that day reminding me of his message.

I don't know.

What I do know—and what really counts—is that my daddy is fine.

~Linda Apple

34

Listen to Your Mother

What greater thing is there for human souls than to feel that they are joined for life—to be with each other in silent unspeakable memories.

~George Eliot

never met my second husband's younger sister, Mae. She had broken with her older siblings more than a quarter of a century before, leaving only bitterness behind. Leonard kept in touch with his other sister Paula and his brother Alex, but none of them spoke to Mae. I learned to accept the situation.

Six years into our marriage, Leonard became terminally ill with cancer. One night he woke from a dream that troubled him. "I was heading down a long hallway," he told me. "And then I saw my mother at the other end. I was so happy to see her alive again, I started to rush toward her, but she gave me an angry look and yelled at me to go back, go back. She was making 'keep away from me' motions with her arms. She didn't want me." He began sobbing at her rejection.

I wrapped my arms around him and tried to put a more hopeful spin on his disturbing dream. "She was telling you to go back because it was not your time to leave us," I said. This seemed to comfort him. He was able to relax and fall back to sleep. We both knew he was near death, yet we wondered about this strange dream. What did it really mean?

A few weeks later, I got a call from his sister Paula.

"I had a phone call from my sister Mae this morning. Not a word from her for twenty-five years and today she woke me up to tell me about a dream," Paula said. "Mae said Mama had come to her and told her to 'Call your sister.' She said Mama was so real she could have reached out and touched her, even though she knew Mama was dead. It shook Mae up, so she felt she had to obey and call me."

A chill ran down my spine. "How did you respond?" I asked.

"I told her about Leonard," Paula said. "Mae was shocked to hear he was dying. She didn't know he had been widowed and remarried and moved to another state. She asked for your address because she wanted to write him a letter and make amends."

It was too late. Leonard was in a near-comatose state, beyond the ability to absorb what Paula had told me and feel reconciled with his sister Mae. Her letter arrived a few hours after he died.

Contemplating Mae's dream, I began to understand the meaning of Leonard's earlier one. They were connected. Both were their mother's attempt from beyond to keep Leonard alive long enough for his alienated sister to correct her mistake, understand the importance of family and reunite with her siblings.

Mae's letter to Leonard did not arrive in time, but Mama's mission was not a total failure. Losing the chance to mend relations with one brother taught Mae that time is precious when it comes to family. As a result, Mae reconciled with her remaining siblings and they remained close for the rest of her life.

~Marcia Rudoff

35

The Dream

There is a fine line between dreams and reality, it's up to you to draw it.
~B. Quilliam

As we sat together, my head on his shoulder and his arm around me, I tried not to think about how short our time together would be and how long it would be until I would see him again. He had the most beautiful smile and anyone looking into his blue eyes could see the love and compassion there. I reached up and touched his face, his neck and then slowly slid my hand away.

I opened my eyes just a bit and could see that a new day had arrived. Reluctantly, I let my dream drift away and rolled from my bed. Tears ran down my cheeks as I faced the prospect of another day without my son. Each night I went to bed eager to enter the dream state, the spirit realm where all was right. Each morning I was thrown from paradise and back into the material world. It was routine for me to greet the morning with tears.

The coffeemaker gurgled and hissed, mirroring my mood. I poured a cup and headed for my computer. Time to read the news and lose myself in the virtual world. I propped my chin on my left palm as I scanned the screen.

Suddenly, a soft fragrance caught my attention and immediately it hit me. It was Jay's aftershave. I sniffed my palm like a bloodhound. Glenn, my husband, doesn't wear aftershave so it couldn't have been his. I was certain it was Jay's. How did it get on my hand? Was it my imagination? About that time I heard my husband shuffling into the kitchen.

"Glenn, come here a minute," I called.

He came into the room all sleepy-eyed, hair standing on end.

"Smell this." I lifted my palm toward his nose.

He looked at me skeptically as if he thought I was trying to trick him before his senses were fully awake.

"Smell it! Just tell me what you smell."

He cautiously sniffed my hand.

"It smells like aftershave," he offered.

"It's Jay's aftershave and I have no idea how it got on my hand."

"It's aftershave all right but I'm not sure I remember what Jay's aftershave smelled like." He shuffled back to the kitchen in search of his breakfast. He was used to my insanity and my signs.

"Well, I remember Jay's aftershave and that is what I smell." I stared blankly at the computer screen.

And then I remembered my dream of being with Jay. I remembered touching his face and running my hand down his neck. I looked at my left hand and realized that I had touched my son that morning—that the spirit world I visited each night is as real as the cursed reality I live in each day. A bolt of exhilaration ran through me—I had truly been with my son!

~Marilyn Ellis Futrell

36

Strawberry Fields

Strawberries are the angels of the earth,
innocent and sweet with green leafy wings reaching heavenward.
~Terri Guillemets

"Look at this one!" I said to myself, holding up and admiring a plump, unusually shaped strawberry. A breeze drifted through the open kitchen window as I stood alone at the counter, knife in one hand, strawberry in the other. There was no one in the kitchen to share my discovery, but I closed my eyes and saw my grandmother's smile. I thought about the times we spent walking barefoot through fields of strawberries searching for the biggest or oddest-shaped berries.

Everyone called her Bone. My dad gave her the nickname after she was diagnosed with Crohn's disease, which left her very thin. "You're nothing but an old bone," he told her affectionately. Rather than be insulted, Grandma Bone took the name proudly, going so far as to embroider a small dog bone on the quilts and pillows she made.

Every year over Memorial Day weekend we'd take Grandma's quilts and pillows to a craft festival three hours away. As we drove along the country roads, she kept her eyes peeled for wild honeysuckle bushes. When she saw one that tickled her fancy, she'd make my father pull over and dig it up to take it home.

The mountains of West Virginia were my grandmother's home. A coal miner's daughter, she was born and raised in the small mining town of Farmington. She would always say, "The ocean is nice, but nothing beats the beauty of the mountains." She was proud of her heritage—even celebrated being a "hillbilly" by almost always going barefoot, even in the town grocery store!

She lost her battle with Crohn's disease when I was twenty-five. Since she had been sick my entire life, I had always feared losing her. And when the time came it was more devastating than I could have imagined. She was the first person I loved who died. I thought I'd never stop crying.

Memories of her consumed me. Springs spent picking strawberries. Summers spent sitting on the porch steps munching on fat dill pickles. Fall evenings spent stirring a pot of her famous spaghetti sauce. Winters spent cuddled together in a rocking chair with a mug of hot tea. I would have given anything for one more season with her!

I remembered all the times she'd been there to soothe me, to wipe away my tears. When I fell and scraped my knee, she was there to sit me on the countertop, clean the scrape and spray it with Bactine. Then she'd give me a round pink chalky candy which she called medicine and which always eased my pain. When my gerbil died, my first experience with death, she was there to hold me and help me to look forward to getting another pet. I needed her to hold me again, to comfort me through this huge loss, but she was gone and I was alone.

After the funeral, I didn't know how I was going to move on. Then one night, a few days later, I had a dream that I was in Grandma Bone's kitchen. Barefoot, wearing a bright yellow T-shirt with ruffled cap sleeves, she was leaning against the countertop, the same countertop where she'd doctored so many of my boo-boos and owies. Her hair was no longer wiry and gray, but dark brown and soft around her face. She was smiling and the picture of perfect health—no tired lines or signs of illness.

"I didn't want to leave you," she said, the smile momentarily slipping from her smooth face. "But there's so many of you. God needs me to help look after you all." Her smile returned and I was struck by how young and healthy she looked!

I was amazed. Even death couldn't keep Grandma Bone from comforting me! She'd come to say goodbye, but also to assure me that she would never really be gone — that she'd always be with me. I woke up from that dream hopeful for the first time since the funeral that my heart could heal.

Seven months later, I was living in a new city with my fiancé's parents while he worked out of town. It was an awkward time for me. I was out of college, but not yet on my own, in a strange place without the solace of family or friends. I felt a little lost and sad. And then, once again, Grandma Bone came to me in a dream.

This time we were in the center of a big empty room. It was dark except for a pool of light illuminating my grandma in a rocking chair and me at her feet. She was wearing her favorite article of clothing — a high-necked flannel nightgown. I laid my head in her lap; the worn and well-washed cotton caressed my cheek. As she rocked, Grandma Bone stroked my hair. This time she didn't say a word, but she didn't need to. All I needed was to feel her presence around me, making everything better.

Over the years our family has grown. Grandma Bone now has ten great-grandchildren to watch over in addition to her four children and twelve grandchildren. Perhaps she's been too busy to visit with me in my dreams, but that's okay because I feel her beside me when I find that especially odd-shaped strawberry or smell the fragrant honeysuckle bush I planted in her memory in my backyard.

I may have been standing alone in the kitchen, but I knew my grandmother was with me. Her love for me survives even death. On sunny spring days when I'm walking barefoot through a field of strawberries, Grandma Bone will be walking beside me, always. It's a promise she made to me from heaven.

~Brianna N. Renshaw

Mark of Friendship

Friendship isn't a big thing—it's a million little things.
~Author Unknown

My mother moved us to Vero Beach in the early 1970s. My grandparents were already living there and she wanted to move her three children out of New York City. We lived in an apartment, so moving into a house with a yard was an exciting experience for us. We learned quickly that to make friends all we had to do was get on our bikes. On the next street over, my younger brother John found his best friend, Mark.

I moved away from home when I was eighteen. I can't remember the last time I saw Mark. I'm quite sure in the ensuing thirty years I didn't give Mark a moment's thought. Then I had a dream.

I was driving into my mother's driveway on a visit home from Atlanta and Mark was standing in the front yard. I got out of my car and said, "Hello, stranger, I haven't seen you in a while." Mark asked if it was okay to give me a hug. "Of course," I replied, feeling his breastbone and the softness of his shirt as I hugged him. He had a big smile. When I asked him how he was doing, he said, "I'm doing just fine. Everything is just fine now." I asked about his daughter. "She's going to be fine," he replied. "She's going to be just fine." I told him John would be home shortly and he'd be glad to see Mark.

During this exchange I felt that he was holding back on some information. I also sensed that my brother needed to hurry or he wouldn't get to see Mark. My mother also had come out the front door as I emerged from the car, but there was no greeting or exchange.

I had the dream three times that night. Each time I would ask Mark how he was doing, because I was never satisfied with his answer. He kept saying, with a big smile on his face, "I'm doing fine now, just fine. Everything's going to be fine." I had the sense that he'd just come through some tough times, but I didn't know what those tough times were.

The dream was so real that when I woke up I wasn't even sure where I was. But I woke up with a smile on my face. I wanted to call my brother right away and tell him that I felt the dream was a sign that whatever Mark had been through recently had finally passed and everything was going to be okay. I felt such a sense of peace that it lit up my morning. On the way to work I abruptly came out of my rose-colored fog.

Something was wrong with this picture. I dreamt about a man whom I had not seen since he was a teenager, and I had no idea if he was married or had kids or where he lived. I didn't even know if John had stayed in contact with Mark over the years. I started to get this nagging feeling that I needed to tell John to call Mark and check on him. But that put me in a quandary. My brother was not going to take me seriously if I told him that because I'd had a dream about Mark, he should call him and make sure he was okay. And, if John didn't take my premonition seriously and something happened to Mark where would that leave John?

There was one thing I knew for sure. Mark had been John's best friend and John loved him like a brother. Regardless of whether they'd kept in touch over the years, I knew if anything happened to Mark it would devastate John. It would especially devastate John if he knew that he could have stopped something bad but didn't. The entire drive to work I fretted whether to tell John about the dream. Would he take me seriously? The longer I contemplated the dream the more sure I felt this was an ominous message.

When I got to work the stress and struggles of the day took over. Then I forgot all about it.

Two days later I ran into the house after work, rushing to catch the ringing phone. It was my mother. "Bonnie, I have some bad news. Do you remember John's friend, Mark? He committed suicide."

I flopped down on the couch as she started to relate the details. "Wait, wait… what?"

"Mark committed suicide the other night. John called a few minutes ago and he's on his way up here for the funeral."

Oh my God. That's when I remembered the dream. "Mom, what night? Do you remember specifically what night he did that?"

"He did it the night before last. John is really upset."

That was the same night I had the dream. I asked my mom if John had kept in touch with Mark over the years, and she said they had and they occasionally got together. She didn't know when John last saw or spoke to Mark, but she did know that Mark had gotten married and had a daughter. I told her about the dream. We talked about whether I should have told John. But even if John had contacted Mark, there was no way to know that he could have stopped what happened. The grief John felt was bad enough without added guilt. I will eventually tell John about the dream, because I believe Mark wanted John to know he's okay.

~Bonnie L. Beuth

Tommy's Visit

Millions of spiritual creatures walk the earth
Unseen, both when we wake and when we sleep.
~John Milton, Paradise Lost

My friend Tommy was a talented writer, cartoonist, and performer. We grew close over nearly ten years, meeting for coffee, drinks, or meals at least once a week. Tommy died suddenly in 1995, and I was heartbroken. But our friendship didn't end with his physical death.

In late November of 1997, my eighty-four-year-old father became ill. Our doctor said he had the flu and would be well by the time I had to go out of town in January. I am a children's author, and had a speaking event and book signing. Tommy knew better, and one night he visited me in a dream.

He was at my father's house, sitting in the living room, talking to me. He told me, "Your father is going to die soon, and it'll be okay. He's coming to be with all of us." However, he said, first, Fath would get very cold, and the only thing I could do was to keep him warm. Then Tommy pointed and said, "Gin, would you grab me that shawl on the back of that chair?" I wouldn't have called it a shawl; it was a black-and-red checked blanket. In the dream, when I covered Tommy with it, he turned into the likeness of my father and died.

I knew that Tommy had somewhat prepared me, and the following day I told my family so that they might be somewhat prepared as well. Some of them believed me. Others chose to put their faith in the doctor's brighter prediction instead.

That evening, I went to prepare dinner for Fath. I went nearly every night. Although my own car was old and unreliable, Fath had given me his new New Yorker to drive. Since he had been so weak, I helped him to the table. As he began eating, he asked, "Gin, would you grab me that shawl on the back of that chair?"

For a second, I froze and I can't remember breathing. He was talking about the red-and-black checked blanket. I got the "shawl" and wrapped it around my father's shoulders, letting my fingers linger for a while.

Instead of improving, Fath got sicker—and colder. He was admitted to the hospital, and doctors explained that the drop in his temperature was caused by a pancreatic disorder. Then his other organs began to fail. He described seeing and speaking with his parents and Uncle Bill; they were all deceased. On Christmas Eve, he told my daughter Hannah and me, "Two more days, then no more nightmares." Then he closed his eyes. I was at his bedside on December 26th when he took his final earthly breath.

My grief was unfathomable. The only comfort was what Tommy had told me: "It'll be okay. He's coming to be with all of us," and the fact that Fath's family members were guiding him Home.

Somehow I mustered up the courage to keep my speaking engagement and book-signing date, but my heart wasn't in it. Fath had often accompanied me to such events, and I feared I might not be able to do this one, especially without him.

As I entered the Thruway and retrieved my toll ticket, I glanced at the car in the lane next to me. It was, of all models, a New Yorker. Even more unbelievable was its license plate: LHK 880. My father's name was Lester Herman Kroll, and he always claimed that his lucky number was eight.

The car soon disappeared into traffic, but I knew without a doubt then that Fath was with me on my trip after all.

~Virginia Kroll

A Grand Visitor

Grandmas hold our tiny hands for just a little while, but our hearts forever.
~Author Unknown

My question took my mother by surprise. We were at the Wright Brothers National Memorial in North Carolina when I asked her, "Mom, did you have a grandmother?"

My mother chuckled. "Everyone has a grandmother!"

"No. I mean, was she alive when you were born? Did you know her?"

"Yes," Mom said, distracted by the monument.

I paused, unsure whether I should continue. My mother seemed happy enough to be walking around the national monument. With her mood so troubled of late, I worried my question might destroy her good mood. But the dream had been so vivid, I had to ask: "Mom, did your grandmother seem kind of like a gypsy?"

"What do you mean?" my mother asked, still half-distracted by the monument.

"I mean when she talked, did she have a thick accent, almost the way a gypsy would sound?" I asked, thinking of old-fashioned gypsy movies I had seen. It was the only comparison I could think of.

"Yes," Mom said, "though I never thought of her accent that way. Why?"

"Did she wear longish skirts, and did she have long hair?"

My mother's eyes widened. "Yes, why?"

"Mom, I think I met her."

My mother stopped. Her face drained of color.

"Describe her again," Mom muttered.

I did.

"Her hair was long."

"Was it white and pulled up in a bun?" Mom asked.

"No," I said. "It was darker, a reddish-brown, and it flowed all the way down her back. Is that what your grandmother looked like?"

My mother put her hands to her cheeks. "By the time I was born, her hair was white. It was long and silky, and she would take it down at night. By day she kept it up in a bun. But she showed me a picture of her once. She was younger, and her hair was darker." Mom's voice trembled a little. "It was a black-and-white picture, but she told me about her hair. It was a reddish-brown, and it flowed all the way down her back."

We stared at each other.

"This is kind of scary," she said finally.

I frowned. There was more, but I wasn't sure whether I should continue. Mom was still pale. I turned away as if to study the monument.

"What did she say?" Mom asked. "What did she want?"

I kept my back to Mom for the moment. My parents had been having some problems lately. With the economic downturn, my father's office was closing, and the threat of joblessness put pressure on their marriage. They fought all the time, often over nothing at all. There was no communication, and the one time I suggested they see a counselor, they both refused. My sister and I had just moved out after college, and when we called my parents focused only on superficial topics. When we asked what was wrong, they would never open up to us. And my mother had been living as if all of life's possibilities and blessings had suddenly ended.

"What did she say!" Mom demanded, regaining her voice.

"She told me that I need to spend more time with you," I said. "She said that you have been upset recently, and the real reason for it is that you have no one to talk to."

Mom frowned.

"She said that the problems you're having aren't that serious, but it seems worse to you because you're keeping it all inside."

Tears started pooling in Mom's eyes. I figured I had better finish what I started, so I continued: "She said that it's too bad you don't have a sibling, that all you've been thinking about lately is how you wish you had a sibling so you'd always have someone to talk to."

"This is very true," Mom managed to say. "Very true."

"There's one more thing," I said. It was the most difficult part, and I wanted to get it out before I lost my nerve. "When your grandmother told me that you wished you had a sibling, she said something strange. Something that didn't make sense. She said it was too bad you didn't have a sibling. But then she took this photograph. She wouldn't let me see it, but she took it out and studied it. She said, 'well, there was the one sibling, but there was the month that pained him.' Then she looked at the picture for a bit more before tucking it away in her skirt and turning back to me."

"The month that pained—him?" my mother asked.

I nodded. "What did she mean?"

"I don't believe this!" Mom said.

"What?"

"I never told you that I had a brother. He was stillborn. They named him and buried him. There was a month that pained him. It was the month he was born." By this time, tears were flowing down my mother's cheeks.

We stood in silence, watching the other tourists at the monument. It was my mother who broke the silence.

"I wonder why she told you that. What did she want?"

"She wanted me to be the one you can talk to about everything," I said. "She wanted you to be able to confide in me. She doesn't think it's good for you to bottle up everything."

"Maybe that's why she told you about the little boy in that picture. Maybe she knew it would convince me that she was real." Mom smiled sadly at me.

It would take time for my mother to process the dream, and it would take more time for her to finally open up to me. But she had always followed her grandmother's advice, and this time would be no exception. But for now, my mother stared off into the distance, warmed by the comfort of knowing that even after death her grandmother was protecting her.

~Val Muller

Chapter
5

Messages from Heaven

An Angel Told Me

40

Two More Years

God pours life into death and death into life without a drop being spilled.
~Author Unknown

t was March 23, 1992, 4:31 a.m. The shrill ringing of the phone jarred me awake but I hesitated. My husband, Art, stirred beside me, prodding me to answer. My father had been hospitalized for over a month during which time I had returned to my childhood home to step into my father's shoes and take care of my bedridden, partially paralyzed mother. As we feared, it was a nurse at the hospital calling to inform us that my father, Joe Bellinghausen, had died of a heart attack at the age of eighty-seven.

An only child, I had no siblings to consult about taking my mother, Dolly, from her familiar surroundings of eighty-eight years and moving her to Texas. I pondered the wisdom of such a decision, worrying that if she died on my watch soon after, I would never forgive myself. But the thought of abandoning her in a nursing home so far away from me was abhorrent. So, after much soul-searching and praying to have her with me for at least two years, we brought her to live with us in Friendswood, Texas.

For the past sixteen years, since her stroke, I had written my mother every day. Lately my father had warned me she wasn't reading the letters and he feared she was "losing it." I sloughed off these observations, since to me she seemed fine. But I soon learned that she had rapidly advancing Alzheimer's.

We had great days and horrible days, weathering many problems.

As Mother's illness progressed, her ups and downs became more extreme. She would be hyper for three days—always happy but unaware—then she'd go into what we called a "coma" for three days where we couldn't rouse her. Hospitalized many times, she always miraculously rallied and returned home to us.

Eventually, Mother lapsed into a coma and then developed pneumonia. The doctors and home healthcare nurses said death was imminent and that I should allow her to die at home. But after a sleepless night of listening to her death rales in the next room, I called the ambulance. She was taken to the hospital, where they said to prepare myself for her impending demise. How many times had I heard that?

Four days later, her doctor suggested we put her in a nursing home for her final days, again stressing the urgency of the situation. I reluctantly agreed; she had now been in a coma for a month. I visited her daily in her bright room and rang bells, shook clackers, even tap danced, doing my best to wake her, but to no avail.

She had been in the nursing home for over a month when I skipped my daily daytime visit. Since Art and I were taking dance lessons near the nursing home, we went to see her that evening after our lesson. When I walked into her room, she was sitting up, laughing and talking to a nurse. I couldn't believe my eyes.

She looked at me happily and said in a clear and distinct voice—one I had not heard for over seventeen years—"What are you doing here?" I couldn't believe my ears.

"We've been to our dance lesson," I stammered.

"Well, then, let's see what you learned."

We were in shock, but Art dutifully cleared the room of chairs and rolling tables, and we danced for my mother. I hummed the glorious foxtrot, waltz and swing ballroom music of her youth, while she kept time on the bed rail with her good left hand and giggled. I couldn't believe it.

After our impromptu recital, I asked her, "Do you know who I am?" She had not recognized me for many months.

Eyebrows arched, sighing, she slowly nodded her head. "Why, of course."

"Well, then, who am I?"

She couldn't understand why I was asking such a silly question. "My daughter, Marilyn," she answered, a "shame-on-you" look on her face.

"Good! Who's this?" I pointed at Art. She had been unable to remember his name for a year, not to mention completely forgetting our last name.

Tired of such easy questions, she answered wearily, "Art Zapata."

We stood staring at her. Art recovered first and, giving her a kiss, said he was proud of her. She glowed. An incredible visit followed, reliving precious memories and family jokes—an unexpected gift.

As we prepared to leave, I said, "It's been great, Mother. I'll be back tomorrow."

She held up her finger and shook it, "Don't bother, honey. I'm going home."

"Sure," I said. "Now that you're better, you're coming back home with us."

"No," she persisted. "I'm going to my home. Joe is coming to pick me up tonight." She seemed really excited about this prospect, so I played along, not to spoil the mood.

"Well," I said, "tell him 'Hi' for me."

That night, the shrill ringing of the phone jarred me awake but I hesitated, fearing the news. Art stirred beside me, prodding me to answer. It was the nursing home calling to inform us that my mother, Dolly Bellinghausen, died during the night of natural causes, at the age of ninety.

I hung up the phone; there was a pause. Then in the darkness, Art softly asked, "Do you know what day it is?" I didn't. He said, "Think hard."

The realization struck me like lightning. I looked at the clock. It was March 23, 1994, 4:31 a.m. I took a deep breath and gathered my thoughts. It was two years to the day, to the hour, to the minute, that we had received the call that my father had died. My prayer had been answered, granting me exactly two extra years with my mother.

I can picture it now. Into my mother's room strides my tall father puffing white clouds of condensation. I see his breath evaporate into the warm room. Like many a scene from my youth, he wears a snow-flake-sprinkled hat and tartan muffler wrapped securely around his neck. His left hand is gloved with a well-worn leather mitt and holds the glove's stiff mate. He blows into his clenched right fist, warming his exposed hand. I hear his car warming up outside. Then, pointing to his watch, he says for the last time, "Come on, Dolly. It's time. Let's go. We don't want to be late!"

~Marilyn Zapata

Pappy's Angel

We are each of us angels with only one wing,
and we can only fly by embracing one another.
~Luciano de Crescenzo

"**G**irls! Wake up! The house is on fire!" Daddy and my step-mom Shirley burst into our bedroom.

I jerked up in the bed.

My sister burrowed under her pillow.

Shirley yanked on Steffie and grabbed my hand.

"Follow me," Daddy ordered as he led us toward the front of the house. We had a clear path to the outside door, but I couldn't help looking over my shoulder at the smoke rolling out of the kitchen. Red-orange flames shot to the ceiling, snapping and spitting like fire-crackers. But we were okay. We were in the living room. The fire was behind us.

My older sister, Tiff, clutching her ten-day-old baby, also fled from her bedroom to the front entry. When she opened the door, letting in outside air, the house erupted into flames. Smoke burned my eyes. Choked me. This wasn't a nightmare. It was real.

Steffie, Shirley and I were together, but we couldn't see Daddy anymore. Only thick, black smoke surrounding us and flames behind us. We couldn't find the door. We were lost in our own home. Were we going to die? I screamed. I think we all screamed, as we groped through the blackness, hunting for the front of the house. Daddy yelled for us, but we couldn't tell from which direction.

"Turn around, Brittini. Go back." Did someone speak to me? Or was I so frightened I was hallucinating? It was like somebody whispered in my ear and I needed to listen to it. I grabbed my sister's hand and we scrambled back over and around furniture until we found our bedroom, the only room in the house the smoke had not entered.

I couldn't let Steffie see how scared I was. "Wait here," I commanded in my big sister voice and forced myself to run back into the smoke-filled rooms calling for Shirley and Daddy. I found Shirley wandering through the smoke, searching, calling for us, but we didn't see Daddy anywhere. I pulled on Shirley until we reached my bedroom. I prayed Daddy had made it through the front door, helping Tiffini with the baby.

Shirley, Steffie and I cried and hugged each other. We didn't know what to do next. The voice spoke in my head more clearly this time. "Shut the door. Don't let the fire in here."

Smoke crawled under the closed bedroom door. I felt the heat, tasted the stench, as those hungry flames ate away at everything my family owned. How long before it would reach us?

"The window over the vanity," Shirley and I said in unison, and ran to it.

The voice came again. It didn't whisper this time. A familiar, stern, demanding voice took over my body. Like a robot, I followed instructions and leapt upon the small vanity under the window. "Pick up the lamp and break the window, Brittini," the voice said. As the smoke curled from under the door, we all coughed and choked. It was hard to breathe.

"I can't. I'm hot. I'm scared." All I had was a small plastic lamp.

My sister depended on me. I had to save us. I beat and banged on the window, but it wouldn't break. "Hit it hard, Brittini. Hit it harder." The voice insisted. "You can do it. You can do it." I picked up that small lamp and banged over and over again on the stubborn glass pane.

"Hit it again," the voice instructed. Using all the strength I had, I drew my arm back and swung the little lamp into the windowpane. The lamp broke. But so did the window. I stared at the hole. It was not big enough for my body to fit through. The smoke twisted into thick clouds. I thought I was going to die. I prayed.

Suddenly the vanity crumbled from under me, and pitched me forward through the broken window. I landed outside on the ground. The glass snagged my leg and it was bleeding, but I was okay. I was breathing fresh air.

The hole was larger now. Shirley hoisted Steffie up, but a shard of glass caught her leg. Shirley pushed her from behind and I pulled her arms, as the glass sliced her flesh. When I helped her to the ground, she was bleeding a lot, and I couldn't tell how badly she was hurt. She might bleed to death if I didn't do something.

Shirley stuck her head through the opening and gulped the fresh air. Steffie and I shouted, "Come on, Shirley. Jump!" But the vanity had collapsed so she had nothing to climb on. We weren't big enough to pull her through the window. We screamed for help and couldn't stop screaming. I'd saved myself and my sister, but my stepmom was going to burn.

Steffie was getting weak. Her face was white and her hands cold. "Hang on Shirley. I've got to get help for Steffie. Please, Shirley, hang on just a little longer. Please God, help us."

Sirens wailed in the distance. Would they get here in time to save Shirley? Were Daddy and Tiffini and the baby safe? I took Steffie to a neighbor and pushed her into her arms. "Please help my sister. Don't let her die." I ran back to Shirley, but by then Dad had heard our screams. He came running around the house and wrenched Shirley out the window before the emergency workers arrived.

Steffie needed eight stitches. Shirley and I needed oxygen. But thank God none of us were seriously injured.

The fire department tried, but couldn't save our home. As I looked into the window and saw blazes ravaging the last room we were in, my bedroom, I said, "Thank you God. We're all alive."

My mother, Beth, came as soon as I got her on my cell phone. She looked at me like I was a piece of gold. "I'm so proud of you, baby girl. Only fifteen and you saved three lives." We clung to each other and cried. My brother and sister, Jacob and Olivia, cried too. My stepdaddy, Jake, squeezed me until I couldn't breathe.

"Momma, that voice that led me out of the house. It was Pappy." I peeked up at her, not sure if she would believe me.

"Are you sure? You were only ten when your grandfather died."

"I still remember his voice. God sent Pappy to tell me what to do."

Momma didn't take her eyes away from me as she kept on rubbing my arm and patting my hand, tears rolling down her cheeks. "I believe you," she said.

"What day is it?" I wanted to always remember this day.

"April 12th."

"Pappy's birthday." He saved me on his birthday! He used to call me "Pappy's little angel." Today he was mine.

~Brittini Jean Watkins, age 16

Saved by "The Look"

I miss thee, my Mother! Thy image is still
The deepest impressed on my heart.
~Eliza Cook

Many of us remember the power of "The Look" with which our mothers showed disapproval. "The Look" could convey such a strong wordless message that it would stop us in our tracks. My own mother used "The Look" rarely, but effectively.

Even though I am far, far away from childhood and my mother died some years ago, I frequently remember her voice or see her face as I navigate through life. But I rarely think of "The Look" anymore. Thus it was a surprise when the image presented itself to me at an entirely unexpected moment.

On a summer afternoon, I was running late to an appointment. As I hurried across town, I looked at the gas gauge and saw the tank was almost empty. Not willing to risk running out of gas, I pulled into a service station. I leaped out of the car, slipped my credit card in the slot and began to fill up the tank. I looked west at the Rocky Mountains, and then glanced around, noticing that only one other car was there.

I had skipped lunch and suddenly realized I was hungry and thirsty. The more I thought about food, the more I wanted to run into the small station and buy some snacks. I argued with myself that I didn't have time, and my empty tummy was about to win the argument when I heard a voice I hadn't heard for a long, long time. I heard a loud "NO!" The power and strength of that word startled me. Still, I reached into the car for my purse when I heard it again, but this time I saw my mother's face with "The Look." With some confusion, I obediently dropped my purse back on the car seat and turned to replace the nozzle. How odd it felt to be chastised so strongly for simply wanting to buy a little snack!

As I replaced the gas cap I felt a rush of movement behind me and heard pounding feet as a man raced out of the station and into his car. With screeching tires he raced away as the cashier came staggering out of the door yelling, "Did you see him? Did you see that guy? He just pulled a gun on me and took all the money from the drawer!"

By the time he arrived at my car he was so shaken that he sank down to the ground. I tried to gather my wits.

"Just now?" I asked. "You were robbed at gunpoint JUST NOW?"

The cashier's hands were shaking, and he asked again, "Did you see him? I've got to call the manager and the police and if you saw him you could give a description."

But I couldn't describe the man who had been a blur as he ran to his car and drove off. I only had a vague recollection of the car. What I remembered was the vivid image of my mother that had appeared and the loud "NO!" All I knew was if I had gone into the station when I wanted to, I would have interrupted the robbery. I would have walked in on a man holding a gun right by the front door. He might have turned it on me. He might have panicked and shot me and the cashier. I sat beside the cashier on the dirty pavement, my hand on his trembling arm, and felt my heart thumping wildly at what might have been. I closed my eyes and gave silent thanks to God for His mercy and a mother whose care extended beyond the boundary of death to keep me safe in this life.

~Caroline S. McKinney

Love Again

*There are things that we don't want to happen but have to accept,
things we don't want to know but have to learn,
and people we can't live without but have to let go.*
~Author Unknown

"I think Jay wants to ask you out," one of my co-workers told me as everyone else left the office for the day. "But he's a little nervous."

I was a little nervous too. Danny, my childhood sweetheart, father of our now twelve-year-old son, and love of twenty years, had been dead two years—long enough for me to have grieved and moved forward—but I couldn't entertain the thought of a new man.

I knew Jay. We shared a few cases together. He was a mental health social worker; I worked in child and adult protection. So occasionally our paths crossed.

Danny and I had vowed to love each other and stay true to each other forever. Our hopes and dreams had been wrapped up in each other and in our child. He would often say, "I have hope, you have faith."

And it was true. He had high hopes that anything and everything would turn out okay. In turn, my faith, in him and in God, was so strong I thought nothing could stand in our way.

When you're young, death is a safe wisp of smoke in the distance. Barely thought about. Barely a reality. You believe you're invincible and that somehow you are immune to that depth of pain and loss.

But in the middle of a cool, quiet September night, one phone call changed all of that.

"It's Danny," I heard a family friend telling my mother on another telephone extension at home. "He died in a car wreck."

He said more, but those were the last words I remember.

I should have done something. Gotten out of bed, driven to the crash scene, called his mother, run around the house clawing into my face with my fingernails, pounded my head against the wall, stabbed my heart with an ice pick... but I didn't. I just lay there in the bed in dark silence, hot tears sliding from my eyes.

What kept me going was our ten-year-old son Travis. He was the reason I got up in the morning, put on a smile when I didn't feel like smiling, thought ahead instead of behind, found a way to push through each day, week, and month. I wouldn't let death cheat him out of a healthy, vibrant, whole mother.

"It's okay," he would tell me if he caught me crying. "It'll be all right."

Work and motherhood helped ease the pain of losing Danny. In the two years following his death, little by little I rebounded. I learned to laugh again, play again, have fun and make plans.

A few guys asked me out, but I turned them down. I wanted to move on, but it just didn't feel right. It had nothing to do with grief. It had more to do with feeling like I would betray Danny if I dated someone.

When my best friend Jolene heard that Jay was interested in me, she said, "Don't be afraid to give him a chance, Tammy. Danny would want you to love again."

Her words clicked into place in my heart like the final piece of a jigsaw puzzle.

She was right. Danny would not want me to waste the prime of my life missing him and pining for him. He would want me to have someone to love and share my life with, and be a part of Travis' life too.

When Jay called, I was alone in the office. Jay sounded bright and sunny, so cheerful after a long day at work.

We made small talk about cases, he asked me how my day had gone, and then finally he asked me if I wanted to go to dinner Friday night.

"Yes," I told him. "I'd like that." I knew Danny would want me to have a chance at love and happiness again.

As I drove home after work, I began to have second thoughts about saying yes to Jay, and for some reason the tears came. I began to talk to Danny in my heart. I needed to make a stop on the way home—a client's house. The family lived up a rocky dirt hollow and across a rickety wooden bridge. I loved driving in the countryside, so it was a nice drive. But all the way there, I had second thoughts.

What if it was a mistake? What about the vows I made to Danny? Would he really want me to date someone else? I didn't know what to do. Should I call Jay back and break the date, or keep it and take one more step into the future? I just needed a sign from Danny. I asked him to show me a sign that it was okay.

That's when it happened. As I was driving up the hollow toward my client's home. A flock of a thousand or more butterflies floated from the bushes at the side of the road and across my windshield, so thick I couldn't see through them and had to stop the car.

I felt rather than heard Danny's soft, calm voice saying, "It's okay, Tammy. Go ahead. Love again."

Somehow. Somehow he sent those butterflies to me as a sign that it was okay to move forward and open my heart to romance, companionship, and love again.

~Tammy Ruggles

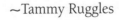

The Visit

In faith there is enough light for those who want to believe and enough shadows to blind those who don't.
~Blaise Pascal

It had been three years since I'd seen my mother. Nine months after my father's death, she had finally found the peace she sought. They'd been together sixty-two years. She tried to pick up the pieces of her life and move on, but she was lost without him. The phone call from the assisted living facility marked the end of her loneliness.

There were so many things I wanted to tell her—little things that wouldn't matter to anyone else, things only a mother and a daughter hold special between them. I'd pass a place we always liked to visit, and I'd want to call her to tell her about it. I'd forget she wasn't there.

Time has a way of healing the hurt. But I felt a gnawing ache, a conscious awareness that she was the only person who ever offered me unconditional love.

I was home alone one morning and doing laundry. With my arms full of clothes, I made my way from the utility room through the den toward my bedroom. As I entered the den, I stopped in my tracks. In front of me, in the recliner in the corner, sat my mother.

She looked up and smiled as I stared back at her. She wore light gray sweatpants and a matching sweatshirt. I noticed she wore the set of pearls she always loved—the same set that supposedly was hanging from a wall sconce in my bedroom. Her new glasses, the kind with clear frames, were barely noticeable, and her hair matched her outfit.

Mom and I shared a brief moment of eye contact, and then she was gone. I felt her presence in the room as I said, "I love you, Mom."

I slowly walked past the recliner and into the bedroom. I glanced at the wall sconce and saw her pearls. I had placed them there just before her service. I threw the clothes on the bed, but I couldn't let the feeling go. I walked back into the den and sat down in the recliner Mom had just vacated.

"Where did you go?" I asked as my eyes took in every corner, every chair, and every inch of space in the room.

My gaze fell upon something beside me on the floor—my study Bible.

I didn't use that Bible often—only when I needed clarification of some of life's questions. It contained three different translations of the Good Book, and it was extremely heavy. I couldn't remember the last time I'd used it, or any other Bible as a matter of fact. With my life in shambles from my recent divorce, I had let my Christian upbringing fall by the wayside as I wandered aimlessly, day by day, trying to figure out what had gone wrong. Two years worth of feeling sorry for myself and blaming everyone else had taken its toll on my faith and my ability to allow God to direct my path. However, the study Bible lay open before me and without hesitation I picked it up.

It was opened to the book of Ecclesiastes, the third chapter—my mother's favorite. She'd read it to me many times during my childhood, and it carried through to my adulthood as one of my most well loved chapters. She liked the poetic flow of the words "to everything there is a season, a time for every purpose under heaven: a time to be born, and a time to die..."

I knew I had not opened that Bible; in fact the cover was dusty.

"What are you trying to tell me, Mom?" I asked as I again searched the room.

The only reply I heard was one she always would say when an answer was obvious: "You figure it out—you're a smart person."

She'd come back for a reason, and that was to deliver a message. I reread the familiar words: "a time to cry and a time to laugh; a time to grieve and a time to dance."

"It's time to get on with it, huh, Mom?" I asked out loud.

I knew it was time to get my life together and get myself back in church. It was time to quit blaming myself and everyone else for past mistakes and move on. I smiled and tried to remember the last time I'd laughed out loud or danced, as the verses mentioned. It had been too long to remember. I reached down and closed the study Bible, then jumped out of the recliner and danced a little jig across the den floor. I laughed so loud that my cat ran behind the couch to hide. My faith in God and His ability to soothe my wounded soul was suddenly renewed and I felt like a new person.

There's definitely a season for all things. Mom was telling me to take life a day at a time and not get bogged down in things that don't matter. I needed to keep looking up and stay focused.

~Carol Huff

Unlatched Doors

For death is no more than a turning of us over from time to eternity.
~William Penn

When my maternal grandmother died suddenly and way too soon, I was unable to imagine my life without her. Grandma hugged everyone coming and going. She hugged so tightly often the huggees were left breathless. She also demonstrated her delight in visitors by her insistence on an unlatched screen door. Working in the kitchen, she entertained me and the other grandchildren with stories of angels, hobos, and bootleggers. We would swivel on the vinyl kitchen stools soaking up the words, aromas, and Grandma's warmth. After she died, I wondered where in the world we would swivel, where in the world we would find warmth.

In the weeks after her funeral, everything felt silly and useless. I found little to laugh about. The haziness of that hot Alabama summer enveloped things more than usual. I stumbled through my graduate school classes. The simple but necessary acts of sleeping and eating took great effort. Sometimes, I didn't bother with either.

Months after I lost Grandma, when I finally started sleeping a little, I had a dream with a message so profound it had to have been delivered by Grandma or an angel or both. I know this because I am not that wise.

In my dream, Grandma and I visited with each other. We sat in what had been her mint green living room. She wore a white eyelet lace dress and white low-top Converse Chuck Taylors, just like the ones I had purchased a week or so before she had passed away.

We sat next to each other, our knees touching, on the old plaid sofa. The same cuckoo clock hung slightly askew to the left of the couch. The dusty old bird popped out of its clock three times. And I began to cry. In her soft, sweet voice, Grandma asked me why I was crying.

"Because I miss you!" I wailed. "I want you here with me, with all of us."

She looked at me and smiled.

"Where I am, we don't miss people," she explained and patted my knee. "We just wait for them."

Our visit ended. She stood and walked to the screen door, unlatched of course, and turned to me. She said, "I love you now even more than I loved you then." She shook her head as if in disbelief. "I didn't know that was possible."

I must admit I did not want the dream to end, but I found my grandmother's brief presence and immense wisdom comforting. In time, I began to sleep regularly again. I also began to supply the salad for my friends' weekly cookouts again. I even began to enjoy the cookouts and other activities. Finally, I began to laugh again.

Twenty years later, I hope I am a little wiser; however, I always will nurse the hole left in my heart when Grandma died. Of course, since that time, I have lost others too, and I have grieved. It's never easy. Anytime someone passes on, it's way too soon for me. But my grandmother's words have remained close to me and have allowed me, I think, to cope with loss better than I once did.

I'm certain that there's lots to do in Heaven besides wait. I imagine as those dear to us go about their eternal lives, they anticipate our arrivals with great peace and happiness. Those of us here should take that to heart and live much the same way, knowing the screen door to Heaven is unlatched and a great big hug awaits us when it is our time to move on.

~Dana J. Barnett

Visiting Hours

It is only with the heart that one can see rightly,
what is essential is invisible to the eye.
~Antoine de Saint-Exupery

"Everything is going to be all right," my mom states after the doctor leaves my bedside. "Jaundice is very common in newborns," she continues. But because there is a blood type mismatch between me and my baby, this case of jaundice is more severe. I know Mom is just trying to allay my worries that I might have to leave the hospital empty-handed after nine months of carrying my baby girl, but it isn't all right. Instead of the joyful homecoming I'd envisioned, my baby will be lying in a clear plastic box with bright blue lights in the hospital nursery, hooked up to an IV until her bilirubin level decreases.

"Everything is going to be all right," my husband says as he kisses me goodbye for the night. Hospital visiting hours are over, but they do not really apply to new dads on the maternity floor. Tom stayed with me the first night our Hanna was born. He awkwardly straddled one leg over the arm of the chair and dozed in spurts, but on the second night, he goes home to be with our three-year-old Lucas. I understand why he leaves, but I just don't want to be alone. When I am alone in the hospital with my fears and worries, I feel weak.

"Everything is going to be all right," a nightshift nurse reassures me in a voice that sounds like a recorded message. I don't believe her. She means well though. When I answer her questions, she can tell by the flutter of emotion in my voice that I have been crying. I am still in a lot of pain, and I am disappointed in myself at my slow recovery. As the nurse wheels the baby's crib out of my room and turns off the light, I am distraught. I want to hold my baby. I want my husband to stay. I want to feel better.

I desperately want to sleep so that I don't have to think or feel anymore, but I cannot. Every fifteen minutes, a nurse quietly comes into my darkened room to check my monitors. The constant beeps and blinking numbers say everything is all right, but like clockwork, a nurse keeps coming back to check anyway. I close my eyes but cannot turn off my mind as I await the next interruption.

The next time someone comes into my room, I don't bother opening my eyes in acknowledgement. Check those monitors again, I think. They're not going to be any different from ten minutes ago. But then, I sense there are two people in the room—one at the foot of my bed and one to the left near my head. I've never had two nurses at once. Maybe they see something wrong on the monitors this time. I pretend to sleep for another minute and hope they will leave, but their presence seems stronger now, more intense. Something is definitely different this time and I begin to feel anxious as this visit lasts longer than the others. Unable to wait it out any longer, I open my eyes, hoping to get an explanation. "Am I all right?"

Silence is the only answer. The room is dim, but clearly no one stands before me. I quickly glance behind me to the left. No one. But I felt them there! I was not dreaming. Someone was here. I close my eyes tightly, hoping to get that same feeling back, but it's not working. I open my eyes again and look around. Emptiness fills the cold hospital room.

I finally shut my eyes again and rest peacefully for the first time all day. In that foggy, weightless place just before sleep, I am no longer confined to this hospital bed. I am sitting on the edge of my mother's bed, a place I've always felt safe. My five cousins sit cross-legged on the country quilt behind me. There's someone they want to see, too. Their father stands by the bedpost at the foot. It's been fifteen years since my Uncle Mike has passed, but I'm happy to see him, looking just as I remember. Kind eyes, wispy hair that looks like feathers, and a big grin under a reddish mustache.

I see my grandma standing to my left. She passed away shortly after Lucas was born, and I am sad that she will not get to hold our daughter. I think she is pleased we named Hanna Catherine after her, but it is me she comes to visit tonight. My grandma always had a serene, caring way about her in everything she did. And in seeing her soft smile before me now, I am comforted to know that has not changed.

In the next instant, I feel my body back in the hospital bed, but I strain to keep my eyes closed, desperately wanting to hold on to this precious time I've been given with my grandma. I want to tell her about the baby. I want to tell her I feel alone and scared. But she already knows. And I know she is really there when I feel the touch of her kiss on my forehead. I take in a sharp breath and let out a brief sob, acknowledging the rarity of the physical connection we just shared. Before I finally drift off to sleep, she leans over and whispers in my ear, "Everything is going to be all right." And for the first time, I actually believe that to be true.

~Erin Solej

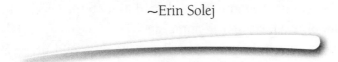

47

Heavenly Counsel

Angels assist us in connecting with a powerful yet gentle force,
which encourages us to live life to its fullest.
~Denise Linn

Our marriage was in a rough patch in 1996, but the children distracted us. We had no time for fight or flight. So, on an overbooked afternoon, as I rushed out the door with our daughter, I surprised myself and went back upstairs where my husband sat quietly reading the paper. He was oblivious to the chaos around him. Uncharacteristically, I reached from behind, wrapped my arms around him and kissed him on the cheek. "I love you," I simply said. He looked at me, an alien.

A mom on a mission, I hurried out the door and drove away with our little girl. Our haste seemed important at the time, but today I couldn't tell you if we were headed for a music lesson or major surgery. A simple cell phone ringtone stopped us. It was my husband according to the caller ID—perhaps a delayed reaction to that unexpected kiss?

"I think you should pull off the road," he said. I was near a friend's house, so I veered into her driveway. "I wish I didn't have to tell you this, but I just got a call from your dad. Your mom collapsed during their walk and she didn't make it," he explained directly, but gently.

Silence. I'd never experienced the death of a family member and I remember thinking I didn't want to go down that dreaded road.

Simultaneously, I realized that all roads from that point would lead to the same destination, and I gasped in horror.

Thus began the Death part of our family's life cycle, and I often revisit the day the phase began. Something about it was profound, and I always remember the kiss.

The uncharacteristic kiss that day came from somewhere outside of myself. After Mom passed, I realized it had happened the exact moment my mother had died. Mom, the wise one, had always tried to explain how marriage required grace, and I had rarely listened. But in death, Mom had stopped me in my tracks, turned me around and made me go kiss my man. Maybe it was her last lesson, and in death she'd found power to make me pay attention.

In life, she'd not been so effective. A typical young bride, thirty-seven years ago, I went crying home to Mommy after our first marital spat. She took my husband's side and sent me home in a huff.

Yes, Mom and I often didn't see life the same, but once in a while, an angel nudges and asks me to revisit her old advice. Decades later, it's as though I've scrambled through the house and finally found my glasses. Now, I can see Mom's ancient wisdom, one corn stalk in a freshly harvested field.

Hopefully, she hears me murmur, "Yes, Mom. I can hear you now, and you were right. Thanks for showing me that there are two sides to every marriage. You have saved me from myself."

~Kristi Paxton

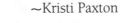

First Born Daughters

The tie which links mother and child is of such pure and immaculate strength as to be never violated.
~Washington Irving

A week before my mother passed away, she gave me her diamond anniversary ring and my grandmother's fiftieth-anniversary wedding band. When I slipped on the first one, chills ran through me. I'm the firstborn daughter, as were my mom and my grandmother. The spark of family connection brought tears to my eyes. I couldn't believe each was the perfect size for my ring finger.

A year later while reading in bed, I drifted off to sleep. In my dream, I drove in an unfamiliar city and stopped for a traffic light. I was headed toward a store that had advertised an antique fainting couch. I had to have one. I drove for miles searching for the store. But I never arrived. The dream faded. I awoke with a real sense of disappointment.

The next day's newspaper featured an announcement about a new antique store an hour away. They sold fainting couches. I gasped. Was this a sign my dream could come true? I laughed and decided it was a mere coincidence. But I'd wanted a Victorian couch for a long time, so I hurried and dressed.

I always wore my grandmother's gold wedding band, but I

couldn't find it that morning. For fifteen minutes, I searched every-where. No luck. It had mysteriously disappeared. Shaking my head, I slipped on my mother's diamond ring and promised to look for it later.

As I drove to the antique store, the steering wheel jerked toward the right. I flinched. Maybe the car had struck a rut? I checked my speedometer and tapped the brakes. I was going ten miles per hour over the speed limit.

"Suzanne, slow down," my mother's voice said loud and clear from behind me. The hairs on my neck and arms rose. I stomped the brakes and checked the rearview mirror. I swallowed hard. The wheel jerked right a second time. Spooked, I lowered my speed even more.

That's when I heard a massive squealing of tires. On the other side of the road, a blue sedan had accelerated to pass a semi-truck. The driver misjudged the speed of an oncoming car. He swerved and jammed on the brakes. Tires screeched as he lost control. The sedan spun toward the median and started to skid towards me. It struck two other automobiles and rolled a couple of times. The car slid side-ways, scraping against the tarmac in a burst of sparks and flames. It crashed into the curb and stopped half a block ahead of me.

I turned my car into a shopping center parking lot. I could hardly breathe. I turned off the ignition and slouched in the seat. My hands trembled in my lap. What just happened? My mother's voice had warned me. Did she yank the steering wheel too?

A pickup truck followed me in and parked a couple of spaces away. The driver bolted from his truck, raced over and rapped on my window. I lowered the window.

"Are you okay?" he asked and frowned.

"Yes," I said. "A little shaky, but that's all."

"What made you slow way down like that? If you hadn't, we'd both have been in that car's path."

"My mother, she... she told me to."

He leaned over and peered into the back seat. His eyes widened and I knew he questioned the emptiness.

"Funny thing is… she's dead. But it was her voice." I cleared my throat.

"Well, thank God for that. I'll say a prayer for her. My family will thank her too." He turned and walked back to his car.

I sat and thought about the previous night's strange dream. Today could have ended in a real nightmare, but I survived because of my mother. I kissed her ring. In spirit, Mom had ridden in the back seat. She still watched over me. I was safe and the fainting couch could wait. I turned around and drove home.

Two days later, I searched for my grandmother's ring. I made it my mission not to stop till I located it. That's when I heard Mom's voice again. "Suzanne, move the dresser."

"What?" I said, shivering. Then an unexpected warmth surged through me. I got my husband. I needed his muscles to shove aside the triple dresser. With him and God as my witness, we found Grandma's wedding band sparkling under the dresser in a small pile of dust. I stared at it, speechless. Mom's spiritual guidance had helped me a second time. I smiled and reached for the precious piece of jewelry. I wiped it clean, slipped the gold band on my ring finger and stared toward heaven. "Thanks, Mom."

~Suzanne Baginskie

49

A License to Love

Our perfect companions never have fewer than four feet.
~Colette

It was love at first sight. The first time I held him in my arms, I knew I had to have him. No, it wasn't a man who won my affections! It was a Peek-a-Poo dubbed Micado by the boyfriend who bought him for me. "Cado" was small in size, but big on attitude. He resembled a gremlin and had an under-bite that made you quietly giggle every time you looked at him. His vocabulary was impressive. He understood words like ride, walk, kids, potty, bed, eat, bath, and especially ice cream! But it was more than that. He intently studied my face when I talked to him, trying to understand what I was saying. Even if he couldn't understand my words, he always seemed to know what I was feeling. We had a deep connection, an unbreakable bond.

Cado seemed to think it was his God-given right to be pampered and I certainly did my best to oblige! After fifteen Christmases, he learned to open gifts and came to expect his own when everyone got theirs. In fact, one year I didn't buy or wrap any presents for him. Not a problem, he just opened mine! Needless to say, he never had another gift-less Christmas!

As he started to age and developed typical senior maladies, I tried to prepare for the eventuality of life without my loyal companion. I told myself that as long as he was happy and not in pain, I would not let him go. I also made a silent promise that I would never let him suffer, but would do the right thing if it got to that point. In spite of arthritis, he continued to play. We took shorter walks. When he lost his appetite, I changed his diet from dry dog food to canned dog food, then to people food like soups, rice and broth.

When he couldn't keep any food down for several days straight, we made the emergency trip to the vet's office. It was a Friday. X-rays and ultrasound showed what appeared to be a large tumor on his stomach. I had three choices—surgery, an agonizing death when the tumor burst (as it was sure to do within days) or euthanasia. Surgery offered no guarantees and I couldn't put him through such an ordeal. There was really only one option. I wanted his last moments on earth to be peaceful. I would be with him to the end. I wanted the last face he saw to be mine and his last memories to be the overwhelming love I had for him. The shot was administered and the vet left the room. Cado's eyes were fixed on me while I softly told him how glad I was to have had him in my life, how much I would miss him and how we would someday meet again. His eyes slowly closed and he was gone.

I can't even begin to describe the sadness and loneliness I felt at the loss of my Micado. For many nights, I lay in bed clutching his favorite sweater and crying myself to sleep. Eventually I started visiting local animal shelters and the pet refuge looking for a dog to fill the huge empty place in my heart. But every visit resulted in the same outcome. None of the dogs, no matter how sweet, how playful, how deserving, were Micado. No dog measured up to him. I just couldn't disrespect his memory by allowing another dog to take his place in my home or in my heart.

I continued to grieve for about a year. Then one night, Micado came to me in a dream. In this dream, I looked out my living room window to see my front yard filled with hundreds of dogs, all sizes, colors and breeds! As I stood there in awe, a voice said, "They are here for you. I want another dog to know the kind of love you gave to me. Pick me up so I can see them too!" It was Micado. I picked him up, and as I held him in my arms, I could truly feel the weight and warmth of his body against mine. I could feel the love he had for me. As he and I surveyed the dogs outside, I reluctantly awakened from the comforting moments I had spent with him. As I thought about the strange and powerful dream, a deep understanding washed over me. The bond between us had transcended death. Micado had come back to ease my pain. He had come back to let me know that he knew how much I loved him and that his special place in my heart would never be threatened, even by another dog. He was there to let me know he didn't want me to be lonely or sad any longer.

A few weeks after the dream, a message went out to all users on our corporate e-mail system advertising a Shih Tzu free to a good home. I was the first of fifteen callers and told the young doctor's wife about Micado, my loss, and finally being ready to get another dog. I made arrangements to meet Xander that very night. Although they had many responses to the e-mail, they told me they had no plans to interview other people. If I was interested, Xander was mine. In spite of Xander's complete disinterest in me (in fact he growled, barked and would not let me near him), I knew he was the one. I knew I would take him home with me and win him over. That was four years ago. Xander is not Micado, but he doesn't need to be. Xander is very special in his own right and I pamper him shamelessly! He has found a permanent home and a lasting place in my heart. He can thank Micado for that.

~Luann Warner

Chapter
6

Messages from Heaven

Love that Doesn't Die

50

Because I Saw Alan

Sometimes being a brother is even better than being a superhero.
~Marc Brown

"I woke up last night," I said, "and there was a soldier standing by my bed."

It was 1960. I was six years old, sitting at the breakfast table one Saturday morning, and, although usually—and for good reason—a very quiet child, I thought this news of my night-time visitor was interesting enough to risk saying out loud.

Sadly, the barrage of scolding that followed was all too familiar.

"Don't be so stupid!"

"Shut up. You're always telling lies."

"How dare you say such a thing."

"You made that up. You're a bad girl!"

"Do you want a good slap?"

It was unusual, even for my dysfunctional family—my parents and siblings—to react quite so strongly to something I said. Although as the youngest I'd certainly had my share of bullying from all of them. Even at my tender age, experience had taught me to keep quiet and stay out of everybody's way as much as possible. This time—I didn't know why—I stuck to my guns.

"I'm not lying," I said, as bravely as I could. "There was a soldier there. I saw him."

My father, a perpetually angry, tyrannical man, leaned across the table and fixed me with a stare.

"If you dare lie to me again," he told me, in a quiet, menacing tone, "I will hit you so hard…"

He let the sentence trail off because it was scarier that way.

There was a moment of tense silence, then a chorus of "She doesn't know what she's talking about" and "She had a dream, that's all."

My mother and my older brother and sisters were trying to nip Dad's temper in the bud, not to protect me, but rather to prevent a bad morning becoming a really bad day.

To everyone's relief, Dad's temper did fade. I was told that I'd dreamt up my soldier and I knew better than to protest any further. But I also knew I hadn't been dreaming. I knew without any doubt that I had awoken during the night and that I'd clearly seen the young man in uniform standing there.

He was facing the window, and although the curtains were closed it looked like a shaft of silver light shone through them. I saw him lift his face up to the light, his eyes closed, as if he could feel its rays on his skin.

He was wearing—though only later did I know the right words to describe it—khaki battledress, and a black beret pulled over to the right, with a silver badge on the front.

I wasn't the least bit afraid—odd for such a nervous child. I know now that I was deeply afraid of my family but too young to understand or express it, and so I developed a whole raft of small fears that I could express. I was afraid of the dark, afraid of shadows, afraid of spiders, afraid of strangers, afraid of so many things. I was crippled by shyness too, and although I was bright and could read well, my timidity made me invisible at school. I had no friends, and teachers would mostly overlook me in favour of the more confident, popular kids.

I looked at the soldier for just a few seconds before he turned his face towards me. The smile he gave me was gentle, and the kindest smile I'd ever seen. He looked at me with love. When I was older and wiser I realised that his smile and his expression were tinged with sadness, but right then, in that little fragment of time, I only knew that I felt more truly loved than ever before.

I was happy and warm and cosy. I felt pure joy for a little while, but then my eyes closed, I was asleep again and the most magical moment of my childhood had ended.

It was several years later—I don't remember the exact circumstances—that I discovered the identity of my soldier. After the angry reaction I got that Saturday morning when I was six, I had never spoken of him again, but I thought of him often and remembered every detail of his all too brief visit.

Eventually the family secret was revealed to me—I had had another brother, Alan, who had died when I was just a few months old.

It was less than ten years since the end of the Second World War, and in Great Britain young men were called up at the age of eighteen for National Service—a period of two years in the military. Alan became a Sapper with the Royal Engineers. He was nineteen years old when I was born, and was home on leave three weeks later. He saw me and held me, and I'm told he was very tender and loving to his baby sister.

Alan's unit was stationed in Germany. He and his fellow Sappers were engaged in a bridge building exercise when the accident happened. Alan was drowned in the river, pinned underwater by a fallen girder.

•••

Life in my family never got any easier. In death Alan became Dad's favourite and best friend, but in reality Dad had been every bit as mean to Alan as to the rest of us. Once I knew the secret, Dad would tell me often that he wished I had died instead of Alan. It hurt, but I had something precious to comfort me, something Alan gave me that nobody could take away—the gift of faith.

Ever since those few treasured moments when I was six years

old, I have never doubted that there is a life beyond this life. I didn't know at first who my soldier was, but I knew in my heart that he came from another place and that although he was not a part of my little world, he was real, and he loved me.

I have never seen him again, but I have felt his presence, gentle and strong, many times over the past fifty years.

On several occasions psychics have told me that a young man in uniform is with me, standing just behind my right shoulder. He has always been with me, they say, as my guardian and guide.

Inevitably, with my experience of childhood, I had many difficulties in my adult life. I battled depression, low self-esteem, and the consequences of making bad relationship choices.

I have buckled sometimes, but never broken. I worked hard, had faith and persistence, and I survived—because I saw Alan. He gave me strength and brought me through.

Now, in middle age, I have a happy life. I found a wonderful husband and left England for a new life in the USA. Alan has been with me all along. He was there on my wedding day and I felt his joy alongside my own.

I shall see Alan again one day, of course. It will be good to thank him for being with me all this time, and to tell him how much I have always loved him.

~Grace Rostoker

Until She Was Ready

Peace — that was the other name for home.
~Kathleen Norris

My grandmother passed away while my family was in transition. I received the news while trapped behind a fortress of boxes as I prepared to move from my college apartment in Pennsylvania to my new home in Virginia. Meanwhile, my parents' house in Connecticut had been on the market for months; my father already spent his weekdays living in a hotel near his new job in Maryland. Two offers on the house had fallen through, and my mother stayed in Connecticut to keep up the property and to visit my grandmother in the special care wing of the assisted living facility. My grandmother had been suffering from dementia for years now. The doctors had only recently discovered the cancer.

We worried about my grandmother during those last months. My grandparents had bought the house in Connecticut when it was new. My mother had grown up in that house, as had I. Our family had special ties to it, and my mother was worried that my grandmother wouldn't understand. During our visits with her, we tried to explain about the move. Some visits were better than others. Sometimes my grandmother tottered on the edge of lucidity; most of the time, she just babbled. As soon as the house in Connecticut sold, we planned to move my grandmother to a facility in Maryland to be near us. But the doctors said her time was near, and my mother and I worried that moving her in such a state would leave her confused and troubled at her time of death.

"The house is holding out," my mother said each time a contract on the house fell through. "It's waiting for your grandmother to be at peace." But the house in Connecticut didn't sell, even weeks after my grandmother's death. My mother said the house felt "heavy," like it would never sell. There always seemed to be something getting in the way of a sale.

We chalked it up to bad luck—that is, until my dream.

A few weeks after the funeral, while sleeping in my new apartment in Virginia, I had the most vivid, lucid dream I've ever experienced. A spotlight shone down from Heaven, and my grandmother appeared. She was elderly, but she was in the prime of her old age: she could walk and talk again, and her long, silvery hair flowed to her shoulders. We walked together, she and I. At first I was so enamored to be with her again that I didn't question the strangeness of the dream. Everything was real: her voice, her eyes, even her scent. I didn't pay attention to where we were walking, and before I knew it we had entered my parents' house in Connecticut—the house in which I'd grown up, the house in which my grandmother had raised her family, the house that wouldn't sell.

The house was dark, and my grandmother wondered where everyone was. I explained to her about my new apartment in Virginia, about my father's job in Maryland. It was probably Saturday, I told her, and my mother had probably gone to Maryland to spend the weekend with my dad.

"I'd better call her, then," Grandmother said. She walked into my parents' bedroom and reached for the phone.

"No," I warned. "If you call her, you'll only scare her. She won't understand."

"But I need to know where she is."

I didn't know how to explain it all to her. Although I could control my actions, I had only limited control of my ability to speak. So instead of trying to explain it all, I gently took the phone from her, hung it up, and began brushing her hair. This calmed her, and I walked her to the bed, tucked her in, and waited until she fell asleep. Just before I woke, I had two thoughts: I was glad she hadn't called my mother, and it surely must have been a dream, for my parents' bed and phone were located on the opposite side of the room from where they had been all the years of my childhood.

A week later, my mother called. She was upset, and her voice trembled. While she was at the hotel in Maryland over the weekend, she said, she'd had a dream. In it, her mother had called her on the hotel phone. She sounded far away and confused, saying, "I can't find you. I need to know where you are." My mother awoke terrified and distressed.

It was then that I revealed my dream. My mother listened as I told her every detail. She asked me to repeat it over and over. What convinced her it was absolutely real was the bed and phone being on the other side of the room. She and my father had moved them after the funeral to better stage the house, she said—a fact I couldn't have known.

We stayed on the phone for hours talking. Our collective dreams had sent us a message. It was just as my mother feared: my grandmother's spirit had been drawn to the house in which she spent the best years of her life. And when she found it empty of loved ones, she became lost. My mother and I agreed: one of us would have to try to make my grandmother understand.

One night while alone in the Connecticut house, my mother felt the same heavy presence that seemed always to lurk in the house. She was sure my grandmother's spirit was present. She sat down on the bed and opened her heart. She thanked my grandmother for all she had done for her family and her granddaughters. She explained in detail the move to Maryland. She told my grandmother that we would always love her. My mother fell asleep with this thought, and when she awoke in the morning, the house felt airy and light. My grandmother's presence was gone; her spirit was at peace.

A week later, I dreamt of my grandmother. She was smiling, her eyes twinkling the way they did in her prime. I knew that wherever she was, she was happy. She told me she would look in on us from time to time, and then she disappeared into a ray of sunshine. When I called the next morning to tell my mother the good news, she had some good news of her own—the house had sold to a family that reminded her of our own family twenty years earlier. There were two children eager to take over the tree house that we'd built in the backyard and eager to play in the game room in the basement, and a grandmother who already lived down the street eager to visit her growing family.

It was as if the house had been waiting for the right moment, waiting for a family that would love it the way we had, waiting until my grandmother was ready. And remembering her smiling face and those twinkling eyes, I knew that she was.

~Val Muller

Last Kiss

Love is something eternal; the aspect may change, but not the essence.
~Vincent van Gogh

The big red numbers on the clock lit the room—6:13 a.m. It was way too early to call Angela. I rolled out of bed, shuffled to the bathroom and turned on the shower. As I stood waiting for the water to warm up, I wondered if I should write down my dream. Would I remember it by the time I talked with her? Something told me I wouldn't forget. As I drove to work, I replayed every detail. It was so real. It had to be real.

But why would Charlie come to see me?

It had been six years since he passed away.

It was the first time anyone I truly cared about had died. I was twenty-four. Charlie was just twenty-six. His death shocked all our friends, but it sent Angela reeling. Charlie and Angie had been in love since they were fifteen. I don't know if any of us fully got over the loss of Charlie. I am not sure if Angela ever will.

When I got to work, I sent Angie an e-mail asking her to call me as soon as she was free. I let out a little laugh when my phone immediately rang.

"Ange?"

"Yea, what's going on?" she asked.

"I had a dream last night."

"Was it about Charlie?"

"Yes!" I said, filled with excitement. I knew it! It was too real. "Did you dream about Charlie last night?"

"No," she said.

"Oh."

"Tell me about it," she said slowly.

I told her: "I was at a water park. Everywhere I went I ran into someone I knew, yet I found myself looking for someone. I felt like there was someone else I should be seeing. But I didn't know who. Just then through the crowd of swim trunks and bathing suits, I saw a guy coming towards me in a white business suit. It was Charlie.

"I ran up to him screaming, 'Charlie! Oh my God! We have to find Angie.'

"He stood looking at me. I grabbed him by the arm and tried to run off with him. But he didn't move. He was with some short man wearing all black.

"The guy in black stopped Charlie and said, 'He can't go with you.'

"'He's going! We need to find Angie,' I said.

"The man stopped him again and said, 'He can't go with you! We have to leave.'

"I looked at Charlie and realized he wasn't talking. Charlie just looked at me. He didn't say a word.

"'He can't talk,' the man said.

"I looked at Charlie again and said, 'We are going to find her.'

"I had Charlie by the arm and searched the park. The man in all black followed behind.

"I found you. I ran up and called your name. I put Charlie right in front of you and stepped back.

"You looked at me and said, 'What?'

"I looked at you confused. You couldn't see him. How could you not see him? But you looked at me and said, 'He's here isn't he?'

"You looked back at Charlie. You couldn't see him, but you could feel him. You reached up and put your arms around him as he leaned in to kiss you. Just as your lips touched, he slowly faded away. I will never forget the way that moment felt. The power of that loving last kiss will forever be with me."

Silence.

"Ange? Are you there?"

"Was his tie light blue?" she asked.

"Yes," I said.

"Did the guy in all black have curly long black hair?"

"Yes! How do you know that?"

"Because two years ago I had a dream about them too," she said.

"Did Charlie talk in your dream?"

"No, the guy in all black wouldn't let him."

I don't know how long we went without saying a word. But finally she said, "Um, there is something else. I don't want to freak you out but..."

"What?"

"In my dream I didn't believe it was Charlie. I didn't believe he was really there. The man in all black kept saying they had to go. Charlie wouldn't say anything. Finally I said to Charlie, 'If you are real, if you are really here, go see Diana.'"

~Diana DeAndrea-Kohn

53

Heaven Scent

Two things make the women unforgettable, their tears and their perfume.
~Sacha Guitry

Mom has been gone more than seven years, but it still feels like she left me just yesterday. The ache in my heart has dulled, but nonetheless is ever-present. I miss her most when I am ill or troubled. Who doesn't long for their mother in times of sickness or distress?

Throughout the first year that followed Mom's death I experienced both grief over losing her and burnout in my career. Bordering on a breakdown, I decided to step down from a management post and accept a secretarial position at the company where I already had nine years tenure.

Taking this step meant surrendering a significant amount of salary and several perks. With all of that at stake one of the things that bothered me most was whether people would think I was crazy. Would they look down on me as if I had been demoted?

Mom had cheered me on throughout my career and once I made manager, no one was prouder than she was. Not even me. Now all of that was about to change. I wondered if she was aware of what was going on in my life. And if she knew, would she approve?

Getting through those last two weeks of tying up loose ends before I started my new position was exhausting, mostly because I stayed awake every night wondering if I'd made a mistake. I wondered if I'd be happy and satisfied without the responsibility of being in charge and managing a staff.

Maybe I should have just resigned. Maybe I should have just kept going in my old job. The "maybe" factor robbed me of both sleep and sanity. Oh, how I ached to talk with Mom. She always knew the perfect words to sooth my frazzled nerves.

At last came the day when I closed my office door one final time and left the building, knowing that I'd return on Monday as secretary to the vice president, and in charge of no one but myself.

As I muddled through the weekend I continued to fret over how things would turn out. By Sunday night I collapsed into bed bushed from worrying. I'd be starting my new job with bags under my eyes the size of poker chips. I laid my head on the pillow and pictured Mom telling me to take a deep breath and ask God to guide me, and then I drifted off to sleep.

A few hours later I woke up to a very familiar scent in the room, though at first I couldn't place it. I breathed in deeply and realized it was "Colleen," my mother's favorite perfume, which she used to purchase at the local Irish shop. As it wafted through the air, I remembered picking up the bottle from her bureau and spritzing it on while sorting through her things one day. Then I inhaled even deeper, comforted by the little mist of all that was left of her—the delicate scent of "Colleen." And now in the deep dark stillness of the night the scent of my mother wrapped around me as soft and cozy as her favorite angora shawl.

In that moment my worries ceased. I knew for certain that Mom was with me, and even better, that she approved of my career decision. Whatever the consequences of this radical change in my life, I now had the courage to sally forth with my head held high. As I laid my head back on the pillow the scent of "Colleen" slowly departed, leaving me calm and confident.

The next morning I started my new job undaunted by the water cooler whispers of "career suicide" I heard when nobody thought I was paying attention. I took that giant leap forward and I've never looked back. I work hard, am well paid, and enjoy every minute of what I do. At the end of the day I go home feeling appreciated and wake up every morning wanting to get started with the new day. If there's a way to improve my situation, I'm at a loss to know what it is.

I am not favored frequently with the delicate bouquet of "Colleen." Perhaps in the last seven years I've encountered it a half dozen times. Over the years I've noticed that Mom chooses her moments with great care—just as she tended her family with great care.

This past year when my sister was diagnosed with breast cancer, I awoke the night before her surgery and caught a whiff of "Colleen" passing through the room. And with it once again went my fear. I knew it would be difficult, even miserable at times, for my sister. But after that night I had confidence that she would overcome this disease, and she did. Her passage from sickness back to good health was a journey peppered with debilitating side effects and emotional stress, but she navigated through every storm and came out on the other side a stronger person for having survived the challenge. Twice more throughout her treatment the scent of "Colleen" roused me from my sleep. Each time my confidence grew.

Even though I don't need the sweet smell of "Colleen" any longer to assure me that Mom is close at hand in spirit, I still welcome its soothing effect on me. Mom had five children. Why she chose me for this very special gift I'll never know, but I'm awfully glad she did.

Mothers are awesome beings in life as well as in that which comes after. We are tethered to our mothers by invisible bonds as strong as steel, and occasionally if we are so blessed, as soft and sweet as the gentle scent of "Colleen."

~Annmarie B. Tait

54

Whispered Melodies

Music is well said to be the speech of angels.
~Thomas Carlyle

wo constants in my childhood were my grandparents and the sweet melodies of the many music boxes that lulled me to sleep. Both gave me great comfort and happiness. And later, as an adult, one would deliver a very special message from the other.

When I was four I developed a fear of the dark and started having nightmares. In their efforts to ease my anxiety and help with my insomnia, my parents gave me a music box. The music box played soothing tunes that would sweep me off into a dreamland where no darkness existed, and would allow me to sleep without fear.

Throughout my childhood, my parents would put me in the car and we'd make the one-hour journey to my grandparents' house, where we spent every other weekend. I spent my days there exploring the fields, chasing after cousins, baking with my grandmother, and spending time with my grandfather. Every day there was a new adventure.

When nighttime fell and I was bundled off to bed, my grandmother would bring in one of her own music boxes to lull me to sleep. My favorite was the dancing unicorn. Sitting on a mirrored pedestal, the crystal unicorn moved in a circle when wound up. The light from my nightlight would hit it just right, casting a magical twinkle around the room.

As I grew up, my need for the music boxes ended. I finished

high school and moved away. And as I changed, so did the world around me. By the time I started university, my grandmother was in a nursing home and my weekend adventures with them were reduced to a few hours by her bedside with my grandfather.

One day in 2004 I received a call that was expected, but no less heart wrenching. My grandfather had passed away. I didn't grieve. I didn't feel. I went through the motions, but it was as if I refused to accept the end of this chapter in my life.

With my grandfather gone and my grandmother in a nursing home, it fell to my family to pack up the house they had shared for many years. It was then that I found a memory from my childhood—the crystal unicorn upon its mirrored pedestal. I pulled it out of the box it had been packed in and wiped off the dust.

The music box had not been used in years. I probably had been the last person to hear its melody when I was a child still afraid of the dark. My hand rested on the lever that would bring it back to life, but I was unable to wind it. This unicorn was not just a memory of sweet music, but of a time when my grandparents were a large presence in my life. I was afraid that bringing the unicorn back to life now, in a time of mourning and grief, would corrupt that memory. So I took it home and placed it by my bed, but its tune remained silent.

Three years had passed when I received another heart wrenching call. My grandmother had passed away. It wasn't until after I had returned home from the funeral that the impact of losing not only my grandmother, but my grandfather too, finally sank in. I crumbled under the weight of my grief.

I grieved not just the loss of two beloved people in my life but also the connection they represented: the stories of their experiences, their wisdom, unique personalities, and the way they enjoyed life with each other and their family. I would miss it all and, as I had come to realize, I would miss that part of myself. I grieved for the person I had become thanks to their lessons—the person I had forgotten in my rush to start my life.

As I buried my face in my pillow, I caught sight of the unicorn. For so long I feared what I would lose if I allowed the music to touch me again. But in that moment I realized it wasn't that I was afraid of what I would lose, but afraid to remember what I had forgotten.

I wound up that music box and let the unicorn dance for the first time in over a decade. As I watched it circle around, the pale light from my window catching the mirrors, my eyes became heavy and I slipped off to sleep as it played its last few notes. I know I dreamt that night, but the details escape me. What I do remember is a sense of innocence and childlike longing to have just one more day with my grandparents.

When morning came I found myself still facing the unicorn—still and silent. The loss was still fresh. Then without being touched, that unicorn danced, its music playing a message from Heaven. My grandparents were with me in that moment, and they were reminding me that they would always be with me.

I will always have my memories, the wisdom I was taught, and the feelings of comfort and family. It took a message from beyond to remind me. I will always have my grandparents, and the whispered melodies reminded me of what matters most.

That unicorn remains by my bed to this day. When I struggle to find my path, feel lost and alone, or just having a hard time sleeping, I wind it up to let it dance and its music carries me away to a place of inspiration and love. Those melodies whisper of the past, but are a reminder for the future—to love without hesitation, to live life completely, and to never forget.

~Tara Scaife

Kadie

When you are sorrowful look again in your heart, and you shall see that in
truth you are weeping for that which has been your delight.
~Kahlil Gibran

woke up that Tuesday with an inexplicable sense of knowing. I
wanted to ignore the feeling so I went about my day as planned.
But when the song came on the radio, I couldn't pretend. I
knew it would happen that day.

Kadie was my cousin. We had the same heart condition: hyper-
trophic cardiomyopathy. The condition had been in our family for
years. When I was diagnosed at thirteen, Kadie and her sister Liz
helped me through it. They helped me realize it was okay to have this
condition. We could do anything anyone else could — we just had to
do it in a different way. We were part of a club. I knew that as long as
they were there with me, this condition would not define me.

Kadie had been in and out of the hospital for months. She had
received a heart transplant a few years earlier, and for a while it seemed
as if everything would be okay. But as time wore on, she worsened.
The week before she died she went into cardiac arrest while at a spa
with her mother.

That morning when I heard "If I Die Young" play on my radio, I
knew it wasn't a random song — it was a message. There was nothing
to do but wait for the phone call.

That night I went to the weekly workout with my stunt team.
My mother knew I would not be able to answer the phone, so if it

happened while I was there I would get the news via text message. Halfway through the workout I took a break and checked my phone. There were two words in the message bubble: "she's gone." I silently handed my sword to my partner and ran for the door.

The rest of the night was blurry. I kept thinking of Kadie's mother, father and sister. And I kept wishing I could have said goodbye to her. I lived in Los Angeles and she lived in Mississippi. I was going home to visit in a week, and had hoped I would make it in time to see her.

As I got ready for bed, memories of Kadie filled my head. I went over and over what I would have said to her if I had seen her one last time. Nothing seemed to express how much I loved her, and how much I would miss her. When I finally drifted to sleep, I had a dream. I was in a gorgeous bedroom sitting beside Kadie in a bed. She was beautiful, laughing and happy. Her mother was sitting on the other side of the bed. She excused herself for a moment and left the room. When she was gone Kadie turned to me, looked into my eyes and said, "I'm sorry I could not wait for you, I had to go." With that I woke up.

Just as I knew the song on the radio that morning was not just a song, the dream I had of Kadie was not just a dream. She came to see me that night, to let me know everything was okay. As hard as it is to accept and as clichéd as it sounds, I know she is in a better place. Kadie's heart condition made it impossible for her to do certain things in this life, things that she can do now she is in heaven. Now she can run and not be weary, now she can walk and not faint.

~Chelsey Colleen Hankins

56

One Last Visit with Lucille

> *Friends are relatives you make for yourself.*
> ~Eustache Deschamps

New to the Navy base in Groton, Connecticut, my husband and I looked for a church to attend. We came across a small congregation in an older part of town. Something about the place attracted us even though our little family of four almost doubled the entire membership.

Lucille played the piano for our services. She pounded out hymns on the old, somewhat tuned instrument with joy. Partially deaf, she slowed the tempo down by the second or third verse. Our pastor would stomp the beat out with his foot so she'd speed up again. Her hair was a wild mane of gray and her clothes, although clean, always seemed a little rumpled.

Lucille and I struck up a friendship. She was past seventy years old and I had just reached thirty, but we shared a passion for Boston cream donuts. I discovered our mutual love one Sunday after service as we fellowshipped in the basement. We reached for the only Boston cream in the box at the same time. If she'd been closer to my age I would have fought her for it, but as she was my elder, I let her take it.

"I love these things," Lucille told me. "I know they're terrible for me, but I can't help myself."

"I'm trying to lose weight." I patted my stomach. "But when it comes to Boston creams, I have no willpower."

She took a bite of the donut and smiled. "Someone used to bring donuts to church every Sunday." She licked a rogue piece of cream from the corner of her mouth. "But now we're so small, it's only once a month, if we're lucky."

"My daughter Annie and I go to the bakery once a week while her brother is in kindergarten. I get a coffee, she gets a hot chocolate and we split a donut." I looked over the remaining pastries in the box. Only glazed and chocolate frosted remained. I took a glazed one. "She likes to pretend she's drinking coffee and we talk about whatever she wants while we're there."

Soon Annie and I included Lucille in our ritual, bringing a Boston cream donut over to our new friend's house at least once a month. Our family even had her over to our house for dinner, no mean feat because of her limited mobility. She became a grandmother to me. I enjoyed spending time with her, reveling in the peace she had in God even through all her health trials.

One Sunday I arrived at church to find Lucille absent. The pastor announced that she'd made a mistake with her medicine and had fallen into a drug-induced coma. Although in intensive care, her daughter had asked for friends from the church to visit. "Just tell them you're family, because we're all part of God's family anyway."

Devastated, I arranged for a babysitter the following day so I could see Lucille. Her daughter greeted me when I arrived, then left so I could have a moment alone with my friend. Tubes ran from Lucille's nose, mouth and arms into machines that beeped and sighed. I stood by her bed and took her hand. "Hey Lucille, it's me, Kim. You need to get better and come home soon so Annie and I can bring you a donut. She misses you and so do I." I stayed a few minutes longer, praying silently, then headed home.

A few days later my husband got up at four in the morning to head out to sea for three months. Normally I had breakfast with him before he deployed, but this morning I couldn't find the energy to get out of bed. He leaned down to give me a kiss goodbye.

Feeling guilty for breaking our tradition, I followed him to the front door and gave him a big hug. "Sorry I didn't make you breakfast."

He gave me a kiss on the cheek. "It's okay. Go back to bed and get some more sleep before the kids get up."

I took his advice. I very rarely remember my dreams, but I'll never forget the one I had that morning. I dreamt I visited Lucille's hospital room. When I walked in, her bed was empty. I turned and saw her sitting in a chair by a large picture window.

"Lucille!" I exclaimed. "You must be feeling better. You look wonderful." I had never seen her look so beautiful. Her hair was combed and her eyes twinkled with excitement. Then she gave me a joyful smile.

"Annie and I are ready to bring you a donut as soon as you get out of here," I told her. "Are you going home soon?"

The sun rose up behind her, bathing her in a golden light. Her smile got even bigger and she nodded to me.

"I'm so glad. I'll see you soon then."

I woke up and rolled over to check the time, it was just after five in the morning. I lay awake, thinking about my dream and wondering if it meant I should visit Lucille again. The kids woke up a short time later and I started my daily routine of diaper changes and breakfast. When the phone rang at seven I thought my husband might have gotten the chance to call before his boat left. Instead, I heard my pastor on the other end of the line.

"Kim? I didn't wake you, did I?"

"No. What's up?"

"I know you were close to Lucille. I thought you'd like to know, she passed away."

I sank down into a chair. "When?"

"This morning, just after five."

I don't know why Lucille chose to visit me before she died, but I'm so glad she did. I'll never forget how beautiful she looked in my dream—radiant, healthy and so happy to be leaving the hospital and going home.

~Kim Stokely

57

Touch from Heaven

Angels descending, bring from above,
Echoes of mercy, whispers of love.
~Fanny J. Crosby

In the lengthening purple shadows of the Oklahoma summer twilight, we rode our bikes toward home, making our own breeze as we pedaled in the still, hot evening. The day was not over for us yet. My friends and I were old enough to stay out after dark in those long, sun-streaked days. "Big kids" at ten years old, and in the haven of our safe 1960s neighborhood.

When the streetlights came on, the bikes were put away, and we congregated on someone's front porch or in a driveway, the strains of Wolfman Jack's WLS radio show all the way from Chicago playing through a tinny transistor radio that someone had brought outside.

At last, one by one, we reluctantly headed inside when our parents called. The bathtub awaited. I was suddenly eager by then to wash off the accumulation of the dust and grime of the sticky Oklahoma day, and get into bed, the attic fan humming as I fell asleep.

Sometime during the night, for as long as I can remember, I would sleepily stir at the touch of a hand on my forehead, then my cheek. Sometimes, after that touch, a light kiss would follow on the top of my head, and a whispered "Mommy loves you."

Like the faraway sound of a train whistle in the night, I came to expect it through the years. So much so, that if that soft caress came much later than usual, I'd feel a restlessness steal over me as if something were missing.

"Why do you come check on me at night?" I asked her, feeling I was certainly getting too old for such a ritual as a teenager.

Mom just smiled. "Because I love you. I just want to make sure you're all right."

"I'm not a baby, you know."

"You may think that," she replied, not looking at me, "but you'll always be my baby."

After that conversation, I felt some satisfaction in the curtailing of those nightly checks. But not as much as I thought I would. As time progressed and I moved midway into my teenage years, rebellion set in. Mom and I were constantly at odds. Still, it seemed that no matter how bitter our arguments were, she had the uncanny ability to know how my conflicted heart needed her while I struggled for my own place in the world.

Sometimes, I'd come awake slowly as the door closed softly behind her, seconds after her fingertips grazed my skin, leaving the remnant of the touch behind like a memory I couldn't quite grasp.

But somehow, it had changed, that touch. The loving care, the gentleness of a mother's love, those things always remained; but in those tension-fraught years, those infrequent caresses seemed stolen and colored with a longing on her part that I didn't understand. Finally, I was on my own and the memory faded. I couldn't remember the last time Mom had come into my room in the night to "make sure I was all right."

The years to adulthood passed for me, and Mom was struck with Alzheimer's. After a two-year battle, she passed away just three weeks after Dad. For the first time in my life, I was completely adrift—an orphan at the age of fifty.

Silly to think that way. I was a grown woman, with two college-aged children of my own. But for the first month after Mom died, I couldn't remember her without dissolving into tears and thinking of the hole in my heart that would never mend. How I wished I had those turbulent teenage years back to do over!

Sleep was generally tough to come by during those days. When

I went to bed at night, I could count on either lying awake for hours, or falling asleep right away only to awaken in the wee hours and stare at the ceiling until morning.

But something happened one magical night that made a huge difference for me. Sleep came to me, deep and dreamless, with no restlessness. Sometime in the early hours of morning, I felt that old, forgotten memory of childhood begin to awaken me, like a magic spell at the appointed hour. The sweet fragrance of gardenias surrounded me, and the familiar touch that I would never forget, from this life to the next, fell upon my cheek.

In only a moment, I awoke fully. "Mama?" My voice was hushed in the deep velvet of the summer night. There was no answer but the lingering perfume of the gardenias that Mama always wore, and the warmth of my skin where her palm had cradled my cheek only moments before.

I told no one about what had happened. I felt the conviction of its reality too strongly to risk listening to any doubters.

A few months later, as I slept, I heard Mama call my name so clearly that I answered her as I came awake in the depths of night. The tone, the inflection, and the voice itself were all so real that I almost got up to look for her. Then, I remembered. She would not be there.

Again, several weeks later, I awoke one night to the feel of her careworn palm just leaving my forehead. This time, there were no gardenias, and I felt somehow that this would be the last time Mama would come to check on me. Sadness overcame me, until I remembered her words of so long ago.

"I just want to make sure you're all right."

Understanding came, and with it, the sorrow vanished. There was no need for Mama to come again. Peace came over me as I realized Mama didn't need to check on me and make sure I was all right. She was letting me know I was.

~Cheryl Moss Pierson

Purple Roses

The past is behind us, love is in front and all around us.
~Terri Guillemets

I have been fortunate to have not lost too many people to death in my thirty-three years. However, two people I was close to have passed away. And I know for a fact they each are watching over me, as they have sent me very specific signs.

My maternal grandmother Ida Weiss passed away at the age of fifty-seven from pancreatic cancer when I was two years old. I do not have any conscious memories of her, yet I feel now, and always have felt, an extremely strong connection to her. My grandfather had bought her a necklace when she was ill—a diamond studded chy, the Jewish symbol for "life." When she died, it was passed down to my mother.

When I was twenty-six, I was struggling with my health. My mother gave me the diamond chy necklace to wear every day, hoping it would somehow help me heal. And I did wear it every day for a long time. Then shortly before my wedding, in the fall of 2004, I went to a woman who provided Reiki and acupressure treatments to people who are ill. She told me, prior to the session, that she was a "little bit psychic" and asked me if I wanted her to tell me if she picked up on anything. I agreed.

As she worked near my neck and head, while I had my grandmother's chy on, she asked if my grandmother was still alive. I did not say yes or no, but "Why do you ask?" She said, "There is a middle-aged woman standing right by your head who claims to be your grandmother." I was shocked.

As interesting, scary, confusing and wonderful as that was, she then asked if my father was still alive. Again, I did not say yes or no, just asked why. She said an older man, with gray hair and a beard, was there and calling me his daughter. She also said he was telling her there would be purple roses on my wedding cake. I laughed at that, because we had made it clear to the caterer and the florist that we did not want flowers on our wedding cake. So I blew that off. But on our wedding day, my new husband and I walked into the reception ballroom to check everything before the guests came in. The first thing that caught my eye, and made my heart leap and eyes water, were the real purple roses on every layer of our wedding cake.

I was not angry. I was a bit confused. The florist told me, "I usually give my brides their 'throw bouquet' for free. But since you aren't doing that, I decided to give you free purple roses on your cake, as my gift to you." It was then I knew those flowers were from Jim, my late father-in-law — his way of letting us know he was still with us, most especially that day.

As far as the "old man insisting I was his daughter" during the Reiki session, I absolutely believe it was Jim. The man she described matched how Jim had looked. And when I first met my husband, Jim was sick with cancer. I was blessed to get to know him and spend over a year with him before his passing. At the end of his life, when he was still speaking a bit, he said to me, "You have been a wonderful daughter." I thought he was confused, that he truly thought I was his daughter. But when I brought it up with his wife, she said, "No, he was not confused. He knows you will end up with his son, and therefore he considered you to be his daughter."

I am not sure what I believe happens after death. As a healthcare professional, part of me wonders if we die and that is the end of it. But part of me also believes in reincarnation — that each soul comes back as many times as it takes to learn the lessons it needs to learn before going to "heaven," if there is a type of heaven. However after these experiences, I believe, no matter what happens when we die, the people we loved the most, who miss us and think of us, do stay with us. They watch over us, sometimes going out of their way to make sure we know they are still there with us.

Perhaps much of this was coincidence, or lucky guesses, or some other logical conclusion. It does not matter. What matters is that I believe with all my heart that my late grandmother and late father-in-law were with me at those times. I wish everyone "purple roses" from departed loved ones, for knowing they are still with us is the greatest gift in the world.

~Tracey Miller Offutt

Editor's note: Unfortunately, Tracey passed away unexpectedly before the publication of this book. Her husband Jason reports: "Whenever I look at pictures of her on the computer, I get a cold, tingling sensation across my shoulders, the same sensation I would get when she used to hug me from behind, as I sat in the same computer chair."

Messages from Heaven

Saying Goodbye

59

One Last Visit Before the Light

Life is eternal and love is immortal;
And death is only a horizon,
And a horizon is nothing save the limit of our sight.
~Rossiter W. Raymond

was driving home from work and I felt troubled. I was thinking that we should have gone to Phoenix on Memorial Day, but I had just started a new job so we hadn't gone. My mother-in-law had been diagnosed with breast cancer shortly after our wedding and given six months to live. But with good doctors and care in Phoenix, she was still alive three years later. Natalie, at sixty-three, was a tiny four-foot-something, gentle, loving woman. Her favorite poem to quote ended with, "Love in your heart wasn't put there to stay. Love isn't love 'till you give it away." She loved her three grandchildren with every fiber of her being. She was thrilled when I had Nicholas; she just couldn't get enough of him.

My in-laws made a habit of summering in San Diego to escape the Arizona heat and to be near us, except this summer. Natalie instead asked us to bring Nicky to Phoenix over Memorial Day weekend. She didn't tell us how sick she was, not wanting us to worry. But if we had known, we would have gone.

It was 4:45 p.m. I had stopped briefly at home and was about to go to the sitter's house to get Nicky when the phone rang. It was my sister-in-law.

"Lisa, I'm glad I caught you," Helaine said in a voice choked with grief. "Mom just passed away at 4:30. Marcia and I were with her at the hospital. Can you guys come?"

"Sure," I reassured her. "I'll call the airline and get the baby. We'll be there as soon as we can."

Minutes later, I arrived at the babysitter's house. Dee-dee, a Navy wife, ran a home day care to keep busy while her husband was away at sea. It was a perfect place for Nicky. Dee-dee was sensitive and caring, treating her day care kids as her own. But today, Dee-dee was pale and visibly shaken when she answered the door.

"What's wrong, Dee?" I asked as I stepped inside. I felt an immediate tingling of panic for my son.

"It's Nicky. He did something strange a few minutes ago," Dee-dee replied nervously. "He was sitting out back in the sandbox, playing with his favorite truck. All of a sudden, he dropped it and looked up—at nothing, just up at the air, the sky, for a minute. And he said, 'Bye-bye, Grandma. Bye-bye, Grandma. Bye-bye,' three times, just like that.

"Then, I got the eeriest feeling," she said, rubbing her upper arms with her hands. "I felt like I was being watched by something. I ran out there and picked him up and brought him inside."

I felt a flush of heat rush over my body and face.

Dee-dee continued, "I knew you were probably on your way because I looked at the clock there in the kitchen and it was 4:30. But why he was saying 'Grandma', I don't know."

"Oh, Lord," I said, rushing over and grabbing Nicky off the floor. "My mother-in-law just passed away in Phoenix. I just got the call before I drove here."

Dee-dee put her hand on the wall to steady herself. She was a devout Baptist and regular churchgoer. "Praise Jesus, Amen!" Dee-dee shouted. "Praise the Lord, Jesus! It was her spirit!"

It was obvious early on that my son was gifted. I know most parents think their kids are gifted, but Nicky always hit his milestones before he normally should. By eighteen months old, he was fully conversational. You could ask him questions and get complete, coherent answers.

I sat the tiny boy on the sofa in the living room. Kneeling beside him, I asked Nicky why he said goodbye to his grandmother. He matter-of-factly explained that she had come to see him because she was going away. He said that she told him she loved him very much and wanted to see him.

I asked him where Grandma was. He pointed, indicating the backyard. "She was outside, over there, floating in the air."

Then I asked if Grandma did anything. Nick said, "Grandma talked, but not out loud. She talked in that little voice inside my head. She said, 'I love you,' and she wanted to kiss me, but she couldn't."

"Why?" I asked.

"Because, she had blood on her mouth," he said. "And then she went up to the clouds."

Dee-dee blanched. I tried to keep a calm exterior, not showing the alarm I felt. I didn't want Nick to cry; I wanted answers.

"And what did Grandma look like?" I queried further.

Nick explained in his "big man" voice, "She was wearing a dress with little flowers all over it and she had wires on her arms."

Dee-dee and I were dumbfounded. Natalie so much wanted to see him before she passed over that she came to him before going to the Light. I believe that distance and time are immaterial for the spirit once it leaves the body. She wanted to see her grandson and let him know of her love.

My husband and I got to Phoenix later that night. We were at my father-in-law's home with my husband's sisters. I recounted the story about Nicky and Natalie. A stunned silence fell over the family. Helaine said that at the time of death, her mom was wearing a hospital gown with tiny blue flowers on it and she had intravenous tubes in her arms. A therapist took her respirator out, tearing her lip slightly in the process. "She had a little trickle of blood on the corner of her mouth," Helaine said, stunned. "But how…"

My father-in-law realized how Nick knew. Nine years earlier,

Bob had a massive cardiac arrest and near-death experience. He spent years reading about and researching these experiences, and taught us all about the spirit's ability to travel and the Light of God that one crosses into at the time of death. Bob made us firmly believe, "Death is the gate of life. It's not an end. The soul goes on." And Natalie showed us that.

~Lisa Wojcik

60

A Kiss Goodbye

Pay attention to your dreams—
God's angels often speak directly to our hearts when we are asleep.
~Eileen Elias Freeman, The Angels' Little Instruction Book

The window in my bedroom slowly opened; I could see the sheer curtains blow ever so gently. I was frozen with fear as a dark figure climbed into the room. He appeared to be wearing a trench coat and fedora hat. I could not make out the face or complexion. He just appeared to be this stalking black shadow of the night, with no identifying features.

The shadow of a man began to walk to my bedside. I was unable to move or speak. When he stopped at my bed something gave me the courage to scream. Awakened by my own screams and shaken, I sat straight up, trying to make sense of the dream. This recurring dream would awaken me many nights over the next three years.

I happened to share my dream with a friend, who suggested that I go to our church and speak with our priest. The priest asked if I had lost someone without having a chance to say goodbye. He suggested that the dream indicated my subconscious needed to say goodbye to a love one and that the next time I had the dream I should allow myself to finish the dream so as to have closure. My dad had passed on when I was fifteen. Maybe I needed to say goodbye to him.

In a deep slumber one night, the dream began to play out. My visitor opened the window, the curtains gently danced in and out from the window. I could actually feel a soft breeze coming into the room.

The mysterious figure began to climb through the window. I could clearly see the silhouette of the trench coat and fedora. Remembering the priest's words, I fought with my fears of the unknown and forced myself to allow him to come close without screaming. He stood at my bedside, standing over me as if admiring me. I tried to make out any features. But it was impossible; the room was too dark. What happened next was so unexpected. He slowly bent over me and tenderly kissed my forehead. Then he turned around and went back out the window. All those years and the strange figure who invaded my nights just wanted to kiss me goodnight!

The next morning, with the memory of the dream still vivid, I realized it was my daddy saying goodbye to me. My parents were separated when Dad took his own life. We never had a chance to say our goodbyes. It was a harsh reality for a fifteen-year-old girl.

I never had the dream again. I had my closure, my final kiss goodbye.

~Lonnie Frock

My Soul Friend

The language of friendship is not words but meanings.
~Henry David Thoreau

Communication between best friends does not always consist of spoken words. I believe that spiritual connections and the language of faith and love between family, friends or lovers transcend physical barriers. I know for a fact that God presents gifts in ways we cannot completely, and sometimes not even remotely, comprehend.

My friend Rose and I had a way of communicating with a few syllables, fractured phrases, grunts, or uh-huhs. We could make inferences and connections with a minimum of conversation, and it drove our kids crazy. We had a connection that stretched through time and place, across miles and over the years.

I visited Rose in the hospital every day for a week as her strength and life were waning. She was heavily sedated and struggling to hold on. One night I sat on the windowsill ledge in her room, thinking, praying, wondering, and reminiscing.

Our twenty-five-year friendship became one-sided when Rose developed terminal cancer. When she was heavily medicated and hallucinating, I would sit in her kitchen and color in Christmas coloring books with her the way we used to with our little girls two decades before. When she had a good day, I took her places she had to go and went with her to places she wanted to go. We spent her last days shopping and eating out. We sat in the car in "our" parking spot at the ice cream stand as we did when we were young mothers struggling to carve time out of our busy days just for us.

Over the course of our friendship, we parented each other's children, leaned on each other in our times of trouble, and encouraged one another through unhappy first marriages. We survived junk cars that broke down, and many weeks we struggled to make ends meet. We attended PTA meetings, home decorating parties, and wished each other a lifetime of happiness at one another's second marriages.

Now, we had just one more struggle, one that could not be won. It is never easy to fight a losing battle. I looked at her lying so helplessly in her hospital bed. I prayed that her transition from this life could be easier. I hoped for a beautiful afterlife.

Her doctor entered the room and asked for a conference. "She's in her last hours, but nobody knows for sure. It could be today or tomorrow."

I cried as I watched my friend's body fade. Her husband, daughter, sister and I said our farewells. At 11:00 p.m. I told her family I would be back in the morning. I walked over to the side of Rose's bed and told her how much her friendship had meant. Then, instead of leaving the room, I felt compelled to return to the window ledge and sit back down. The television was on for background noise; all of us were seated around the room, lost in our own thoughts.

Then, in a strong, clear and younger voice, I heard Rose call my name as she had many years before. I couldn't believe my ears. I looked over at her bed, thrilled, and wondered how she had gotten the strength to speak. I wondered why everyone in the room wasn't on their feet rejoicing. Actually, my friend was comatose.

I sat and tried to make sense of what had happened. I was completely lucid, not hallucinating. I wondered if someone in the hall had called to someone with my name, but it was after visiting hours, and no one was around. I looked from one to the other of her family members, but no one had seemed to hear what I heard. I didn't mention it. I watched as my friend's breathing became shallow. Then in amazement I witnessed the most incredible sight. I saw a gauzy, white apparition rise from Rose's body and float to the ceiling. I watched it hover in a corner, and then it slowly faded away. I opened the curtain and rationalized that I must have seen a reflection of car lights, but behind me there was a brick, windowless building.

A few minutes later my best friend officially passed from this world. I know her soul headed heavenward, because I watched her spirit leave her body.

A year later my adult son had a serious motorcycle accident. I rushed to the hospital. He wept in the emergency room. "Mom, Rose came to me as I lay on the road waiting for the ambulance. I could see her. She held my head. She was with me, Mom, and she told me I would be okay."

And he was okay. He recovered. I believe my son's "other mother" came to comfort him. I also believe that when people are connected spiritually, they don't need a rational explanation for the unexplainable.

~Linda O'Connell

It Is Well

Spiritual force is greater than material force — thoughts rule the world.
~Ralph Waldo Emerson

Paul Carmine and I met when I first started with IBM. We worked together, off and on, for more than twenty-five years. He was my colleague, my boss, my mentor, and my friend.

Paul was a manager with the company, and, in 2001, he recruited me into his department. We tackled challenging assignments side by side. When a project was completed, Paul was quick to laud me for a job well done.

Paul nurtured my career in a way that no other manager had. He encouraged, even badgered, me to pursue the position of Senior Technical Staff Member (STSM), a distinguished advancement in IBM. "Finish all the work I give you, then stay up nights to pull that STSM certification packet together," he kidded.

For six months, I pored over the STSM submission. Behind the scenes, Paul sang my praises to company executives, and likely called in some favors, in order to garner the sponsors I needed. When I earned the STSM appointment, Paul took me out for a celebratory lunch.

Paul and I shared many lunches through the years. Over good food, we brainstormed about problems at work and did a bit of griping. We told jokes and laughed about our children's antics.

IBM awarded us both with a trip to Palm Springs. Paul brought his oldest son along to join in the fun. During the day, there were cable car rides up Mount San Jacinto and bicycle treks. At night, we had dinner together. Paul's son was kind, just like his father. He would regale us with tales of his filmmaking studies. As he spoke, I noticed Paul smiling with pride.

Paul had a knack for balancing work and family. He was equally a diligent manager and a loving husband and father. I, on the other hand, had trouble striking a balance and was known to put in seventy-hour weeks. Paul would chide me for my work obsession. "You need to cut back on your overtime," he told me. "Enjoy life!"

"I'll try," I assured him.

About a year ago, Paul telephoned me. His voice sounded somber, and I knew something was wrong. "I have a suspicious growth on my thyroid," he said. "My doctor ordered a biopsy."

"I'm sure everything will be fine," I said. I hung up the phone and said a silent prayer that the test would be negative.

Paul and I met for a meal several days later. His voice was raspy from the procedure, but I could still detect his relief. "It's benign," he said. This would be another celebratory lunch.

Just two weeks passed when Paul contacted me to say he hadn't felt well since the biopsy. He had been suffering pains in his abdomen. The doctors performed a full battery of tests. "I've been diagnosed with late-stage pancreatic cancer," he said quietly. "I'm going to retire immediately and spend time with my family."

I sat stunned. "I'll keep you in my prayers," I said.

Soon after, Paul's oldest son e-mailed to let me know that his dad had been hospitalized.

"I want to go see him in the hospital," I told my wife.

But Paul died before I could visit. I hugged my wife and said, "I never got the chance to say goodbye."

The morning of Paul's funeral, my wife was preparing breakfast. She loves to sing as she does her chores. She buttered bread and sang:

When peace, like a river, attendeth my way,
When sorrows like sea billows roll;

Whatever my lot, Thou has taught me to say,
It is well, it is well, with my soul.

"That is a beautiful hymn," I told her. "I've never heard it before."

"I haven't sung it in years," she said. "It just popped into my head."

That evening, Paul's church was overflowing with mourners. During his eulogy, the pastor told us how bravely Paul had faced death, "Paul knew that he would see Christ in heaven."

The pastor said that in Paul's last days, he was in and out of consciousness. One afternoon, he opened his eyes and muttered, "It is well." The pastor patted his hand, "Yes, Paul, all is well." Paul shook his head no.

"I finally deciphered what Paul wanted," said the pastor. "Would you please all stand and sing Paul's chosen hymn?"

The lyrics scrolled on the screen behind the altar: "When peace, like a river, attendeth my soul..."

I looked at my wife in amazement. It was the same hymn she had sung that morning.

She smiled and whispered, "Paul found a way to say goodbye to you."

~John E. Miller as told to Marie-Therese Miller

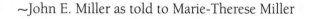

The Dark Lady

The past is never dead, it is not even past.
~William Faulkner

Yes, agreed the seller of our dream home in Michigan, she would sell us some of the furnishings if we would allow her to leave behind two generations worth of stuff stored in the basement. My husband Dick and I were stretching our budget to the limit to acquire the spacious Tudor-style house and happy to accommodate her.

The young woman selling it had inherited the house from her father and stepmother, and she had grown up there. Her mother had died years before; her father remarried and his new wife had consigned a large number of items to the basement. Our seller had added more in recent years. Now she, her husband and children were moving to the West Coast and they didn't want to take much with them.

When we moved in, thrilled to be in a house after years of apartment living, we ignored the full basement. We had plenty of time to sort all that in the future. That winter I made space in the main basement room so our sons, then two and four, could play indoors. I sold large items ranging from a Ping-Pong table to a printing press. I would explore the boxes heaped in every corner at my leisure.

One snowy morning, when I was tackling one of the cartons in the main room, my toddler Mike pointed to the open door of the storeroom and said, "Lady."

I looked up and thought I saw something move beyond the

storeroom door. Then I decided it was a shadow. Later I noticed that the boys avoided playing at that end of the basement. Imagination is catching, I thought.

It was more than a week later, on a cold February day when I was doing laundry in the basement and the boys were playing with their Matchbox cars on a rug that Dave, my four-year-old, suddenly called out, "Look!" and pointed to the storeroom.

Startled, I looked past him into the cluttered storeroom and there, indeed, seemed to be a dark woman bending over a large box! Tall, slim, short black hair curling against her cheek, wearing a white dress too flimsy for winter! My heart thumped and I stepped close to the boys, ready to grab them and run upstairs if we had a prowler. As I moved, the figure disappeared.

Frightened now, I pushed the boys ahead of me up the basement stairs quickly and locked the door behind us. No one followed and there was no sound from the basement. Dick was out of town. This was before 911 service, so I dialed the phone operator, told her we might have a prowler, and shortly after that a policeman arrived. He checked out the basement and the whole house. He found nothing and we concluded, laughingly, that our imaginations had played tricks.

Spring came and I decided to thoroughly clean out all the unwanted stuff left behind by the former owners of the house. I started with the large carton over which I had "imagined" seeing a dark lady hovering on that wintry day. The box was filled with old dresses. At the bottom of the carton, however, I found a leather-bound photo album. Opening it at random I found myself looking at—you guessed it!—a photograph of our dark lady of the basement! Tall, slim, the same short black hair, the white dress, she was hand in hand with a little girl in the picture.

I promptly mailed the album to the woman from whom we had bought the house, although not mentioning in my accompanying note any word about our vision.

Back came a letter of profuse thanks. "How wonderful that you found Mom's album," she wrote. "I am so glad to have it, especially the photo of me with Mom. She usually took the family pictures and somehow this was the only one of us together when I was a child, just before she died."

We never again saw "the dark lady" and my boys played freely all over the basement. I cannot swear to it but I believe the dark lady had accomplished her mission.

~Marcia E. Brown

The Last Gift

A friend is a hand that is always holding yours, no matter how close or far apart you may be. A friend is someone who is always there and will always, always care. A friend is a feeling of forever in the heart.
~Author Unknown

The elementary school library was crawling with little ones, grabbing books and crowding around the table where we worked. We were the adult volunteers, moms mostly, helping at the book fair. I sat next to a pretty mom with blond hair, a foreign accent, and an infectious smile. Her name was Lone, she said, from Denmark. I had to ask her several times how to say her name because here in Georgia, we don't come across too many Danish folks. A year later, Lone and her family moved a few houses down from me, and despite the difference in cultures, we became fast friends. It was hard not to be friends with Lone; she was funny, and smart, and she'd do just about anything for you.

She was the person I could call, day or night, when I was in a bind. It didn't matter what I needed: butter or milk for a recipe, tin foil for a school project, hair-braiding for my daughter, or sewing up a Halloween costume. Lone was one talented and generous friend, always happy to help. But it was her plant assistance that I especially relied upon.

You would think, coming from Denmark, that Lone's knowledge of plants would be limited to cold-weather varieties. But she knew everything about plants, what would thrive, what would wither, how and when to transplant, even Latin names! It was awesome to behold, to see Lone's yard and all her overflowing pots. She single-handedly turned my black thumb into a green thumb. We often went on plant-shopping expeditions, looking for the best deals. "Put that back and get this," she'd say. And I would. She had a knack for finding jewels among the dirt.

It was plants that brought her to my house one early October afternoon. I had a bed full of salvia and called to see if she'd like some of the plants I'd thinned out. She was in a hurry, but dashed down, and as usual, we started talking. We laughed, we talked some more, just an ordinary afternoon.

But a few weeks later, when her husband showed up at our door, asking to speak with my husband and me, I knew that the situation was anything but ordinary. That's when I found out that Lone was desperately ill.

She hadn't been feeling very well, said her husband. Though she'd never mentioned a word to me, not that afternoon or ever. Finally, she'd been in so much pain that she'd gone to the hospital. She was diagnosed with pancreatic cancer and there was little the doctors could do. She would try whatever treatment was available, he said, but the situation looked grim. For the present, she didn't want to see anyone. She had asked her husband to let me know.

"Can I call?" I asked, in tears.

"Not now," he said. She'd call when she felt better. November came and went. I brought food and cards, but Lone never felt well enough to see me. She never called. And a week before Christmas, on a bitterly cold night, she died. One of her daughters called and asked me to come down. There, at last, I saw my friend of fifteen years. But of course, she'd already gone.

It was a shock to lose Lone. And worse, I never had a chance to say goodbye, to tell her what a wonderful friend she'd been to me, to thank her for her kindness and generosity, to let her know how honored I'd been to call her friend. I knew she'd read my cards, where I'd tried to express those feelings, but I'm not very good at that sort of thing. I ached with the pang of words gone unsaid.

The family took her body back to Denmark for burial; a small memorial service was held for her here. The weeks passed, and like the snow we had here in Georgia, my acute grief began to melt, too.

And then the weather warmed and the spring rains fell and I looked out to the yard where green grass poked through the dead leaves and suddenly I missed Lone so! We used to check with each other on the progress of our plants in the spring, as if our hostas were engaged in some kind of growth competition. But this year, I could barely bring myself to go outside. Spring had returned in all its glory but it seemed bleak without Lone by my side.

Then one morning, I awoke close to tears. I immediately went downstairs to tell my husband about a dream. Though even then, I knew what I'd experienced had been more than a dream.

I'd seen Lone at a crowded train station, her figure shadowy and distant. I couldn't believe my good fortune! There she was, if I could just catch up to her. But as I looked around, I began to realize that perhaps I was the only one who could see my friend. People rushed about around her, oblivious to her, all running to make their train. I knew she'd died, yes, I remembered that as I watched her thread through men and women. But still, here was my opportunity and I was determined to speak to her. I saw her duck into a shop and browse through overcoats, and it occurred to me that Lone was being her practical self. It's so very cold in Denmark! I crossed over to the other side of the tracks and walked into the shop.

"Lone!" I cried.

She turned and looked at me, with that infectious smile I knew so well. I ran to her and wrapped my arms around her.

"I love you so much!" I blurted, and I started to cry.

Now, I'm not a terribly demonstrative person. Neither was Lone. The truth is, we'd never say that to each other, in words. But in this dream, no, in this visit, I could say what was in my heart: "I love you so much!"

She hugged me, too, then looked at me with such understanding and a little half-smile.

"I know," she said.

That's when I awoke, and rushed to find my husband. I broke

down and sobbed as I recounted what I'd shared with Lone. My husband didn't understand, didn't know quite what to do. He thought I was upset, but in truth, I was overwhelmed with joy and gratitude. Because that visit was just so typical of my friend.

I'm absolutely certain that Lone knew how desperately I needed to speak those words. And she came back to me, for only a brief moment, so that I could move on. You see, she couldn't go without helping me, one last time.

~Cathy C. Hall

Heavenly Chocolate

If there's no chocolate in heaven, I'm not going.
~Author Unknown

I was only thirteen when I began corresponding with Corporal Steve Conboy, a young U.S. Marine stationed in Cambodia during the 1970s. His letters pulled me into the war that surrounded him. While there, Steve was determined to use his free time wisely. He worked with nuns who cared for children orphaned by the war. I was touched by his compassion and vowed to devote myself to orphans someday too.

When Steve was reassigned to another part of the world, we lost touch. I married Patrick after college and planned for a family. We decided to adopt orphans from Romania.

It was not until I adopted my two children that I realized how influential Steve was in that decision. With just a little searching, I found Steve again after so many years. He was an active duty Marine stationed in Quantico, Virginia. The military was the focus of his life, yet he found time to listen to reports about my daughters. It might have been because he never had children of his own, or perhaps there was a soft spot in his heart for orphans after working in Cambodia, but he always made my children a priority. The conversations we had helped me through many rough days. We kept our friendship alive through letters, e-mails and occasional phone calls.

Steve and I only saw each other twice, but I felt close to him and appreciated our unique friendship. When my daughter Juliana turned thirteen, the same age I was when I began corresponding with him, Steve was scheduled to visit us. I circled that date on my calendar and planned a few things we could do together. I could not wait to see him.

On the day he was supposed to arrive, I received a call telling me Steve had died unexpectedly. I was shocked that a fifty-three-year-old Marine who lived through war could die so suddenly without a good reason. The only justification that I could accept was that it was more important for Steve to go to heaven on June 20th than to visit me. He was now Heaven's angel.

My father and I drove to Washington, D.C. to attend Steve's funeral. It was during the mass that Steve appeared to me. He did not say anything. He merely stared at me with a solemn expression. I was afraid to take my eyes off him for fear he would disappear, and after just a few minutes, he faded away. I wondered if my brain was recalling past images of him, but I realized I had only seen him twice before and the image I saw was new and undeniably Steve.

When I returned home, Patrick and our daughters rallied around me offering support as I grieved. One thing that bothered me about Steve dying so unexpectedly was that I never got the opportunity to say goodbye to him. Even though I saw him in the coffin and the vision of him during church, it was not the same as talking to him alive and face to face. In the thirty years I knew Steve, I had only "seen" him two times! I was disappointed that he died on the day he was planning to visit me.

One night, shortly after his death, I dreamed he called me on the phone. I could hear his breath through the receiver so vividly it made the conversation feel real. He explained that he had to go away for a while and although it was not his choice, he had to do what he was told. I understood the Marines would send him to places throughout the world that were not to his liking, but he always did what he was told. That was the life of a Marine. So, hearing Steve tell me that he was going away seemed almost natural and I accepted it.

I wanted to keep talking to him, but the conversation seemed awkward, and in my dream, I looked out the window and saw Patrick walking up the driveway with Juliana and Andrea. They were carrying a huge bag of M&M's and I could see the excitement on their faces. They knew how happy that would make me. I told Steve I had to get off the phone because the girls and Pat were at the door.

We hung up the phone and then I woke up. I began to cry when I realized it was just a dream. Then, I noticed the phone on the dresser across the room was out of the cradle. I thought that was odd and I wondered if I was losing my mind. Did I just dream that I had a conversation with Steve or did I really have a phone call from him? I looked out of the bedroom window at the sky full of twinkling stars and asked God to tell me if that was really Steve I was talking to. At that instant, a falling star streamed across the sky. I was stunned, unable to comprehend it all.

The next day at work I told Michelle, my co-worker, about my dream and the falling star.

"I think it was God," she said.

I sighed deeply. "If someone gives me M&M's today, then I will know it was God."

Michelle burst out laughing. She pushed her work aside, looked straight at me and said, "All of those signs were not good enough? You seriously want more?"

"Yes. I am a woman and I want chocolate."

We chuckled. And then a drug representative approached the small glass window at the doctor's office where we worked. I slid the glass door open and greeted her. She handed me a small plastic container and said, "Here you go." Then, as quickly as she appeared, she was gone. I carried the container back to my workstation and set it on top of the files I had been working on.

"What's that?" Michelle asked.

"I have no idea," I responded.

"Who was that?" she asked.

"I don't know," I said.

Michelle reached over, lifted the lid and gasped. It was a container full of M&M's!

God works in mysterious and miraculous ways.

~Barbara Canale

Just What I Needed

I believe that imagination is stronger than knowledge —
myth is more potent than history — dreams are more powerful than facts —
hope always triumphs over experience —
laughter is the cure for grief — love is stronger than death.
~Robert Fulghum

My favorite movie as a child was *The Wizard of Oz*. There was something mysterious and thrilling about Dorothy's dream of Oz. Was it possible to truly visit somewhere else in our dreams? Or was I simply a child who had way too much imagination?

When I was twenty-one and due to have my first baby, my father became gravely ill. It was a hard time for my family. And my good news was overshadowed by the harshness of life — my father's impending death. My mother was having a difficult time accepting the situation and our relationship had not been smooth to begin with. With the added pressures of my father's condition, we were not getting along.

My father passed away when I was in my sixth month of pregnancy. It was a very difficult time for me. Things had been so strained between my mother and I that at the end of his life I was not welcome to visit my father, who was unconscious more than conscious. I loved my father, and I knew he knew that. But I had wanted to talk with him just one more time. Not being able to do that nearly drove me over the edge.

However, life goes on and my beautiful baby girl was born on a hot day in August. Motherhood was a great balm for my grief and I poured all my love into my precious little girl. The days went by quickly. Nevertheless, it was the nights, when all would be quiet, that I allowed myself to wallow in my grief. I still held onto my irrational hope of having one last conversation with my father.

One night as usual, my husband and I went to bed after the baby, who was already eight months old. My husband fell asleep while I stayed awake thinking. I started reviewing all the events leading up to my father's death, and I cried myself to sleep.

Then I began to dream. I was in a gray place. All around me I saw shadows of people walking past. Then my father came out of the shadows. He didn't look gray. In fact he looked good. When he approached me, he was smiling and held out a hand to me.

I automatically took it and blurted out, "I can't believe this is happening. I don't feel like this is a dream. You seem so real."

He smiled and said calmly, "For now this is real. And we have to talk. It's very important."

Amazed that his hand felt real and warm, I couldn't contain my excitement. "This is wonderful! You are real. I missed you so much. I don't want to stop holding your hand!" I placed my other hand on top of our clasped hands. It felt wonderful.

"Amy," he said seriously. "We need to talk. I don't have much time and I have to tell you something."

"Okay, go ahead."

"I need you to know that everything is okay between us. There is no reason for you to be upset. I know you love me and I love you. It's all okay. Everything that happened, I understand and it's all okay. You don't have to worry anymore. I love you."

I was crying with relief and I clung to him saying over and over, "Thank you, thank you, I love you. I really do…"

Then he stood up, said he had to go and that I had to go back. I was angry and I wouldn't let go of his hand. I told him I needed to stay with him a little longer. But he insisted we needed to part. He pulled his hand from mine and again told me he loved me. He disappeared into the many shadows walking past. I sobbed so hard that I woke up.

All of a sudden, my husband yelled out. "Oh my gosh, what was that? What was that?" He was pointing over my head. When I looked nothing was there.

He flipped on the light and I could see he was really shaken. He told me that something woke him and when he looked towards me, he saw a white light glowing over my head. Then it vanished. It really scared him.

I felt the most amazing peace. "Don't worry," I told my husband. "It was my father. Everything is okay now." And it was.

~Amy Schoenfeld Hunt

67

Seven Twenty

Sometimes the poorest man leaves his children the richest inheritance.
~Ruth E. Renkel

y dad and I had always had a rocky relationship. To many in our small community, Dad was a hero. From years as a volunteer firefighter, to an EMT who had earned more than one certification for saving a life, to a jail officer who had saved an inmate from hanging, Dad always seemed to be at the right place at the right time. Except with me.

When I was four and playing a coveted game of *Candy Land* with Dad, the fire whistle would take him away from me. One Thanksgiving, Mom, my grandparents and I spent it without Dad as he left to take an ambulance call because the assigned EMT refused to take the call on a holiday. It's no wonder that I felt I came in second in Dad's life.

Dad was a diabetic who refused to take care of himself. As he approached sixty, his eyesight began to fail and it became necessary to amputate toes and parts of his feet. He could no longer drive fire trucks or volunteer his services during the annual fundraising Fourth of July celebrations. He had to take disability and quit his job. This was really hard for a man whose life was committed to helping others.

Old hurts ran deep and I seldom talked to him. When he called and told me he was in a nursing home, I felt sorrow, but not enough to attempt a reconciliation.

Over the next few years, I visited Dad occasionally and had brief conversations. We were wary of each other and careful to sidestep important issues and not bring up any old wounds.

In April of 2006 Dad called one Sunday afternoon and told me he was in the local hospital. He had suffered a heart attack and would be transferred to a larger, better equipped medical facility in the nearest city. The ambulance would not arrive for an hour for the transfer, so I jumped in the car and drove the twenty minutes to be with him.

Maybe it was then, seeing him so vulnerable and sick and alone, that my perception of him began to change. He had told me not to come — not to bother — it would be such a short time before he was transferred. But I could tell by the mist in his eyes he was grateful I had ignored his request.

Dad recovered from the heart attack and returned to the nursing home, but his kidneys failed. Three days a week he had to be transported to the city for dialysis. Once Mom and I took him when the facility's van was being repaired, and I saw firsthand how difficult the trip and maneuvering in the wheelchair was for him.

He developed an unbearable pain in his back and ended up in the hospital. I went there one beautiful autumn day. Somehow the walls began to come down and Dad told me he was sorry that I felt he placed others ahead of me. I told him I was sorry I hadn't understood how much his generosity to his community meant to him. Thirty years of resentments melted away and the walls that had built up crumbled. Then and there Dad became my hero and I knew he loved me more than all his "projects."

The pain and dialysis became too much for him. He decided to stop the dialysis treatments. We both knew this meant two weeks or so for him to live. I hated to lose him, but it was his choice. I told him I loved him and gave him my unconditional support.

He slipped into a coma. I had a feeling he could still hear me, and sat by his side and talked to him about everything and anything. I even sang "Found a Peanut," over and over. This was a favorite song of his that he would regale me with endlessly when I was a child. I smiled, as I imagined him telling me to knock it off.

That evening at home, I sat at my computer when all of a sudden the pungent aroma of his aftershave, combined with the distinct antiseptic smell of his nursing facility, filled the room. Dad was there. I knew what that meant.

A few minutes later a call from Dad's nurse confirmed what I knew. Dad had just passed away. He had visited to give me a final goodbye. He had died at 7:20—the date of my birth—July 20. I can't think of any better way for a father to reaffirm his love to his daughter.

~Jennifer L. Short

Messages from Heaven

Heaven Sent

68

A Little Nudge

To live in hearts we leave behind
Is not to die.
~Thomas Campbell, "Hallowed Ground"

It didn't seem right that the sun should be so brilliant or the sky such a deep cloudless blue. Only six months had passed. Not near enough time to blur the image of my mother's thin form lying beneath white hospital sheets, or to forget the cloying smells of antiseptic and chronic illness. Yet no one's tragedy stopped Mother's Day, a grim reminder, from arriving. At the age of fifty, I had become a motherless child. Uncertain of how to handle my changed place in the world, I decided to do what I had always done for Mom. I purchased a dozen red roses. Then I took them to the cemetery.

During the drive, I reviewed bittersweet memories. Mom walking me to school my first day of kindergarten. The pride that sparkled in her eyes when I graduated from college. Her joy as she cuddled my son, her first grandchild, soon after his birth. At every important event of my life, she'd been with me. My heart ached. I couldn't imagine a future without her. I thought I'd never again feel complete.

My thoughts stilled once I passed through the cemetery gate. I stopped the car and swallowed hard. I hadn't been here since the day of Mom's burial. Hundreds of tombstones were lined up in neat rows. Where was she? After more than thirty minutes of fruitless searching, my melancholy gave way to rising panic. I could no longer pick up the phone to call Mom. Or go to her house on Sunday afternoon to visit. And now it seemed I couldn't even find the place where we had laid her to rest only half a year before. My throat constricted. Before tears could form, I shook my head and willed myself to stop thinking negative thoughts. I needed to concentrate on the search.

I stopped the car, and then, although it was undeniably futile, I couldn't help but say, "Mom, where are you?" It was a question that haunted me on many levels.

Of course no one answered. I swallowed hard and reached toward the key to start the car and leave. I suppose it really didn't matter if I delivered roses on Mother's Day or not. Mom would never know the difference.

But before I could turn the key, movement caught my eye. Two gray doves swooped by. They drifted and circled gracefully until one, then the other, landed softly on a nearby headstone. The pair strutted across the stone, heads bobbing with each step. I watched them for a moment until my gaze drifted to the name carved on stone. My eyes widened and goose bumps rose on my arms.

The birds had landed on my mother's headstone.

I got out of the car and walked toward the grave. My hand clutched the roses so hard a thorn pierced my thumb. With a whirr of wings, the doves fluttered away. I watched them fly high into the sky until they disappeared from view. Then I dropped to one knee in the soft ground at the foot of a deep pink granite stone. My fingers brushed across her name.

A feeling of wonder and hope swelled in me for the first time since Mom's illness and death. Someone sent those birds to guide me and I knew it had to be her. I needed my mom and even death didn't keep her from responding. And if she could respond to a moment of grief in a quiet cemetery, it meant she still remained as vital a force in my life now as she had ever been. I realized that all it took to find her again was to open my eyes and look around. I could see Mom in my memories, in the faces of my children, and in the woman she had helped me become. The words I whispered came straight from my heart.

"Thanks, Mom."

I put down the flowers and rose to my feet. My body felt lighter than it had in months.

Mom found a way to reach out to me through the veil that separated this life from the next. I'd always be able to find her.

And all it took to convince me was a little nudge.

~Pat Wahler

The Post-it Note

God not only sends special angels into our lives, but sometimes He even
sends them back again if we forget to take notes the first time!
~Eileen Elias Freeman, The Angels' Little Instruction Book

My bond with Papa grew stronger after he and Mom moved in with us after her fall. Two families living together wasn't easy, but soon I appreciated the blessings associated with day-in, day-out togetherness. Maybe that's why his death hit me so hard.

It seemed like no time since the strong, quiet man with the big smile was diagnosed with asbestosis, had lung surgery, and then moved into the nursing home for twenty-four-hour rehab care. One day, he said to me, "I'm never going home, am I?"

"I hope so, Papa," I answered, but we both knew it was unlikely.

He never asked again, and our lives revolved around Mom spending her days with him. I'd pop in for the night shift. Many times, I brought work with me. He'd snooze, and I'd meet marketing deadlines—all within his curtained section of the room.

One night, Papa said, "You shouldn't work so much." He pointed a bony finger at my pile of notebooks, Post-it notes, proposals, and works-in-progress. Everything I needed to complete my projects except my laptop, which remained in the car. I didn't want to be so obvious about working. But Papa knew each time my BlackBerry dinged a message.

"You've got Post-it notes stuck on everything," he said, grinning.

"My memory isn't what it used to be," I said to him with a smile. "They remind me what's important to do."

"Just remember there's a difference between important to do and what's important." He patted my hand and lingered a beat.

To lighten the mood, he spent the rest of our visit teasing me about my Type A personality traits, something he swore I got from my mama. At the end of the night, he said, "Take it one day at a time, and you'll be fine. I do, and it works for me... with help from our Lord." His bright blue eyes twinkled. "Maybe you should make a note about that."

"Maybe I should," I said and laughed. "I'll remember... Don't be so serious. Be happy. Be happy. Be happy." I giggled, drew a smiley face, and printed his name, Delmar Ayers, above it. I slapped it against the pocket of his pajamas. He chuckled, and then he reminisced about dates with Mom. I updated him about my daughter Meredith's college life. He shared WWII stories. He said he'd like to go fishing again.

When I got to the car, I wrote on a sticky note: fishing trip for Papa—doable?

But the Coastal Georgia January weather turned cold and windy. The fishing trip had to wait.

On a cloudless, blue-sky Friday, Papa's lung specialist called Mom and me into his office. We studied a large mass on the screen. "There's nothing we can do," he said. "I've operated on folks older than eighty-six, but Mr. Ayers isn't a good candidate." We agreed not to tell him. "It will only depress him," the doctor said.

Instead, we spent the afternoon planning the fishing trip. We ate a burger. We talked about everything except lung cancer.

Over the weekend, EMS brought Papa to the hospital with sirens blaring, and he didn't regain consciousness. He struggled to breathe. "We'll try to keep him comfortable" resounded through the room. Mom and I huddled together, shell-shocked, after learning the cancer had spread into his stomach. The doctor contacted hospice. We stayed with Papa day and night.

The hospice nurse said, "His pulse reacts to your voice. He can hear you, so talk to him and share what's in your heart."

We poured out our love and memories while Papa's chest thrust up, then plummeted with raspy, ragged breathing. I turned to the nurse and said, "He was the best dad." And Papa breathed his last breath.

He died on Wednesday, and I had no idea how hard the finality of it would hit me. Why hadn't I made his fishing trip happen? Spent more time with him? Why hadn't I...? The list went on and on.

Family and friends rallied around us. "He's in a better place," someone said. "He's not suffering now." Another friend shared a story about how a bird started showing up after her father's death. "Daddy was a florist," she said. "We decorated for Christmas together, and I missed him more than ever during the holidays. Still do," she admitted. "But I started noticing a bird hanging around. Once, I took the truck to get a large potted tree, and the bird landed on the back of the truck. It wouldn't get off. I knew Dad was with me."

I prayed for my own message from heaven.

A week later, we'd planned to spend Meredith's twenty-first birthday at her North Carolina college, a six-hour drive for us. I said to Mom, "I don't have enough energy to drive, but we have to go... I want to."

So I stood by the car and studied my list. I'd picked up Papa's belongings from the nursing home at daybreak, sobbing so much I had to pull off the road. I marked it off, but my heart sank. How could Mom and I get it together enough to celebrate this major milestone? I sighed and focused on the list: birthday cake, candles, Meredith's presents, camera, and other items waiting to be placed in the just-vacuumed car trunk.

I heaved our suitcases and pushed them to the back of the trunk, leaving ample room in the front part for our toiletry cases and birthday paraphernalia.

"Check the mailbox," Mom called from the door. "I forgot yesterday."

I walked down the driveway, shivering against February's biting wind. A bird flew in front of me, landed on our mailbox, and didn't move when I approached. I walked around the gray-brown bird, staring, but he ignored my movements. All of a sudden, he sang. Was it Papa? I grabbed my camera from the car and took picture after picture from every angle before I went to get the rest of our stuff.

When I returned to the car, the bird landed in a nearby tree. I lifted the trunk lid, and gasped, staring at the empty space I had left in the trunk. The yellow sticky note with Delmar Ayers and a smiley face beamed like a ray of sun from heaven. My heart thudded. Memories of a younger, smiling Papa flowed through me, bringing a sense of peace. I looked around and the bird flew away as I slammed the car trunk shut.

"One day at a time," I promised. "Mom and I will be fine. I'll make a note of it."

~Debra Ayers Brown

70

The Birthday Present

He who has gone, so we but cherish his memory, abides with us, more potent,
nay, more present than the living man.
~Antoine de Saint-Exupery

s a girl, I didn't know my paternal grandfather, Sam, very well but I grew closer to him as an adult, after he had a heart attack and moved into a small, one-bedroom apartment with his dog Brutus. Brutus was a spoiled, overweight, toothless Chihuahua that barked constantly. His dog, a houseplant, and my dad Charlie, were my grandfather's only companions so I worried that he was lonely. I started making weekly visits and frequent calls. Our relationship grew and soon we were exchanging recipes, laughing, and talking every chance we could.

My new husband Mike loved him too, and we'd take him and Brut lunch on Sundays. Everybody's favorite was Philly cheesesteaks with fresh brewed sweet tea. It was a big event for us all. Brut would beg, dance and spin in return for pieces of meat and bread. After lunch we'd sit watching the sparrows, redbirds, and squirrels at his feeder while Pawpaw told stories.

Pawpaw's bad knee got worse, so I began doing everything from housekeeping to grocery shopping for him. We had several precious years together, but one night he had a stroke, never returning to his homey apartment. He went into a nursing home to get the care he needed and Brutus was given to a new family.

Months later, my birthday approached and my husband planned a romantic getaway. Pawpaw was adjusting well to his new residence, encouraging us to go on the trip. The night before my birthday I called him from the beach for one of our long talks. He informed me he was hospitalized. Before hanging up, he joyously shouted: "Happy Birthday!"

"Thanks Pawpaw," I said, "but it's not my birthday yet. Promise you'll celebrate with me." He and I both had the feeling he would not make it until the next day, but he promised anyway. A few hours later, at 5 a.m. on the morning of my birthday, I got the call. He had died in his sleep.

A few days later my maternal grandmother June and I visited an outdoor shopping mall. "I saw something yesterday that reminds me of you and your grandfather," she said. She took me into a store and showed me a small wall plaque that said: "Perhaps they are not stars in the sky, but rather openings where our loved ones shine down to let us know they are happy." Although touching, the writing was chicken-scratched into a grayish, headstone-looking slab. She urged me to buy it but I couldn't; the ugly memento did not remind me of Pawpaw.

The next evening, in another town, my husband and I finally celebrated my birthday. My husband spent an hour in a quaint gift shop before dinner. Sitting in the car outside the restaurant, he handed me a present. "I can't wait to give you this," he said. "It's really special." I opened the lid of the decorative brown box, beholding a beautifully painted Tuscany gold candle holder with delicately painted hearts and stars and calligraphy script that read: "Perhaps they are not stars in the sky, but rather openings where our loved ones shine down to let us know they are happy."

I was awestruck. I asked my husband if my grandma had told him about that quote after she showed it to me in the other store. "No," he said. "I looked in there forever, like there was something specific I needed to find. When I saw this, I knew it what I was looking for."

My eyes filled with tears. Pawpaw had kept his promise to celebrate my birthday with me, leading my grandma to the message and then Mike to the same message in the form of a beautiful gift. I treasure that candle as a message and a gift from heaven. Pawpaw found a way to tell me he was happy. I knew then that he had not died on my birthday, but rather made a special journey that morning to someplace amazing. Each year on our special day, August 15th, I light that candle which reminds me that I have a grandpa in heaven who loves me.

~Deborah Sturgill

71

Sure Bet

When you make a bet, you're saying something.
~Al Alvarez

In the last few years of his life, my father loved going to the horse races. My brother, Mike, and he would discuss that day's racing form and off they'd go to one of their favorite tracks near Cincinnati. At the time, my son Zach and I lived in northern Michigan, and we'd join them every time we came to town.

A few days before Valentine's Day 1993, Mike told me that Dad was dying from stomach cancer, with no more than a month to live. I sent Dad a dozen red roses with a note that read, "To My Favorite Valentine." When Dad called to thank me for the flowers, he asked if I could make the trip to Cincinnati to help my stepmother Jane take care of him for the next few weeks.

"We need you, sweetheart," my father said in his gentle, matter-of-fact voice.

"Of course," I said. "I'll be there as soon as I can."

When I arrived at Dad and Jane's apartment several days later, a nurse was giving them an overview of at-home hospice services. Her name was Mary Angel. True to her name, Mary filled the room with compassion and gave us the confidence we needed for the difficult days ahead.

During the first week of my stay, Dad could still sit up in his favorite chair and carry on a conversation. His chair occupied a space just a few feet from a glass patio door through which we watched the snow fall, collecting flake by flake on the trees that lined the ravine below. A bright red cardinal often perched on the tree branch closest to the window, the one bold spot of color in an otherwise gray and white landscape. The cardinal seemed to peer intently through the glass, singing his heart out just for us. To this day, I cannot see a cardinal without thinking of my father.

Eventually, a hospital bed was set up in the living room to maximize Dad's comfort at night and to help us in our care for him. I slept on the couch beside him to assist with trips to the bathroom. During the last few days of his life, Dad had whittled his vocabulary down to two essential phrases: "It doesn't matter" and "I love you." The first usually referred to some human drama going on around him; the latter was spoken to anyone who came into his presence.

One morning, we moved my father to the hospice center near the hospital. We left him later that afternoon resting comfortably, watching a golf tournament. Jane and I kissed him and said "Goodbye" and "I love you," never dreaming those would be our last words to him. The weather channel forecast a winter storm that night, so we thought it best to get home.

In spite of the inclement weather, my brother Mike made it to see Dad later that evening. Mike recounts sitting by Dad's bed, stroking his thin white hair at the temples. Drawing from their times at the racetrack, Mike sighed and said, "Oh, Dad… This is one 'long shot' I don't think we're going to win."

That morning around three, the phone rang. It was a hospice nurse telling us that Dad was about to make his transition. "He seems very peaceful," she whispered. "His breathing is slow and shallow."

I told her to tell Dad how much we loved him and that we would be there as soon as we could. Before we could make it out the door, however, the phone rang again.

"Mary," the gentle voice on the other end of the line said. "He's gone."

Several days later, after finishing some preparations for Dad's memorial service, Jane sat down to read the paper while I went into Dad's study to work on an article for a local magazine. I was staring at blank paper when I heard Jane's startled voice coming from the living room.

"Mary? Is this yours? Where in the world did this come from?"

I rushed to see what she was talking about. There she stood in the middle of the living room, holding a two-dollar bill.

"No, this isn't mine," I said tentatively as I took the bill from her hand and examined it. "In fact, I haven't seen one of these in years."

The bill was crisp, clean and absolutely flat, as if it had just come off the printing press. Neither she nor I could imagine how it got there. The only other person who had been there that morning was a man who delivered a plant from a nearby florist shop. No currency had been exchanged.

I laid the two-dollar bill on the table next to Dad's chair and didn't give it another thought until Mike called later that afternoon to see how we were doing. After discussing dinner plans, I remembered the two-dollar bill.

"Mike, the strangest thing appeared in the middle of the living room floor today," I said and proceeded to tell him about Jane's mysterious find. "It's brand new," I added, "like it's never seen the inside of a wallet."

There was a palpable silence and then my brother finally spoke. "It's a two-dollar bet."

"Oh, my God," I said, breathlessly. Every nerve in my body tingled. If our father were to choose a sign out of all possible signs, this was the one the whole family would understand. Two dollars is a traditional bet, two being the common denominator at the racetrack.

"It's a sign," Mike said. "Dad's telling us he's okay."

As we grieved the physical loss of our father over the months that followed, that two-dollar bill became a touchstone of comfort for everyone.

Life after death is not such a long shot after all, Dad was telling us beyond the grave.

It's a sure bet.

~Mary Knight

Breaking Through Barriers

There is no surprise more magical than the surprise of being loved.
It is God's finger on man's shoulder.
~Charles Morgan

She was just your average runner, a middle-of-the-pack jogger with modest goals. She was also a businesswoman, a mother of two young children, and my wife. But more than anything, Linda was an inspiration to anyone who has ever pushed beyond personal limits and broken through barriers they once thought insurmountable.

Linda was forty-six and had spent the last fifteen months of her life battling a rare form of cancer called primary central nervous system (CSN) lymphoma. She underwent countless sessions of radiation therapy and chemotherapy. She had endured a bone marrow biopsy, the insertion of a portacath into her chest, and an Ommaya reservoir into her head. She had been given methotrexate, Neurontin, MS Contin, and dozens of other drugs and medications. Doctors had done everything but douse her with holy water from Lourdes.

During her stay at University of California San Francisco's oncology ward Linda suffered hair loss, weight gain (from steroids) and a nightmare roller coaster ride of stomach-churning emotions.

Not once, though, did she lose her spirit. Don't focus on the negative. That was always her philosophy. Take your problems and make them challenges.

Fighting cancer took its toll on her. One of her first challenges was to regain her strength. To do so she turned to running. Linda's training routine started at the hospital, sandwiched between chemo treatments that left her sapped, hollowed out and violently ill. Along with a few other hearty souls, she would climb from bed and drag her IV stand around the oncology ward.

The goal was sixteen laps, or one mile. A seemingly easy distance, but one that would cause the average cancer patient to crumble like an old Tinkertoy fort. Some jokingly referred to it as the UCSF endurance run. A race filled with sick and bald and pasty white athletes pushing themselves to greater distances, working outside their comfort zones.

The hospital workouts were just a warm-up for Linda. During her brief visits home, she would run with me on the steep trails in the woods behind our town.

"It's a chore," she admitted. "Every day is an excuse to wimp out. It's hard to get my breath and maintain my stride."

I asked her, "If it's so hard, why bother?"

"It's good for my heart, for my strength," she replied. "I feel happy when I make myself do it."

Linda knew there were no guarantees. Her cancer had already gone into remission, and resurfaced, Hydra-like, dozens of times. The tumors had disappeared and reappeared, almost overnight. Battling the disease was paramount to climbing Mount Everest or winning the Tour de France.

Just ask Lance Armstrong.

"During the journey I've found out many things about myself," she said. "By having this, I've learned to live life one day at a time, and to be thankful for what I have."

The future was uncertain but Linda was prepared for anything. When she ran, she reached for the impossible. In my heart I knew she was going to beat her cancer. Our family simply didn't plan on losing her.

When Linda died we suffered greatly. Looking back on that shipwrecked period, I remember the kids telling me how much they missed their mother. I found myself thinking about Linda constantly. I would catch sight of her portrait or hear one of her favorite songs and just lose it. I would dream about her and sometimes wake up with her on my mind.

In the following months my life seemed to be spiral downward. I drank heavily and became increasingly depressed. For a time I was hanging on by a thread.

My struggle ended one morning when Linda broke through another impossible barrier and came back to visit. I was in the back-yard when I felt a hand on my cheek. Then I smelled the scent of her skin. It was heaven ethereal. I glanced up and saw a cloud directly overhead, one solitary heart-shaped cloud in an otherwise flawlessly blue sky. It was a message from Linda, of that I have no doubt. She was sending her love.

My life changed that day. I found strength in knowing that I was not alone. Linda was watching over us. She is still here today, giving me the willpower and the courage to go on.

~Timothy Martin

73

Amanda's Jonquils

Every flower is a soul blossoming in nature.
~Gerard de Nerval

I do not have a green thumb, nor do I possess so much as a green pinkie. In fact, plants and flowers seem to have an aversion to me. Despite all my earnest endeavors, most of my plants and flowers exhibit a varying array of colors, none of which is normal. One plant on my brass flower stand is now mostly yellow. Another plant is a lovely green, except for the tip of every single leaf, which is black. I water too often, I am told, or too much, others say; I'm not sure what I'm doing wrong, but I seem to keep doing it.

The truth is, my plant collection is not one of my own choosing. All of my plants were gifts during a time of traumatic grief in my family. I still have one living from the time we lost my father-in-law to cancer, another from the year a stroke took my mother-in-law, three from the loss of my nineteen-year-old daughter eight years ago, and one from the death of my sister-in-law two years later. My plants have truly been watered with tears.

There was a time that I attempted to plant a flowerbed in my front yard. When my two girls were small, I ordered beautiful varieties of tulips and planted them each fall. Then each spring, I would eagerly watch for the first signs of growth. Each tulip that pushed its way through was a victory for me. However, I soon found that the neighborhood dogs and cats seemed to enjoy destroying my flowers as much as I enjoyed watching them grow. Some animal liked to eat the tops off my tulips; another liked to pull them up by the roots.

About nine or ten years ago, I quit planting the bulbs in the fall, and I gratefully turned the flower gardening over to my husband. He plants mums, which do not need several months of dormancy, and which the neighborhood cats and dogs do not find as much fun to destroy.

Eight years ago, my nineteen-year-old daughter was killed in a blinding rainstorm. On a hot August afternoon, she hit a patch of high water, hydroplaned, and spun around into the path of an oncoming car. The state trooper said she was killed instantly. My family was inundated with grief and despair, neighbors and friends, food and plants. In the months that followed, my thoughts turned to creating a legacy for Amanda. She died too young to have married; no children would carry on her genes. How could we ensure that her memory lived on?

One of our first efforts was the establishment of a perpetual scholarship fund, because Amanda had been an outstanding student in high school and during her one year at college. We also assisted the Wesley Foundation at East Carolina University in constructing a prayer garden in her memory. Her boyfriend named a star for her and brought us the star chart. Her best friends and their families built and maintain a cross at the accident site. Her Girl Scout troop planted a tree; her high school friends dedicated library furnishings to her—so many people understood and aided us in our attempts to create a legacy for Amanda.

Amanda's birthday is in April, and that first April after the accident we decided that we would place flowers in church every year in honor of her birthday. After church, we carried them to her grave. When we returned home, however, we were shocked to see a group of cream jonquils with yellow centers in my flowerbed, right outside Amanda's bedroom window. We had never planted this particular type of jonquil, nor would we have ever planted them in just one spot. Our flowers were always evenly spaced across the front of the house. We looked at them in awe but we could not explain their appearance.

The following April, the jonquils once again made their magic appearance, blooming beautifully outside Amanda's window. Every year now, for eight years, the jonquils have appeared. They always bloom right before her birthday, always in the same spot, without any assistance on our part. We recognize them as what they truly are — Amanda's birthday present to us — and we simply accept them with gratitude and wonder. And amazingly, the neighborhood dogs and cats leave them alone. And so do I.

~Kim Seeley

74

Mary's Song

There is nothing in the world so much like prayer as music is.
~William P. Merrill

I was with my husband the day he was diagnosed with cancer. I accompanied my mother four summers later to the physician's office where she was informed she had terminal lung cancer. She died a few months later, on my fifty-first birthday. Less than two months later, I witnessed the same doctor tell my daughter Elizabeth that her five-year-old son, my grandson Jacob, had Wilm's tumor, a rare form of cancer that would necessitate the removal of the affected kidney.

When the doctor reached for the doorknob to leave the room, his eyes met my stricken ones. He shook his head sadly, laid a comforting hand on my shoulder for a moment, and then left the room, closing the door with a loud click behind him. At that precise moment I heard a beautiful female voice sing just two words, "Ave Maria," from the radio speaker above us. Stunned, I turned to my daughter, but seeing her face buried in her little boy's back, her shoulders shaking with sobs, I wisely said nothing. The song had already ended anyway, and a generic Christmas song was playing. Later, I would ask Elizabeth what she'd heard when the doctor closed the door, and the answer was the same; just the two words, "Ave Maria."

"That was your grandmother's favorite song," I told her. My mother had even mentioned it in a memory book she'd filled out years ago, noting that as a young girl she'd loved playing the piano and singing that song. For weeks I searched YouTube videos for the voice, but to no avail. It wasn't Celine Dion, Charlotte Church, or any other famous singer's voice.

Having seen two other loved ones through cancer, we could barely stand the thought of all that Jacob's little body would have to endure. First there was the invasive surgery to remove the tumor and the kidney, a surgery Jacob would spend Christmas Day in the hospital recovering from. The days following the surgery were long and difficult, especially for my daughter, who stayed at the hospital night and day. Jacob was in obvious pain, and cried for the catheter and IV to be removed. The news from the doctors kept getting worse. The tumor was of the unfavorable type, with a lower survival rate. Jacob would need months of radiation and chemotherapy treatments. Elizabeth repeatedly asked me, as if pleading for it to be so, "Can Grandma watch over him? Help him in some way?" Her grandmother had so recently died; it seemed natural to wonder that.

We both yearned for a sign, any sign, from my mother, desperately grasping onto the smallest of things: a few faint whiffs of cigarette smoke at odd times, small feathers we'd find on Jacob's coat, and that "Ave Maria" at the doctor's office.

My mother had lived for less than three months after her diagnosis. She'd faced cancer bravely, determined to live to the fullest in whatever time she had left. When her children asked her what was on her "bucket list," her reply was immediate. "I've always wanted to ride in a small airplane. Or fly one," she added.

My sisters made arrangements with a local pilot to fulfill that wish. Before she got on the airplane, Mom turned, and with a huge smile on her face and a twinkle in her eye said, "Wouldn't it be something if this was the way I went?" My son made a film of that ride, choosing the Coldplay song "Viva La Vida" to accompany it. I often watched that video on my computer to remember her like that, so happy and excited. But I also knew the song was not one she would have chosen herself; it wasn't even a familiar tune for her. Instead, she would have picked something more traditional, more religious. Something like "Ave Maria."

In August of 2011, a year after my mother's diagnosis, I interviewed a man and his daughter for the local newspaper. Mariah, a twelve-year-old, had recently advanced to the State Fair as a vocalist. The fact that she'd advanced to the finals from local competition three out of the last four years was quite a feat. Her father, Rick, mentioned that this year she'd won with the Miley Cyrus song, "The Climb." The previous year she'd won with "The Star-Spangled Banner." And the year before that? It had been "Ave Maria." A little chill went down my spine with that information. Apparently, Mariah had chosen that particular piece then because it had been her grandmother's favorite song, a grandmother who had recently died of cancer.

Rick promised to send me video clips of Mariah singing. He e-mailed me that evening, telling me he'd checked out my blog and giving me a link to his own. Another chill went down my spine when I saw the pages of his blog were filled with photos of small airplanes. From the entries, it was evident he loved flying. He'd even flown the small airplane that my mother had ridden in, which he informed me when I asked if he knew the man who'd donated the ride for my dying mother.

I reminded him of his promise to send the video link of his daughter singing "Ave Maria." When it arrived in my inbox, I hesitated before clicking on it. I didn't think I could stand to hear a butchered version of the special song. Closing my eyes, I clicked on the link, listening closely.

"Ave Maria." I was startled out of my reverie by a woman's lovely soprano emanating from the computer speaker. I opened my eyes and stopped the video. I started it from the beginning again. And then once more. Over and over, I clicked on the beginning of the video, shaking my head in disbelief. The rest of the song sounded like a very young girl, but not those two words. After months of searching for the voice I'd heard in the doctor's office, I was certain I was hearing it again. And for the first time since that day at the doctor's, I listened all the way through to the end of the song. It was only then that I realized those words, "Ave Maria," were only at the beginning of the song, and not repeated at the conclusion. Elizabeth and I couldn't have been hearing the tail end of the song before the next generic Christmas tune began playing.

At that very moment, watching that video of a young girl singing a song that her grandmother had loved, I knew without a doubt; those words sung in that doctor's office had been a message from my mother, and the message was: I am here, and Jacob will be okay.

Ten months later, he is.

~Mary Potter Kenyon

75

My Butterfly

I am convinced that these heavenly beings exist
and that they provide unseen aid on our behalf.
~Billy Graham

I've never claimed to know what happens to us on our way to the final destination, whatever it may be. Probably unlike most, I find a sense of solace in not knowing, in accepting that our time on this planet entitles us to nothing. The natural order of things dictates that it is best some things go unsolved. But something extremely curious happened recently.

I am a teacher, and I've spent the better part of a decade discussing literature, grammar, and writing with middle school students at a private school in the South. In my classroom, I've always subscribed to the notion that a good teacher plays no favorites.

But Emma was special.

She perpetually exuded a youthful exuberance and a steady ease with all aspects of the world around her. When she looked at you with her dark eyes and flashed her trademark smile, you walked away knowing she genuinely cared. She dedicated her life to helping anyone she could, from her own brother, to a first-time acquaintance, to a ladybug that might have found itself caught in a spider web.

When a car accident killed her at age sixteen, I spent a good day or two in outright denial. How could anything possibly extinguish the spirit that was Emma? And I was not alone. The sheer outpouring of stories from colleagues, friends, former students, camp counselors, coaches, about the many ways this young girl had touched their lives was both astounding and admirable. They helped to soften the blow a bit, but none of us could truly express the impact Emma had made during her short time on this planet.

And then I was given that final opportunity, when Emma's family asked me to deliver the eulogy at her service. My first thought was, of course I'll do it. I'd do anything for Emma. My second thought was, how in the world will I be able to pull this off? My third, and many subsequent thoughts thereafter, was a cataclysmic, unintelligible jumble of outright panic.

It wasn't the words that worried me. I knew that such a unique and vibrant girl would basically write the piece for me. Instead, it was the prospect of speaking about such an emotional topic before a packed church. And there was the underlying fear that, despite wanting to deliver a few minutes of perfection for Emma, I simply didn't have the strength or the fortitude to give her what she deserved.

But I pushed on anyway and, after writing the eulogy, I began practicing the hard part. I read and re-read the words throughout the day prior to her service. I performed it in front of the mirror. I read it to my dogs, to my girlfriend. I even dialed up loved ones in distant states to deliver Emma's eulogy over the phone. And each time, I was met with the same fate: a few unimpeded lines followed by noticeable cracks in my voice and long bouts of uncontrollable sobbing. I found it impossible to separate my emotions for sweet Emma from the words I wanted to share with the community. I was never able to reach the final lines.

The folly continued into the next day, and with each re-reading it became clear my efforts were an exercise in futility. I simply didn't have the strength to pull it off, and my anxiety level was reaching the boiling point. With only an hour to go before Emma's service, I decided to give it one more shot. Silently I asked Emma, possibly the most resilient person I'd ever met, to lend me some of her strength. But secretly, I had doubts even she could help me.

I was wrong.

I headed out to my patio for the final practice round and began reading the first few lines to my girlfriend. The sun was warm but pleasant on my back. About a paragraph into the piece I felt the familiar scratchiness in my throat and the sting of tears forming behind my eyes.

And then suddenly, as if in perfect response, I saw her fluttering.

Her black wings danced through the air like patches of velvet and skimmed across the top of my page. A blue and purple blotch on her back, the shape of a large, round eye, seemed to wink at me briefly as she lit on the myrtle flowers and listened to me. I paused for a moment—just long enough for the recognition to sink in—and then a feeling I can only describe as pure serenity washed over me. I finished the reading without flaw and folded the pages into my jacket pocket, for I knew everything would be okay.

When I arrived at the church and examined some of Emma's belongings, which had been displayed in her memory, I couldn't help but smile when I noticed one of her drawings hanging high above a collage of photos dedicated to the loss of her first tooth.

It was a purple butterfly.

And when I rose in the pulpit to deliver my words to the parish, that same feeling of serenity given to me by my butterfly washed over me.

My knowledge of the true nature of eternity still falls short, and for as long as I'm given the privilege to grace this Earth I shall never strive to understand that which is not meant for my understanding. But every time a butterfly flickers and sways through my yard on the warm summer breeze, I will know without question that Emma has dropped by to check on me.

~C.G. Morelli

76

Six-Inch Ruler

We are never so lost our angels cannot find us.
~Stephanie Powers

My son Danny was unexpectedly taken to Heaven by an attack of spinal meningitis three months short of his tenth birthday. That happened thirty-four years ago, and God has brought me through the pain remarkably well. He was a healthy well-adjusted little boy who loved football. He also loved his family and never hesitated to show concern and affection. I really miss that part of him. He would often tell me on our way to school, "Mom, you sure do look pretty today." When I think of that, it still brings a lump to my throat.

Fast forward to last summer. I had taken up a little ministry of making small tip boxes out of greeting cards. I included an encouraging note and gave them along with the tip to waitresses and other service personnel. They seem to enjoy receiving the box more than the tip. Many have told me they keep the little box, sometimes with the tip still inside.

I use a six-inch ruler to measure the folds while making the boxes. One day while making them I realized I had lost my little ruler. I tried using a longer one but it was too awkward for the task, so I started shopping for the six-inch ruler. I was having a hard time finding one.

One day after struggling to make the boxes with a larger ruler, I took a break and walked to the outside building where my husband was working. There are shelves on one wall that house containers of things that have been there since we moved in ten years ago. As I walked through the door, my husband was standing there doing something near a table under the shelves. I was about to ask him something when a small object on the table caught my eye. It was a piece of a broken ruler. I asked what it was. He looked at it and said he had never seen it before. I picked it up, turned it over and remembered. It was the first six inches of an old wooden ruler that had been broken in half over thirty years ago. It still had the cellophane tape remnants of an attempt to mend it. I turned it over and my eyes instantly welled up as I read the child-like writing carved into the wood. "Danny D." It had been my son Danny's school ruler. My memory shot back to the time he had broken it in two and I tried to fix it for him. I knew that I had never thrown it away, but how it suddenly showed up baffled me.

I turned to my husband with tears streaming down my face and said, "Look who this belonged to." His eyes also welled as he looked at me and said, "He has been here."

The ruler had been broken when Danny was in the fourth grade, not long before he died. It somehow was packed away in the boxes on the shelves, but never showed up until thirty-four years later when I needed a six-inch ruler. I still cannot explain how it got there, but it is now one of my tools for my little ministry of encouraging people with tiny tip boxes. Thank you Danny, I love you.

~Linda Benfield

77

Art Lessons

The golden moments in the stream of life rush past us and we see nothing but sand; the angels come to visit us, and we only know them when they are gone.

~George Elliot

When I saw my mother's little red car parked at the curb as I returned home from work, I knew I'd find Mama Anne inside giving my five-year-old son Anthony an art lesson. The kitchen table would be covered with watercolors, jars of water and brushes. Mama and Anthony would be bent over their sketchpads creating colorful scenes.

At sixty-seven, Mama finally had time to get back to what she enjoyed most: teaching art. Although even she would admit she could not draw a straight line, or any recognizable creature, she somehow had the gift of inspiring others. Since she had successfully taught elementary students art, she now would teach her grandson.

Arriving in her red smock topped with a beige beret, she looked like a Parisian artiste. She would help Anthony put on his sneakers and they would head out for a walk, sometimes around our neighborhood and often at the beach. During their walks, she would ask Anthony what he was seeing, such as a bird of paradise flower or a seagull. She would ask him what shape it was, what color. Back at the kitchen table, she would talk about what they had seen, and ask him to make a picture. On the back of each picture she would write the date and describe what Anthony had observed on the walk. I could expect to find the latest rendition taped to the refrigerator.

One January evening, I came home to no Mama Anne, but instead a message from her on the answering machine. In her Georgia drawl, Mama reported her whereabouts.

"Don't worry. The doctor had me check into the hospital for a few days to get over this chest infection. Don't bother driving in to come see me tonight. I'm fine. Tell Anthony we'll finish working on his bird picture when I get better."

A few days in the hospital turned into eight and her condition worsened. She was transferred to ICU where no children were allowed. The doctor told us the prospects weren't good, but there was hope. "Hope springs eternal" was Mama's favorite saying. For her, I tried to remain hopeful. Anthony drew and painted cheerful scenes for me to take to her, but what she really wanted was to have him visit.

A friendly nurse helped us smuggle Anthony into ICU to see her. We donned surgical masks and walked in. He carried a picture of flowers he had drawn for her. Wearing a serene smile, Mama Anne took the picture from him and praised his work. She asked if she could hang it on the wall along with his other drawings and paintings I had brought in previously. I asked the nurse for some tape.

Perhaps knowing this might be her last time seeing her grandson, she made a special effort to appear upbeat, although I could see she was weak. When we returned home that day, Anthony spotted her red Toyota parked at our curb.

"Look, Mama Anne is here," he shouted. In his five-year-old mind, he assumed Mama Anne had simply checked herself out of the hospital and was once again waiting inside at our kitchen table with sketchpads and paint. He was very disappointed when I explained my sister had parked the car out front, not Grandma. She was still back in the hospital.

A few days later, Mama stopped breathing and the doctor had to put her on a respirator. In the next twenty-four hours, we prayed and hoped she would get better. Just after sundown on a Sunday, Mama died. I went in to see her after. She lay on her bed clothed in white sheets and looking radiant. She no longer had to struggle to breathe.

She looked free. Back at home, I tried to explain her passing to my son.

"Where's Grandma?" he asked.

"She's in heaven now," I told him.

"Will she still come see me?" he asked.

"No," I answered. We both cried and hugged each other.

We took her south to Jackson, Georgia to bury her in her native red clay. When we returned to California, I was overcome with grief. Not a day went by that I did not feel the pain of Mama's death. I kept hoping the phone would ring and she would somehow be there so we could talk again. I wanted to tell her how much I missed coming home to see her in her beret giving Anthony art lessons at our kitchen table.

On a chilly February day a few weeks after the funeral, I walked at the beach with only a few wandering sandpipers keeping me company. Mama had loved the sandpipers, the beach and the sight of the sun sinking into the sea. I glanced up to take a look at the setting sun, a sight Mama would never see again.

The clouds had transformed into pink cotton candy, not only to the west but to the east, north and south. The sky behind was awash in shades of gold and rose. As I looked at the brilliant sky, I knew Mama was sending a sign. My sadness lifted, and I began to feel hope again. I rushed home to show Anthony.

"Mama Anne is in heaven painting with God," I told him as we stood under the glowing dome.

"Mama Anne sunset?" he asked. I nodded and hugged him.

From then on, every time we saw a sky streaked with warm colors dotted with pink cotton candy clouds, we called it "Mama Anne Sunset." We talked about Grandma Anne's walks and art lessons. Even though she no longer wore a beret or sat at our kitchen table, she still continued with her art lessons. Not with paint and brushes, but with a much larger palette, the infinite sky.

~Janie Dempsey Watts

78

Thank You, Dad

When you're a nurse you know that every day
you will touch a life or a life will touch yours.
~Author Unknown

I never had a chance to say goodbye to my dad. My father, Alfred Gaspar, was only seventy-four years old when he died unexpectedly. He and my mother lived together at home in Rochester, New York. He had been disabled by a stroke sixteen years earlier, his left side paralyzed. Overall, he was a healthy six-foot tall man who sat upright in his wheelchair. My mother helped him and encouraged his independence so he could remain at home.

I lived in Florida with my husband and two daughters. I had just returned home from the beach when I listened to the message on my answering machine. My brother's voice on the recording was urgent: "Dad was taken to the hospital by ambulance in the morning. Please call back!" As soon as I heard the message, I called my brother. Dad was already gone. He had died in the hospital earlier that afternoon. I never got to say goodbye. I had visited my parents months ago, and had booked a flight to be with them later that month. I went to New York for the funeral and a sorrowful family gathering.

Eventually I had to return to Florida, to my home and to my nursing administration position. I worked with geriatric patients. My brothers and sisters asked me, "How are you going to go back to work and see older men sitting in wheelchairs?" "I don't really know," I replied honestly, "but I need to."

More than once I felt a lump in my throat and tears forming when I approached a tall man sitting upright in a wheelchair. Little gestures and facial expressions of older men made me pause. I would gently say out loud, "There's something about you that reminds me of my dad. He's gone now, and I miss him." In response, the older men would offer a smile, a hug, or express gratitude that I shared my feeling with them. Some men asked me my father's name, and offered to say a prayer for him.

Years passed. I missed my dad's voice and his chuckle and his one-armed hugs. I wish he had been alive to meet my loving second husband Ed, to see my daughters get married, and to enjoy our new granddaughter. But I have accepted losing my father and I try to apply lessons of honesty, love of family, simplicity and integrity, which he modeled all his life.

I resigned from nursing administration and returned to "hands on" clinical nursing practice. I became supervisor in a 110-bed skilled nursing facility. Half of the patients were admitted after a brief stay at the local hospitals. Some patients had complicated surgeries or massive infections or new disabilities. They came to my facility for a short-term stay, to stabilize, and benefit from therapy and skilled nursing care before returning home. The turnover of patients was high. As soon as one patient was discharged, another patient was admitted to that bed.

One of my many responsibilities was to meet and assess new patients as soon as they arrived from the hospital. I listened and answered questions from family members. I examined the person literally from head to toe, inspecting every inch of skin, and listening to lung sounds, heart sounds and bowel sounds. Physically the assessment process demands thoroughness; it is tedious and time-consuming. The subsequent paperwork is even more extensive and time-consuming. Work was stressful, managing many ill people — some critically ill — their anxious family members, and an array of problems that always seem to arise with pharmacy deliveries, physicians' orders, and the dynamics of working with people.

On one such stressful evening, I prepared to admit a very

old man from the hospital who was blind, deaf, full of infection, extremely weak and malnourished. His elderly wife accompanied him as the hospital transport team transferred him from their stretcher to his bed. I introduced myself to him and to his wife, and then started my head-to-toe assessment. I took my time and was very thorough, making notes. He was very thin and very frail, and I moved him gently in bed to examine him. Nonetheless, my mind raced with all the tasks I needed to complete before the end of the shift was over.

When I finally concluded my lengthy assessment, I carefully repositioned the frail man on his back. He reached over to my right hand, held it to his lips, kissed my hand, and held my hand in his over his heart. My eyes welled with tears at the intense familiarity of that gesture.

"I'm crying," I said softly to the man and his wife, "because my dad used to kiss my hand and hold it to his heart just like that."

"Oh, honey," his wife reassured me. "Don't you know your father is in this room right now?"

I still tear up at this memory. The loving gesture from my dad through that stranger was a gift. In that moment, my dad was tenderly holding my hand to his heart. I realized I needed to see the person in that bed, no matter how busy or pressured I felt. I was a conscientious, committed nurse. But at times I focused on my tasks rather than on the people who needed me. I allowed myself to be sidetracked from the powerful spiritual connections offered in "hands on" nursing. Staying in the moment, really present with the patient in front of me, was a gift to myself as well as the person in the bed.

Over and over, I have felt my dad's presence at work. I sense him always during moments when I feel overwhelmed with my responsibilities. I halt my activity, quiet my mind and feel that my father is with me. Then I know I need to slow down my thoughts, focus on the person in front of me, really listen, and take time to be truly present and attentive.

I never had the chance to tell my father goodbye. But I do get to tell him, "Thank you."

~Mary Beth Sturgis

79

Amazing Grace

Faith makes the discords of the present the harmonies of the future.
~Robert Collyer

My mother's singing left a lot to be desired, but her lack of talent didn't stop her from belting out the songs from our church hymn book loudly and off-key. While I'd seen her scare a few crows away from the corn patch, I personally loved it. When she was hoeing a half-acre of weeds in the garden, her screechy but cheery voice convinced me that although she was working hard she enjoyed the time spent in meditation.

If I happened to go through the barn while she was milking the cattle, her rendition of "Rock of Ages" might reverberate through the rafters. I'd hear her on the way to the hen house to collect the eggs, and the strains of "Standing on the Promises" echoing across the knolls were almost musical.

Without a doubt, her favorite was "Amazing Grace." She not only sang, but believed, that hymn. She sang it so heartfelt and gratefully there was no doubt she placed herself within the words when she sang "When we've been there ten thousand years, bright shining as the sun, we've no less days to sing God's praise, than when we've first begun." I often woke to those lyrics as she cooked pancakes at the coal stove in the kitchen and went to sleep with them ringing in my ears as she tucked me under the comforters at night.

When she passed away, at her request we played "Amazing Grace" at the funeral. I thought my heart would burst with all the memories it brought back. But as the final notes faded away, I felt joy knowing my mother was a woman of great faith who knew that grace had brought her though her "danger, toils and snares" and grace had led her home.

Many years later, I waited nervously in the cardiac clinic at my local hospital to have a stress test. I was not physically able to perform the standard treadmill exam, so my increased heart rate would be chemically induced.

The small room was crammed with other patients and their supportive family and friends. I suddenly wished I had allowed my daughter to accompany me. I had stubbornly insisted on doing this alone.

As the minutes ticked by, my nerves frayed even further and I longed for my mother. I realized what she meant when she said no matter how old you get, you never quit worrying about your kids. And you never stop wanting your mother. Especially in scary situations.

I tried to fix my eyes on the television. Cheers and applause from *The Price Is Right* game show filled the air. I turned away, trying not to think of Bob Barker, new cars, and the fact that my entire future (or lack of it) hung on the results of the stress test.

Suddenly the unmistakable strains of "Amazing Grace" filled the room. With the song came a deep sense of peace and solace. Had someone switched channels? No, because the screen showed a young woman jumping up and down, having just won a trip to some exotic beach. The other patients in the waiting room were riveted by the game show.

This melodious rendition of my mother's favorite hymn was for my ears only. I felt calm as I realized I was not alone after all. I clung to the words from the seldom-sung fourth stanza "The Lord has promised good to me, His Word my hope secures." And I realized, as my mother had, that "He will my shield and portion be, as long as life endures."

This all happened more than ten years ago. My heart was so

filled with my mother's love and my Father's grace there was no room for blockage.

~Shirley Nordeck Short

Messages from Heaven

Messengers and Angels

Heaven's Mail

A dream which is not interpreted is like a letter which is not read.
~The Talmud

I dialed the phone while wondering if it was too early to call. My sister, Jennifer, was away on vacation with her family and might not like my 8 a.m. interruption.

"Hello." A groggy voice answered.

"Jennifer, it's me, Joanne."

"What's wrong?" she asked, sounding more alert.

"Nothing is wrong," I assured her. "Sorry about calling you so early, but I thought the kids might have you up by now." My little sister was used to my pushy nature. Being the oldest of our four siblings, I enjoyed teasing them and pulling the bossy-older-sister card from time to time.

"None of us are up. The girls are still in bed." She sighed and continued, "I don't know about them, but I had a hard time getting to sleep last night. Lots of things going through my head…" She trailed off.

My sister was struggling to come to terms with our mother's death months before. After a two-year battle with cancer, Mom left our world for Heaven at the age of fifty-four. We were still reeling from the shock of her illness, and the fact she wouldn't be there for us to lean on, or to watch her grandchildren grow up.

Two years had been a bittersweet gift for me. I took advantage of the time to talk with Mom about as much as possible, including her death. I could see how it helped to speak with her, about things like what songs she wanted played at her funeral and how certain possessions needed to go to specific loved ones.

Sadly, my sister had none of these conversations with her. For two years Jennifer had been in denial.

Sure, she sat by like all four of us did and watched cancer transform our beautiful homecoming queen mom into a hollow shell of a person, but sadly, she never once spoke with her about dying. Mom worried about my sister and her anxiety about the whole situation. And in sparing her second child the tough conversations, Mom stunted grief's healing process.

I went on, "I have to share a dream I had about Mom. Now that I have you on the phone, it seems quite silly."

Actually, I'd debated about calling at all. The dream was so random it was borderline ridiculous. But it had been so vivid, so real, I felt compelled to share it.

I had Jennifer's full attention. "What did you dream?"

"Okay, well…" I hesitated, feeling kind of foolish. "Mom walked up to me and was smiling. She looked beautiful. She said just one thing: 'Tell Jennifer I loved what she wrote.'"

I rattled on, "I told you it was silly. Pretty out of the blue, huh? She really seemed to want me to give you that message." I softly chuckled, and then realized there was only silence on the other end of the line.

"Hello, Jennifer, are you there?" I pressed the receiver against my ear and heard a soft hiccup and gentle sobbing. "Are you okay? I'm so sorry. I should've waited to call you later." I figured my dream touched a tender place and quickly regretted my call. "I know you miss her, Jennifer."

"It's not that…" She sniffled and hiccupped again. "You're not going to believe this, Joanne."

Now she had my full attention.

"Last night I was having such a hard time falling asleep. I was tossing and turning, thinking about Mom and how I'd never talked with her about the important things."

I stayed silent, letting her get out whatever it was that had her so upset.

She went on, her voice thick. "After Mom died, I wrote her a letter. I really poured my heart out to her and told her how sorry I was about some things. On the day of her funeral I placed that letter inside her coffin." She softly blew her nose and continued. "Last night before I fell asleep, I prayed she could somehow read the words tucked away beside her."

Tears ran down my cheeks as my dream came rushing back to me. It all made sense now—my mother's gentle smile, her pleading eyes and request that I pass on a message to my little sister. I realized my mom's words were far from random, and now it was me who was sobbing.

"Tell Jennifer I loved what she wrote."

My mother's message to her hurting child—a bittersweet gift spanning eternity and inspiring hope in both of her children.

~Joanne Kraft

My Fairy Godmother's Gift

*A friend knows the song in my heart
and sings it to me when my memory fails.*
~Donna Roberts

anye befriended me when I was eight years old. For most of the next twenty-five years, we had fairly constant contact. Something of a Fairy Godmother, she took me out to lunch at least once a month during my teen years. We frequently attended the ballet and the opera together. When I was older, I stayed at her beach house on weekends, and we'd share the time cooking or reading to each other or just chatting. After I relocated to New York to study opera at Juilliard, our visits were more sporadic—but whenever she was in the Big Apple, she'd call and we'd get together.

Fanye had begun life in abject poverty. She had been raised in an orphanage, and as her fortunes improved, she took great delight in acquiring knowledge of the finer aspects of life—fine dining, beautiful clothes, the ballet, the opera. Especially the opera. It thrilled her when I became a singer, and several times I was happily surprised to find her at my dressing room door, backstage at New York City Opera after one of my performances.

I hadn't heard from her for quite a while when, one day, I got a call from my brother. "Fanye's son Mark phoned. He didn't know how to reach you. His mother died. He knew what great friends you were, and asked me to let you know."

And just like that, my Fairy Godmother was gone. Forever.

Fifteen years passed. Sometimes, at the ballet or the opera, the thought would come to me: Fanye would have loved this. Out of the blue, a wave of sadness would wash over me. And always the questions: How had I not known of her long illness, her looming death? Why wouldn't she tell me? How could she have left like that, giving me no chance to say goodbye?

One morning as I was waking up, I heard her distinctive voice. "Call Mark," she said.

Call Mark? I hadn't seen or spoken to Mark in over forty years. But Fanye had sounded firm, imperative. I looked up Mark's architectural firm online and called his office.

"Ummm… Mark? It's Penny."

"Penny? Penny Orloff?"

We chatted for a short time, and he finally asked me the reason for my call. I took a deep breath.

"Ummm… your mother told me to call you."

"I'm not surprised," said Mark. "She makes herself known from time to time."

I had dinner with Mark and his wife, Eloise, a few days later. Ellie was worried about their younger son, Zach, who lived in New York. An aspiring opera singer, he was having a hard year and facing a major crisis of confidence. The hairs on the back of my neck quivered.

"I don't know how to help him—he's seriously considering giving up. We feel so helpless."

I told them my story. They were astonished. Mark hadn't known I attended Juilliard nearly forty years earlier, and that I had been an opera singer. He couldn't have imagined that I had come up against that same crisis of confidence that Zach now faced, and considered throwing in the towel many times, myself. He never knew that his mother had transformed my life, by encouraging and inspiring me many times during the darkest days of my early career.

In a flash, it dawned on the three of us—Fanye had come to me after fifteen years of silence to help her young grandson.

The next day I phoned New York.

"Zach, I've known your dad since we were kids. Your grandmother was a great friend to me," I said. We talked for a long time about his passionate love of singing, his months of discouragement, and his fear that he wouldn't be able to make a career in opera. I told him about my similar feelings as a young singer, decades earlier, and how passion and persistence had been the magic ingredients that had allowed me to realize my dreams.

And speaking of magic, I told him how his grandmother had come to me in a dream.

"I believe she wanted to introduce us. She seems to have thought we might have a lot to say to each other."

In the months since that first call, I've become Zach's Fairy Godmother, as Fanye was mine. He and I have spoken many times and e-mailed regularly. I visit him from time to time in New York. His renewed optimism and enthusiasm have taken him to new levels of accomplishment. As his rich baritone voice has blossomed, so has his career. In the short span of four months, he experienced a great success singing in Italy, and returned to New York to pursue graduate studies in the opera department of the renowned Manhattan School of Music.

I felt so blessed to be able to deliver Fanye's gift of hope to her grandson. But there is more to the story. It would appear that Fanye had a gift for me, too. With a wave of her magic wand, she has transformed my life once again. Her encouraging words, coming out of my mouth, have resonated in my heart. Now in my sixties, and too long silent, I am singing again.

~Penny Orloff

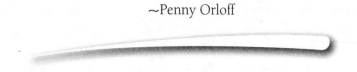

Crossroads

Dad, your guiding hand on my shoulder will remain with me forever.
~Author Unknown

When I was twenty-five years old, my father died from a massive heart attack. He had turned sixty-one only two months before. It was the saddest day of my life. Not just because I lost one of my parents, but because I had lost my role model, my advisor, my friend—someone who had always been there for me, no matter what.

My dad was an early riser. Growing up, I could always count on him to have a cup of cocoa, a hot breakfast, and a helping of wisdom ready for me before I left for school. We were on the same wavelength; he would amaze me by knowing what I was thinking even before I said anything.

Fifteen months after my dad died, my husband and I celebrated the birth of Valerie, our first child. Almost three years later, our second daughter, Lisa, was born. My mother was overjoyed to have two beautiful granddaughters, and they loved her, too. What a pity my father and his granddaughters never got to know each other.

Years passed, and our daughters were in elementary school. It was a beautiful fall afternoon in southwestern Connecticut. Lisa, who was seven, had gone to a friend's house after school. I finished work, picked up Valerie from school, and drove her home. This was Valerie's last year in elementary school. Next year—middle school. Where had the time gone?

After having a snack, Valerie went outside to play with some of the children in the neighborhood. I did a few chores in the house and then went outside to rake some leaves. Down the street, I could see Valerie walking back home. As she spotted the freshly-raked leaf pile, she started running and took a flying leap right into the middle of it, scattering leaves everywhere. I flopped down in what was left of the pile, and we both enjoyed a good laugh.

I still needed to run to the store to buy a few things for dinner. "Let's brush ourselves off. I need to go to the food store. After that, we can pick up Lisa."

Valerie loved to sit in the front passenger seat when we went places together without her sister, so she hopped into the car for the five-mile drive to the supermarket. As we drove through our neighborhood, we chatted.

"Me and Lisa collected acorns yesterday. When Daddy gets home from work, maybe he can help us make 'acorn men.'"

As I turned onto the road leading out of the neighborhood, Valerie chattered on about her plans for the rest of the day. I tried to listen, but something muted her voice. It was a strong and clear message, and it echoed through my mind: "When you get to the light, stop. Even if it's green, don't go."

I approached the traffic light at the end of our neighborhood. The intersection was very dangerous and had been the scene of many car accidents. The light glowed green, but I slowed, the weight of the message pressing on my mind.

The light turned yellow and then red, and I came to a full stop. When the light turned green again, the message from earlier echoed: "When you get to the light, stop. Even if it's green, don't go." I sat there, pressing hard on the brake. Nothing short of an act of God was going to move that car! Only seconds passed, but they felt like minutes. Out of the corner of my eye, I could see my daughter looking at me as if I had surely lost my mind.

"Val, I know the light's green, but I'm not moving this car."

"Mom!"

"No! We're staying right here!"

Just as the words left my mouth, a black Jeep Cherokee went speeding through the red light. We could see the driver holding her cell phone, oblivious to everything except her conversation. Again, my daughter stared at me, but her expression had changed from exasperation to shock.

"Mom, oh my God! How did you know? That car would have hit us right where I'm sitting!"

No one was behind us, so I continued to sit through two more light cycles as I composed myself and waited for my hands to stop trembling.

Finally, I said, "Val, you're probably going to think I'm crazy, but I got a message while we were turning onto this street. The message said not to go through the light, even if it changed to green."

"Mom, how could that be! Who do you think gave you the message?"

I didn't even have to think about it; I knew exactly who it was. "Your grandfather. He's still there for us."

As I spent the evening watching my daughters play in the leaves and make acorn men with my husband, I looked up at the sky and knew that my dad was watching, too. And once again, I didn't have to say a thing because he knew exactly what I was thinking.

~Michelle Tompakov Muller

Picture This

When someone you love becomes a memory, the memory becomes a treasure.
~Author Unknown

I told myself not to look but the temptation was too great. The scene was exactly as I feared it would be and my heart sunk under the burden of anger and resentment.

How could they? I watched as teenagers laughed at each other's jokes, horsed around, or leaned casually against the brick wall of their high school waiting for the first class of their first day back to school. I fought the urge to pull into the parking lot and run to each of those students, grab them and remind them that their fellow classmate, my daughter, had died.

I shook my head as the anger turned to sorrow; I was too consumed by my grief to feel grateful when I finally made it through the congested morning traffic leaving the high school behind. On the drive home a panic began to overtake me. Kyley had been gone for a little over a year and the longing to hear her laugh, to just feel her presence at that moment was overwhelming.

I tore into my driveway and rushed to the front door, fumbling with my keys as I desperately tried to open the door. When I was finally inside I grabbed the stepladder and took it to my closet. I pulled down the two large boxes from the top shelf and settled down on the floor. I stared at the boxes for a few seconds. They contained the thousands of photos I had taken of my children over the years. I hadn't looked at them since my daughter died. I needed to feel close to her, to be reminded of every freckle and every strand of hair.

I took a deep breath and removed the lid from the first box. I grabbed a handful of about twenty pictures. They weren't in any particular order and a five-year-old Kyley smiled back at me. I felt like the air had just been knocked out of me. With each picture the tears fell faster until my body shook from my sobbing. I couldn't look at any more. I went to place the pictures back in the box when the last picture in my small handful fell to the floor. I picked it up and for a brief moment I smiled and was surprised at my own spontaneous laughter as I gazed at the image. I laid the picture gently on top of the others and closed the lid, exhausted.

The next few days were excruciating. Life refused to stand still for me and I made feeble, half-hearted attempts at my daily routine. My inbox was overflowing and as I scanned through my e-mails, I stopped at one from my daughter's aunt. She lived a few towns over and I hadn't seen her since the funeral. I opened the e-mail and this is exactly what she wrote:

"Ok, last night I was going to sleep and Kyley came to me, she said to tell you she loves you. I don't know if I was completely asleep, I felt sorta awake. She also wanted me to tell you something about a freezer? Not sure. I would have played it off, but she kept saying it. Not sure if it was 'put something in the freezer' or something about a freezer. She just said tell her, she'll get it or know. Just thought I would let you know. You may think I'm crazy, but at the end she said, 'You won't tell her.' so I had to tell you. Don't think I'm nutzo, Ky made me do it. ;-)"

I sat there in disbelief. I read it one more time to be sure I wasn't imagining it and then, when I felt it was safe and what I was experiencing was real, I began to cry. A happy cry, a cry that released so much of the hurt I had been holding onto.

I went to the closet and brought down the picture box. I lifted the lid and there it was sitting right on top where I had left it just a few days earlier. I smiled as I looked at the photo once again.

Several years ago, I had booked a camping trip for our family right in the middle of August, a blistering hot time of year in Texas. I rented a cabin at the park and figured we could always go indoors to cool down if we needed to. When we arrived I was horrified to discover the cabins were not air conditioned, nor did they contain any type of fan. We were miserably hot and after one sleepless night decided to cut our trip short. Before we left, being the comedian that she was, my daughter opened the freezer door of the refrigerator unit in the cabin, and stuck her head inside in a mock attempt at cooling down. I managed to snap a picture of her posing with her head in the freezer, the very same picture that days before had turned my cries into laughter, the very same picture I was looking at now.

"I love you, too, Kyley," I whispered with a smile and a newfound lightness in my heart. "I love you, too."

~Melissa R. Wootan

84

Hot Dogs in Heaven

All that is in heaven... is also on earth.
~Plotinus

When I was a little girl I began to see apparitions—translucent figures or shadows whisking by. Sometimes I'd hear their occasional whispers as I fell asleep. Like most kids, I'd pull the sheets over my head and immerse myself within a cotton-blend fortress. I don't think my visitors intended to scare me but on occasion they did. As I grew older I became less fearful, but the early years were tough.

The first night I saw a spirit I was terrified and bolted from my room as fast as my six-year-old legs would carry me. My anxiety was quickly dismissed with a kiss on my forehead and a "go back to sleep." Since my folks didn't believe me the first time I told them, I knew sharing additional experiences about Casper's friends was out of the question. I never told anyone: not my pastor, not my closest friends.

No one knew until thirty-four years later.

Dad and I were at lunch, munching on chilidogs and having a heart-to-heart talk about one of the most difficult subjects in the world.

Dying.

He had advanced emphysema, and time wasn't on his side. In spite of a ravenous appetite and a fondness for deep fried junk food,

Dad couldn't gain an ounce of weight and was painfully thin. The doctors told us that every calorie was used for breathing.

"I'm worried about Mom. She's never been alone and may have a hard time getting used to it," Dad said while toying with the straw in his root beer. "When I'm gone I'm counting on you take care of her for me."

"I'll be there Dad. I promise," I said, reaching for another chili-dog. "And if I mess it up, just materialize like all the others and tell me how to fix it."

Then I stopped mid-bite.

Maybe he didn't notice.

"Materialize like all the others?"

He had noticed.

"Daddy, you'll probably think I'm crazy but I see and hear spirits. Not all the time, but every now and then."

His eyes widened.

"For real?"

"Yes, ever since I was a child."

"Why am I just now learning about this?" he demanded.

"Once I tried to tell you both but no one believed me. So I didn't talk about it." I sighed. "The reason why spirits appear to kids is because they don't question what they see. Grownups do."

There was a long pause as we both took another bite.

He spoke first.

"I suppose we've all seen and heard things that we dismissed because we're frightened of the truth. There are millions of mysteries in God's universe that we can't begin to comprehend. No doubt this is one of them. I'm truly sorry that you had to shoulder this burden alone," he said, wiping the chili from his chin.

He studied the food on his plate.

"Not to change the subject, but I wonder if they have hot dogs in heaven. I certainly hope so."

We laughed.

"So how does this ghost stuff work?" he asked.

"Fortunately my visitors appear to be passing through. I think they just want to be noticed. A few try to speak but I can't understand what they're saying. It's like listening to someone talking underwater."

"I'll bet you'd understand me." He chuckled.

"I'll bet I would too."

A few months later Dad was in a coma and not expected to survive. As he struggled for every breath in an Indiana hospital, I was in Florida waiting for news. I longed to be there, but he was adamant that I not witness the inevitable.

So there I sat one day, feeling utterly helpless.

Then I heard his voice, clear as a bell.

"This is Dad. You need to be brave and take care of Mom. Remember your promise."

Just then the phone rang and I nearly jumped out of my skin.

It was Mom.

"When did he pass away?" I asked, choking back tears.

"A few minutes ago," she sobbed.

I flew to Indiana the following day. Mom was inconsolable so I was unable to give in to my own grief. If I did I'd be no good to anyone. There was work to be done; locating paperwork and policies, making phone calls and funeral arrangements. In spite of Dad's advance preparations, I still found myself fumbling through desk drawers.

"For Pete's sake Daddy, where did you hide this stuff?" I groaned.

Then I began hearing "open that" or "look in there." And I found what I was searching for.

A few weeks later I was back home in Florida still trying to hold myself together, but the dam was crumbling. Mom knew so little about how to handle her home and finances. Dad hadn't done her any favors by taking care of everything for so long. Until she was self-sufficient I was on-call looking after her long distance.

One afternoon I heard Dad's voice again.

"Shelly, you need to call your mom."

I was emotionally drained. No doubt Dad's directive meant that Mom had another brushfire to stomp out.

I tried ignoring him.

A few minutes later he said it again using his "do it or else" tone.

"Listen to me. You NEED to call your mom."

I dialed the phone.

For the first time in ages Mom was genuinely cheerful, which encouraged me. Maybe whatever was wrong wasn't a big deal.

"You don't usually call in the afternoon. Why are you calling this late?" she asked.

"I don't know. For some reason I thought you might need me or want to talk."

There was a long pause.

"You're right I do want to talk and for once I want to talk about you. I've been such a mess lately that I've been blind to the fact that a very sad girl has been looking after me. My wonderful son-in-law told me that you haven't shed more than a few tears since Dad died. You've been so busy propping me up that you haven't allowed yourself to mourn your own father. It's not healthy to hold it in, even though I know you've done it out of love for me."

My lower lip began trembling, and my eyes filled.

"I can't imagine how much you must be suffering. I'm so sorry. Please forgive me and let your mom help you for a change."

With just a few words the dam burst and the tears gushed.

I didn't think the human body could hold that much water. From 1,200 miles away Mom spoke words of comfort as I wept with abandon.

Dad didn't tell me to call Mom because she needed me. It was I who needed Mom. She was turning a corner, starting to adjust to life without my father.

It was my turn to do the same.

Since that day Dad has been silent. Perhaps he knew it was time to let go, that we'd be okay. And we are.

I just wish I'd remembered to ask him if they served hot dogs in heaven.

For his sake, I certainly hope so.

~Michelle Close Mills

Our Little Angel

Angels can fly directly into the heart of the matter.
~Author Unknown

I have always believed things happen for a reason. My faith tells me God has a plan. I may not understand at the time what it is, but I know at some point it will be clear. When my husband Ryan and I had our first child, Jenna, we never expected anything bad to happen. When she died three days after her birth we were grief-stricken. Through my tears I kept telling myself there was a reason for this. Later, we would have two more children, Tony and Brittany. As the years passed I found myself repeating "things happen for a reason" whenever life threw me a curveball. It always seemed to make it easier to accept the unexpected.

On November 9, 2009 my faith would be tested. My husband suffered a ruptured brain aneurysm while at work as a firefighter. He was rushed to the hospital. I called our son and daughter. The thirty-minute drive to the hospital was agonizing. Ryan was conscious when I saw him in the ER. He was later moved to the neurosurgical ICU. By this time his assistant chief and good friend, Jake, had arrived. We were told they would try to repair the aneurysm in the morning with a procedure called "coiling" in hopes of avoiding major brain surgery.

We arrived at the hospital early the next morning hoping this procedure would work. Unfortunately it was not successful and Ryan would need surgery to stop the bleeding in his brain. They brought him back to the ICU. We were allowed to see him, but only two to three people at a time. Jake went in with me.

The ICU rooms have glass front walls and doors. There is a nurses' station outside each room. As I approached Ryan's room I looked in and saw a nurse by his bed adjusting one of his IVs. I waited a few minutes before going in. Jake was right behind me. As I walked in, I didn't see the nurse. I scanned the room, but she was gone. I knew she didn't come out the only door in the room. Jake had seen me looking around. "Where did she go?" he asked. I was stunned. "You saw her too?"

He said he had seen a nurse standing by Ryan's bed adjusting his IVs. We both described her the same way. We knew it wasn't a reflection in the window, and there wasn't a nurse on duty that matched our description. It was then I realized who she was. She was our daughter Jenna, who had died thirty-two years ago. The nurse we saw was about that age and looked like what I would expect Jenna to look like as an adult. Of course Jake knew nothing about this. Very few people except family and close friends knew about Jenna, so I told Jake about her. He also has a deep faith and knew it must have been her. A few hours later they took Ryan into surgery.

I know in my heart that Jenna was there to help her father. Perhaps to ease his pain and comfort him before the surgery. I believe she was sent to look after him. I was comforted knowing that she would be there with him when I could not. After the surgery, Ryan was in a coma for three weeks. I wasn't sure if he would wake up or if he would remember any of us. When he woke from the coma I asked him if he knew who I was and who his children were. He knew me and our two children but he also talked about Jenna as if she were still alive, which was something he had never done before. I am convinced he also saw her that day, even though he says he doesn't remember.

On Jenna's gravestone we had engraved "Our Little Angel." She was our angel then and still is today.

~Carol Reed

Our Little Angel : Messengers and Angels   293

Yes, I Believe

Faith is a knowledge within the heart, beyond the reach of proof.
~Kahlil Gibran

"Mrs. Nichols, your father has taken a turn for the worse. We suggest that your family come to the hospital as soon as possible." I made note of the time on our bedside clock: 5:30 a.m.

Just seconds before, I had woken from a dream both disturbing and comforting. I saw my father's hospital bed, not in a sterile hospital room, but atop a grassy hill illuminated in early morning light. My husband, a resident physician, was positioned on one side of my father, who lay peacefully in the bed. Dave was listening to my father's heart with his stethoscope. Opposite Dave was a handsome young man that I "identified" as my twin brother Frankie, who had died at age six in the polio epidemic. In my mind, Frankie had aged as if death had never snatched him away. I had imagined that face for many years. Both Dave and Frankie were dressed in green surgical scrubs but only Dave spoke to me: "Jan, it's almost time." I knew that my father's death was imminent. I prayed that his death, when it came, would be merciful.

When we arrived at the hospital, we rushed to Dad's room only to learn that he was not there. Returning to the nurse's station, the charge nurse took us aside and announced that my father was already dead; she escorted us to a room down the hall where my father's body had been placed for private viewing.

Though Dad's death had been expected, his condition had remained stable as we kissed him goodnight the night before. I had expected to be prepared for his passing in much the same way that I had been forewarned of my twin's death some twenty-five-plus years earlier. Though a dream had not preceded Frankie's death, I had sensed his passing when my parents visited me at my paternal grandmother's home, where I was staying while Frankie was hospitalized. When my parents attempted to avoid my question as to Frankie's condition I had blurted out, without hesitation, that Frankie was dead. How did I know that? My parents continued to ask that question for the rest of their lives.

Since that event so long ago, I have had an unsettling dream, featuring the loved one who will soon die, each time I am about to lose someone close. It has never failed. There have been times when the person has not been ill, or at least not seriously ill, yet death has always occurred within a matter of hours or days.

Even as a little girl, I had reasoned that it was Frankie's gift to me — a twin way of always preparing his birth partner for loss and sadness. Though the dreams have frightened me, I am thankful that I have never been unprepared. I was therefore certain that I would have a dream before Dad's death, just not the dream that startled me on the morning of March 31st. I had actually prayed that my dream would be a less terrifying version of gloom, a dream that in the past had always featured a hooded figure with black cape. Had Frankie heard my plea? Can those who have crossed over anticipate our needs and intervene?

A few weeks later, my mother received mailed copies of my father's death certificate. It was then that I saw the time of Dad's death — 5:30 a.m., immediately after my warning dream.

What am I to make of my dream or its timing?

Since my father's death, I have recalled the dream and its possible significance many times. A few people have even suggested that I had been somehow teleported to my father's bedside with my husband's and twin's faces and bodies superimposed on the faces and bodies of medical personnel. Though I readily acknowledge that I seem to possess some kind of sixth sense, I'm not ready to contemplate the concept of psychic transport.

I prefer thinking that it is just my twin's way of softening the sadness and grief that always accompanies death. Frankie, if he is my heavenly messenger, could not have chosen a better way to prepare me. Both my husband and twin were there to provide comfort to Dad and me. Dave's soft soothing voice was a voice that I not only recognized but one that I relied upon in times of trouble. The setting was not clinical, but pastoral. My father's face was not the drawn face of a dying man, but the robust face that I had recognized my entire life. I like to think that Frankie was featured in my dream not only to comfort me, but to show me that Dad would not be alone as he crossed over. His only son would lead him to eternal life. He would be forever reunited with the son whom he had missed for so long.

Long ago, I came to believe that my twin would always be by my side even though my Earth eyes could not see him, that death cannot destroy the twin bond, and that those who have crossed over continue to provide care and comfort if we choose to believe in con-nections—even the power of such everyday occurrences as dreams.

Yes, I believe.

~Janice Flood Nichols

Guide from Beyond

For every soul, there is a guardian watching it.
~The Koran

On my fortieth birthday, I was surrounded by a wonderful group of friends. I had been on bed rest for nearly two months, pregnant with twins and unable to rise due to complications with the pregnancy. Since I couldn't go out, they came in. At 5 p.m., I received a telephone call from my mother. While I expected congratulations, I instead received news of my dear nana's passing. It had been a long struggle, and I was glad for her relief, but I was also devastated.

Less than three days later, I went into labor and brought the twins into the world—ten weeks early. Two months later, we were finally able to bring them home from the Neonatal Intensive Care Unit.

Three months passed and I received the second call. My grandfather, after sixty-seven years of marriage to his sweetheart, had left to join her. Despite his advanced age, my grandfather was playful and engaged. His death was almost incomprehensible to me. I had been close with my nana, but my grandfather and I shared a special bond—one so deep in Spirit that at times I would be dialing his number, and he would be dialing mine simultaneously!

The memorial service and the year after were a blur. My life had lost its foundation. I focused all of my energy on tending my family and my practice, as my marriage tore apart and I began to lose myself in my grief. I knew that something had to give—I couldn't keep going without some help.

I spoke to friends, family, therapists, and even to God. Then, the most amazing thing happened. During the process of caring for one of my therapy clients, I started to get signs. And the signs led me to unwavering faith.

I attended a conference to review new research in the treatment of trauma. I met a terrific clinician who told me about a trauma facility she was helping launch. A week later, I opened my e-mail to a flyer announcing the opening of that facility, accompanied by a bio of its Executive Director, Lee McCormick. The following day, I admitted my client to a similar facility, owned by none other than Lee McCormick! And, while my client got acclimated to her new surroundings, I toured the grounds with the Intake Director. For two hours, he told me about the place and then asked me about myself. I told him of my practice, of my reality, of my dreams. He stopped, looked deeply into my eyes, and said, "I've got someone you need to meet!"

A week and three e-mails later, Lee and I spoke at length on the phone. It was uncanny how much we had in common, if not professionally, then personally. He was eager to see how we might work together. And he invited me to join him on a journey to Teotihuacan, Mexico—the place where it is believed that men become gods.

Teo is an interesting place. The city is more than 4,000 years old, and no one knows who actually built it. It was completely abandoned when it was discovered. It houses two major pyramids, several major temples, and thousands of residences. And, Teo is alive.

I first noticed the vibration as we walked towards the site on our first morning together. I actually had to stop and catch my breath several times because my heart seemed to be beating out of control. One of the shamans came beside me, placed her hand on my back and said calmly, "Recalibrate."

We entered the site and made our way to an altar in front of the Pyramid of the Sun. We removed our backpacks and hats and seated ourselves on the ground. Lee instructed us to close our eyes and breathe in this magical place. Then, in the gentlest of voices, he led us into our own hearts. He encouraged us to feel the space, to embrace its sorrow, to feel its pain. He guided us to invite an avatar to assist us — a spirit, our God, a loved one — to hold our hearts during this journey.

Tears streaming down my face, eyes closed, face basking in the sun, my grandfather came to me. He was surrounded by a magnificent light — so bright it was hard to focus on him at first. He came from the room at the base of the Pyramid and strode towards me, arms open, a smile on his face. He embraced me. Then, as he stepped away, I saw that he held my heart, now shimmering with iridescence.

"You do what you need to do. I will care for your heart while you heal. You've been through so much. You need to become whole again."

And, with that, he turned and was consumed in the light of the Sun.

I was brought back by the sound of Lee's voice, inviting us to open our eyes and begin our journey. Sobbing, I tried to regain my composure until I realized many others were also crying, laughing, smiling — all at the same time.

"The journey's begun," Lee said.

Four days later, I had made my way through a maze of rituals, ceremonies, memories, songs, and guided imagery sessions. I was lighter than I had been since my childhood, and had found a road-map for the future. I had found myself, and within, an unwavering faith.

On our last night together, in reverent silence, we invited back our avatars and guides. Once again, my grandfather appeared in all his glory and placed my heart gently back into place. I felt an amazing burst of energy, matched by an overwhelming sense of peace. The smile that came from my depths surprised me. I opened my eyes as he waved goodbye and reminded me, "I am with you always, my dear."

~Sage de Beixedon Breslin, Ph.D.

Joni's Revelation

Friendship is one mind in two bodies.
~Mencius

Joni's husband was getting married again. What? So soon? My mind couldn't wrap itself around that thought. Joni had been gone for less than a year. How could he re-marry?

When Joni left this earth, she left behind a grieving husband and two small children who needed a mother. My guess is that he was looking for a mother for the children. He chose one of Joni's friends, someone who already loved the children.

I was really confused about this so I began a dialogue with Joni. Just because she no longer lived on this earth didn't mean the communication between us had ended. "So, Joni, how are you feeling about this? Because I will feel how you want me to feel, but I've got to be honest with you and admit I am a tad confused about this."

The following week, I began finding things with a Joni theme in strange places. I found a photo of us at my wedding. We were both so pretty, she with her bright red hair and me just looking like me, cute. She was one of my bridesmaids. A few days later, in my garage of all places, I found the professional photo of me at her wedding, as one of her bridesmaids. Really, God, in my garage?

I took a break to sit on my porch, holding the two photos and pondering what Joni was trying to tell me. "Okay, I'm sensing a wedding theme here, Joni. Are you trying to tell me that you are okay with John getting married again? Is that what this is about?"

I kept the photos with me and continued to question the message. About a week later, I found a little card that Joni had written to me after the birth of my second son. On it she wrote, "My sweet friend you know how much I love you! Remember Revelations 21:5." I ran for my Bible and read these words:

"And He who sits on the throne said, 'Behold, I am making all things new.' And He said, 'Write, for these words are faithful and true.'"

"You want me to write, Joni? What? Tell me!" Through His word, Joni was telling me to write, to send a message, that God's word is faithful and true. "Is that it? Anything else?" I read on. In the same chapter, one verse above, the Bible says, "and He shall wipe away every tear from their eyes; and there shall no longer be any death, there shall no longer be any mourning, or crying, or pain; the first things have passed away."

"Oh, Joni, are you telling me that you are okay with John getting married again?" I could feel her smiling as her message penetrated my thick head. "Okay, so then I'm supposed to write about this to your family. You want me to tell them you are fine with John's plans."

Not knowing how my letter would be received, in faith I wrote to Joni's mother. I didn't know that her family had been struggling with this turn of events as I had been struggling. When I told her mother how this message came to me, she felt a sense of peace. A few days later, Joni's sister called, and she too felt peace from Joni's message.

I'm not sure why I was her messenger, except that we had been friends from infancy. We'd been pen pals and participated in chain letters throughout our lives, and she knew I was a writer. We were still pen pals; I was just the only one with the pen.

~Jeri Chrysong

Samuel's Promise

Faith is reason grown courageous.
~Sherwood Eddy

My mother had already suffered five miscarriages when she got pregnant with me at the age of forty-one. Two months into her pregnancy she began vomiting and spotting, and she worried she'd lose me too. It was 1945 and Mother's previous doctors had suggested no medical treatments except confining her to bed. Her new doctor suggested Mother also try shots of a drug called diethylstilbestrol. Dad gave her the daily shots of DES and Mother only left her bed to use the bathroom. She quit bleeding and vomiting, and as the months passed she could feel me move inside her. She and Dad were thrilled when the doctor heard my strong heartbeat.

But Mother grew weaker and weaker and lost weight despite the pregnancy. "At least we'll have our own child," she comforted herself.

Then Mother's father, Samuel, suddenly died. All her life, Mother had leaned on him for comfort and strength. As a child, she often went with him to wash the windows of his real estate office. Afterward, they would go for ice cream and he would tell her, "Helen, you are the best little girl in the world. I'm so lucky you are my daughter."

Once, when Mother was five years old, she couldn't stop crying because her older sister wouldn't play with her. Samuel came to her with an empty goldfish bowl.

"Here, Helen," he said. "When you've filled this bowl with tears we'll get you a goldfish."

As Mother tried to catch her tears in the bowl, she started to giggle. For years she kept the bowl on her dresser as a reminder to look on the bright side of things.

When she went away to college, Samuel kept in close touch through letters and phone calls. He continued to write and call after Mother and Dad married, and my parents spent summer vacations with him in Utah.

Now Samuel was gone. There would be no more infusions of his positive energy.

"I can't even go to the funeral," Mother sobbed. She grieved day after day and lost still more weight.

Frantic about her health, her doctor suggested a C-section to save her life, even though her pregnancy with me hadn't reached full term.

"Think about it," Dad said. "We've done our best. You're getting so weak."

I can't imagine the turmoil Mother must have experienced. I was her chance for a child of her own flesh and blood. But was having a baby worth risking her life? And what if I lived but she died and left me motherless?

Mother closed her eyes to pray for guidance and a vision came to her. She saw herself, heavy with child, standing on a bridge over a mountain stream. Slender aspens lined both banks. The sky was a cloudless blue and the spring air smelled fresh. Samuel was there, walking toward her, as if they were on one of the family outings she'd enjoyed as a child in Ogden Canyon.

"Papa," she cried in the vision and held out her arms to him. "I thought you were gone."

He gathered her in a hug, and then took her arm and they crossed the bridge together. On the other side he turned and looked into her eyes. "Helen," he said. "I promise you that you will have a healthy baby, and that you will live to raise your child to maturity."

"Are you sure?" she asked.

"I'm sure," he said.

As Mother lifted her face to kiss his cheek, the scene faded and she was back in her bedroom.

Mother immediately told Dad about her vision. "I'll be all right and so will the baby," she assured him. "We'll tell the doctor we're going to wait."

Dad might have thought Mother's vision was a dream born of wishful thinking, but Mother knew differently. She held onto Samuel's promise in the core of her being, and gathered enough strength from his words to carry me to full term. When I was born I weighed in at a healthy six pounds.

After my birth, Mother had reason to fiercely hold onto Samuel's promise that she would live to raise me. During the months she'd been confined to her bed, she had developed phlebitis, an inflammation of a vein near her right ankle. Despite following the doctor's instructions to keep her leg elevated all the time, she developed a blood clot.

While I lay in the hospital nursery, hours old, snuggly warm in an isolette, Mother fought for her life in a room down the hall. If the clot broke loose from the wall of the vein it would travel to her heart. A large clot would choke off all the blood to her lungs and kill her. At that time the doctors' only weapon against a thrombus was heparin, a blood thinner.

Despite medication for pain, Mother suffered terribly. Dad sat by her hospital bed all night, Mother gripping his hand so tight it grew numb. Doctors and nurses came in and out of her hospital room, checking Mother's vital signs.

"My leg is on fire down by my ankle," she sobbed, her face pale and twisted with pain. And then, taking a shuddering breath, she said to Dad, "We have to remember my father's promise."

Mother's doctor took a seat across from Dad as the night brightened into day. "The next hours will be critical," he whispered.

"My chest. The pain," Mother moaned. "I can't breathe." She cried out again. Then her body jerked and was still. Her skin took on a deathly pallor.

The doctor searched for a pulse and then leaned close to her chest, placing his stethoscope over her heart.

Two nurses standing in the doorway took each other's hands.

Dad fixed his eyes on her face, willing her to live, praying for her life.

He blinked his eyes, and blinked again. Was color coming back into Mother's face? Had her labored breathing resumed?

The doctor checked her pulse. "She made it," he announced, wiping his forehead with a handkerchief.

Dad choked back tears of relief. "I thought we'd lost her."

"It was so strange," Mother said when she had the energy to talk. "I was on the ceiling looking at my body. I could see the sweat on Dr. Cobb's forehead." She closed her eyes and rested, then said, "The chest pain is gone. My father was right."

Several times over the ensuing decades Mother suffered significant health problems including pancreatitis, and diverticulitis so severe that hemorrhaging threatened her life. "Remember my father's promise," she would always say. "Sammie isn't raised to maturity." Holding on to her vision, Mother recovered from every illness, returning to the care of our family and to her active career as a writer and writing teacher. She died of a stroke at age eighty-eight.

I believe people when they say they've had a visit from someone who has passed. Mother's belief in her vision gave her the strength to fight for and save my life as well as her own.

~Samantha Ducloux Waltz

Chapter
10

Messages from Heaven

Answered Prayers

Money from Heaven

Angels are never too distant to hear you.
~Author Unknown

*I*t is possible to grieve for someone you've never known. My maternal grandmother, Eva, died when she was only fifty-two. I was given her name as my middle name when I was born more than a year later. I heard many stories about Eva, and felt a strong connection with her. She was a central figure in the rural community where she was born and lived. She was the hard working farm wife, postmaster, store manager, schoolteacher and mother. During the hard times of the Great Depression, when her family was struggling to keep their farm, she still managed to feed the passing hobos, looked the other way when drifters lifted food from the store, and found work for the occasional itinerant. She was also renowned as a strong defender of proper grammar and an advocate for higher education. I was sad that I'd never had the chance to know her. I did, however, have a very special communication with her.

It was August 1978 and I was in graduate school in Hawaii, over 2,400 miles from my family in California. It was the summer between my first and second year of school and I was surviving on a student loan and odd jobs. Early that month, I had the opportunity to attend a workshop in the Ira Progoff Intensive Journal Method based on Jungian psychology. The journal had several tabbed sections including one titled, "Dialoguing with People." The workshop leader picked that section to demonstrate, and asked the participants to create a list of people with whom they would like to have a conversation. The list could contain historical figures, fictional characters, celebrities etc. We were then asked to select one person from that list and have a written "dialogue" with him or her. From my list of about twenty people, I selected my grandmother Eva. I told her about the stories I'd heard about her and how I genuinely missed knowing her. In my imagined dialogue, she "responded" that she was with me and aware of my life, my interests and my challenges. This was a powerful experience, as during the process of writing, it did feel very much like a real and intimate moment with my grandmother.

The following day, I was in the student loan office and learned that my next check wouldn't come for another month. Having only a few dollars left, I panicked and wondered how I would manage until then. Although there were friends who would feed me, and family who would lend me money if I asked, I was twenty-five and very proud of my independence. I was walking home wondering what to do. I actually looked up at the sky and said aloud, "I wish it would rain money!" Then, very unexpectedly, I physically experienced a profound sense of calm certainty. Some people might refer to it as faith. Still looking at the sky, I extended my arms, relaxed and said with absolute knowledge, "I don't know where it will come from, or in what form, but I know my needs will be met."

A few days later, I received a letter from my mother's sister, my Aunt Mary who lives in Oregon. I hadn't been corresponding with her regularly and was somewhat puzzled as to why she was writing, seemingly out of the blue. As I walked from the mailbox, I opened the envelope and a check for $50 dropped out along with a brief note. It read:

"A very strange thing happened to me today—I was talking with your mother on the phone and as usual we were talking about our kids. After we hung up, I was still thinking about you. Then as clear as if she were standing right next to me, I heard my mother say, 'Well, why don't you send her some money?' So here is a small check. Don't thank me; it's from your grandmother."

My mouth dropped open, I stopped in my tracks and I literally shook. I immediately wrote back to my aunt telling her about the journal workshop, my "conversation" with her mother, my temporary financial anxiety and my absolute knowledge that somehow I would be okay; though I never expected it to be through help from my grandmother who had died thirty years earlier!

Many years later, I spoke again with Aunt Mary at a family reunion about this connection with her mother. She added a last bit of information I hadn't known. She told me that her mother was "always scraping together money for people she knew who wanted to go to college." Mary added that when her mother told her to send me some money, she had replied, "Okay. I'll send her $25." Mary said her mother remonstrated, "Don't be so stingy! I would have sent her $50!"

~Joan Eva Engelbart

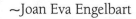

The Poem

Put your ear down close to your soul and listen hard.
~Anne Sexton

My mother was a poet and quite a good one, although I didn't always fully appreciate her talents. Her poetry at times seemed dark to me, and even a little morbid. When she wrote about family and things that touched her heart, I truly loved those poems. But she also wrote about things that I didn't care to think about, especially in my younger days—things like death and dying. And she wrote one particular poem that I flatly refused to listen to. I didn't care to hear long sad verses depicting my own mother's death. So for years I balked at her reading this poem to me, as if by listening to it and giving credence to it would somehow make it come true.

This one particular poem was called: "Oh Death Where Is Thy Sting?" But Lord knows she never stopped trying to make me listen to it. She used to say, "I want you to hear it because I want this read at my funeral." As a teenager I would rebel and bark back at her, "Mama, I do not want to hear about what you want read at your funeral!" And with that I would stomp off to my room and slam the door.

The truth was I did not want to hear that I would ever have to face that day. Usually by the third line in the poem I would be reduced to a blubbering mess. The adolescent, independent "me" would rather die than let my mother see weakness, so I would cover it with anger and run off to my room in a huff.

Over the years she tried many times to read the poem to me. And with each failed attempt, the conversation ended with the same burning words: "I mean it. I want this poem read at my funeral." And I have to confess that in all those years I never actually read or listened to her read the entire poem. I only knew the title and bits and pieces that I had heard over my protests. But I did know that although we never talked about any other "final wishes"—that she absolutely wanted this poem read at her funeral.

Thirty years passed and the day I had dreaded all my life was upon me. My mother had succumbed to an aortic aneurysm at seventy-three. Sixteen hours warning, hardly time enough to even say goodbye, and here I was with my three siblings planning her funeral.

Though she never talked about her flowers, we all knew when my brother Kelley picked out yellow roses for the family blanket that they were perfect. Though she had never seen a polished cherry casket, my mother had a deep love and appreciation for beautiful wood furniture and we instantly knew it was right. The songs were hymns I'd heard her sing at the top of her lungs in the car on every road trip we ever took. And the officiate was a dear friend of the family who she loved and respected. All was set—all, that is, except the poem. And I had no earthly idea where it could be.

Mama never kept her poems together in any kind of book or typed in a file on her computer. Most were memorized and the rest were scribbled on scraps of paper scattered in dresser drawers or buried beneath old photographs in various shoeboxes.

"Oh no," I cried to my sister Joan, "she made this one thing abundantly clear to me and I am going to fail her because I was too stubborn to listen and keep a copy."

Four and a half years before she had downsized from a ten-room house, where she had lived for twenty-five years, to a small two-bedroom apartment we had built for her adjacent to our house. She had pared down her furniture and purged a ton of paper prior to that move. It could be anywhere or it could be gone. I had not seen that poem in more than ten years.

"Calm down. We will find it," my sister Renee said.

"You don't understand! Boxes of her overflow are still stacked in my garage and the funeral is tomorrow!" I wailed. "There is no time to look for it." I buried my head in my hands and sobbed about that too. Emotionally drained and physically exhausted from four hours sleep in the past seventy-two hours. "There is nothing I can do about it now." So I dropped my head in bitter resignation and headed off to bed.

My house was full of extended family in town for the funeral and so Mama's youngest sister, my husband, and I were going to have to stay in Mama's apartment. As I lay down in my mother's bed I said to myself more than anyone, "I'm so sorry Mama, but I have no idea where that poem is. I know you really wanted it read tomorrow. I so wish you had told me where it was." And with that I closed my eyes and dropped into the restless sleep of pure exhaustion.

At 4:00 a.m. I awoke from a fitful sleep and sat straight up in the bed. I proceeded to get up and walk to her living room. Lit only by a tiny nightlight in the bathroom, I felt my way to the old comfortable rocker/recliner where Mama spent probably fifteen hours a day. Without even knowing why, I reached my hand down deep in the cushion on the left side of the chair and pulled out a folded piece of notebook paper, yellowed with age and nicotine stains. I slowly unfolded the single wrinkled page. I was hardly able to believe what I was seeing—there in my mother's own, familiar handwriting was the poem.

I did not get up with the intent to go look for the poem. I never even checked the other side of the chair. I just walked straight to the chair, reached down, and pulled out the poem. It was as if she had quietly whispered to me in my sleep and told me exactly where it was.

~Andrea Peebles

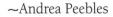

Finding Sea Beans

Our memories of the ocean will linger on,
long after our footprints in the sand are gone.
~Anonymous

I survived the car accident that took the lives of both of my parents. I turned five in the hospital while recovering from merely a broken ankle.

I would only have five year's worth of memories with my parents; unfortunately most of those would be forgotten because of my age. However, I am grateful to have one favorite memory of spending time with them at the beach. We took annual trips to Florida to escape the cold Wisconsin winters. On these trips we spent much of our time combing the beach for sea beans. These were a favorite of my mother's and were hard to find. The ones we found were plump, round and dark in color, resembling small pincushions. Little did we know of their rain forest origin or of the lengthy journey they had endured to arrive on the beach.

Our collection of sea beans had grown over the course of several trips, giving my mother enough to have them polished and made into a matching set of earrings and necklace. They were her favorite pieces of jewelry; in fact, she was wearing them in the last photo taken of her a week before the accident. In the years to come I would cherish her sea bean jewelry as it represented a time when we were all together.

Many years later, with a four-year-old daughter of my own, we too would travel to the beach in Florida. Being there with her made me acutely aware of how life had come full circle. At first I was disappointed to see that our beach was barren, offering little for us to collect. So instead we were content to stroll the beach. Occasionally I had the opportunity to go alone. During these private walks I experienced an overwhelming sensation that my parents were there with me. I dismissed this as nostalgia until the feeling became so strong I couldn't ignore it. As a result, I found myself drawn to the beach where I would feel closer to them. Late one afternoon I simply couldn't resist any longer. Sensing they were with me, I spoke aloud, "Okay, if you're there like I think you are, then send me a sign. Send me a sea bean."

That same day the wind shifted and a strong, steady breeze blew all night and all the next day. The waves were pounding the shore and depositing an abundance of seaweed and seashells. After an entire day of this blowing we woke up to a beautiful, quiet day and a beach covered with treasures from the ocean. After breakfast, we started our beachcombing and I stopped at one point to watch my daughter chase the waves, taking delight in watching her trying to outrun them. Before continuing, I gazed down to see where I was stepping next, careful not to be stung by one of the numerous stingrays now strewn on the beach. That's when it appeared. Lying in the sand, at the very tip of my big toe, was a sea bean. A perfectly placed sea bean, matching the ones we had collected so long ago. I knew immediately, without any doubt, they had heard me. I was overwhelmed with emotion and love. Tears filled my eyes and I knew this was my sign. I excitedly explained to my daughter that I had asked for this sea bean and that Grandpa and Grandma had sent it to us. She had never seen one. It had never occurred to me to show them to her but now was the perfect time.

We spent the entire day searching the beach, finding only one more hiding beneath some seaweed. Out of curiosity I decided to show our sea beans to some local residents to ask if they had ever seen one before. The answer was always the same; no one had, no one knew what they were.

That night back in our room, we placed the sea beans beside each other, noting one was smaller than the other. I said to my daughter, "I think the bigger one stands for Grandpa and the smaller one stands for Grandma." My daughter confidently corrected me and pointed to the smaller one and said, "No, this one is for me, Mama, and the big one is for you." Either way they were meant for us!

~Wendy Delaney

Goodbye Tears

Love is stronger than death even though it can't stop death from happening,
but no matter how hard death tries it can't separate people from love. It can't
take away our memories either. In the end, life is stronger than death.
~Author Unknown

I found myself standing partly hidden in the back of a church. The lights were low. My eyes were drawn to the middle row of pews. To my amazement my husband Roy stood in the second row. How could that be? It was not possible! Someone standing to the right behind me spoke. "It is alright. You must go sit by him. Go, it is alright," he urged.

Slowly I made my way to the front and slipped in beside my husband. Just then the preacher said, "Let's bow our heads in prayer." I slipped my arm around my husband and he drew me close in a warm hug. In wonder I looked up into his face. Tears were streaming down his cheeks as he held me tightly.

Why was he crying? We are together.

The next instant I was lying on the couch in front of the fireplace. It was the middle of the night. My daughter was awake, curled up at the foot of the couch. "I just had the most marvelous dream," I told her. After I had related the dream to her I asked, "What do you think it means? Why was your dad crying?"

"Oh, Mom, don't you know?" she said. "He was saying a final goodbye."

She was right. I still felt him close by. Sometimes I would think

I saw him out of the corner of my eye. Every day while driving to work I could almost feel him sitting next to me. I just could not get my mind around the idea that he was gone forever. I was not ready to live this life without him. Was it possible that he also was having a hard time letting go?

My daughter and I hugged and cried together. Later as I drifted off to sleep, I could still feel Roy's arms around me so tender and warm. My heart was filled with his love. My husband's final goodbye lives on in my heart and memory.

I still struggle with my loss. But I know God cares and understands my pain. I'm so glad he chose to comfort me with a dream.

~Norma Favor

Granny's Quilt

A quilt will warm your body and comfort your soul.
~Author Unknown

When I was nine, I was very ill. After a long stay in the hospital, I faced three months of complete bed rest at home. With two other small children to look after, Mom sent for Granny. We knew everything was going to be all right then.

My Granny was a small, plump woman with gray hair. She never left the house without a strand of pearls around her neck. She was great at baking biscuits from scratch and making you feel special with hugs that smelled of Bengay.

"Idle hands are the devil's workshop," she would say as she rocked the hours away, her arthritic fingers flying and her needle joining colorful scraps of material together, turning them into something beautiful. She lived her faith and honored God with her talents. Her quilts were greatly sought after by family and friends.

"Wouldn't it be easier to just buy a gift?" I asked as she finished a baby quilt and began to start another. It seemed my aunts were always having babies.

"Maybe," she said. "But it wouldn't be made with love."

Each night she would tuck the blankets tightly around me, kiss me on the forehead and then kneel in prayer. "Everything will be all right," she would assure me as she turned out the light. "God is watching over you."

I was sixteen when she gave me my own quilt. It was edged in purple, my favorite color at the time. The quilt was made up of thirty-two white squares trimmed in purple and appliquéd with old-fashioned girls, pantaloons peaking out from under their colorful dresses. Sunbonnets atop their heads, the girls were outlined with black blanket stitches. The edges were quilted in a butterfly motif.

I could see the love in each of the small uniform stitches surrounding the pattern. Whenever I felt bad or sick I would wrap myself in the quilt and her words would come to me, "Everything will be all right. God is watching over you."

It was the only quilt she ever made for me. Her time on earth was up before she could start on my baby girl's quilt.

Forty years later, I was diagnosed with colon cancer. Having no symptoms, it came as a complete shock. Surgery was scheduled. Sitting in the hospital parking lot, car keys in my hand, I cried and prayed for over an hour before I found the strength to drive home.

On the hot, muggy July night before surgery, I tossed and turned, afraid of what the day would bring and fearful of the outcome. I retrieved Granny's quilt from the foot of the guest bed where it lay. The edges were a bit frayed and worn, the colors slightly faded, but the love was still there.

I gathered an armful of quilt to my chest, the majority of it flowing to the floor. I looked like Linus from the Peanuts gang, holding onto it for dear life. I prayed and suddenly felt a warm soothing presence. A wisp of cool air touched my forehead, like a familiar kiss. I fell asleep, comforted by the fact God was watching over me and that everything would be all right.

The next morning, waking from a restful sleep, I looked down and found Granny's quilt was no longer draped over the side of the bed, but had been tucked tightly around me.

I asked my husband if he had covered me with the quilt. "Are you crazy?" he asked, "As hot as it is?"

On the way to the hospital, my daughter told me not to worry. During the night she had also felt a comforting presence that assured her all would be well.

But I wasn't worried. Granny had sent me a message from heaven, "Everything will be all right. God is watching over you."

And He did.

~Jeri McBryde

95

Azalea

Earth has no sorrow that Heaven cannot heal.
~Author Unknown

When our first son was about sixteen months old, we learned that I was pregnant again. The baby was due September 15. We were thrilled to be expecting another baby, and I was excited to be pregnant again at the same time as my best friend. Our first children were born one month apart, and now the due dates for our second babies were one month apart again.

But just shy of twelve weeks of pregnancy, our baby's heartbeat could not be found. Within a week, I had a miscarriage. Even now I struggle to find the right words to describe the devastation I felt. Many women in our church and our circle of friends reached out with cards, meals, and kind words, yet I still felt lonely and grief-stricken. I discovered that there is a secret sisterhood of women who have suffered miscarriages, but I would have preferred not to belong.

Names are important to my husband and me, and we wanted to find the right one for this baby we'd lost. There was no way to know the gender, but we felt like she was a girl and named her Azalea, which means "spared by Jehovah."

Months passed and early in the summer, we received some good news. I was pregnant again. Unfortunately, within a few weeks I had another miscarriage. I was more devastated than ever, afraid we would never have another baby. My best friend had her baby in August, and I was so sad that we would not be having our baby soon. By the time

September rolled around, I felt fragile and alone. I dreaded Azalea's due date, but I couldn't talk about it with anyone. I just wanted time to pass, the month of September to come and go.

In mid-September I was outside playing with our son, and I noticed a pink bloom on one of our azalea bushes. Azaleas, of course, bloom in the spring, not the autumn, and this was just a lone bloom in the midst of several azalea plants. In that moment, I felt such relief. I didn't feel alone anymore. I knew God remembered us. That bloom felt like a message from Azalea and from God himself, reassuring us that we indeed had a daughter and she lived in heaven, the safest place of all.

~Nina Taylor

96

Please Forgive Me

We have two ears and one mouth so that we can listen
twice as much as we speak.
~Epictetus

In his last years, my father suffered from a kind of dementia that caused him to associate with people who took financial advantage of him. When my sister and I discovered he was deeply in debt and had no way of paying off the credit cards others had tricked him into using, we knew we had to act.

We contacted an attorney and had him file for bankruptcy. Then we brought him to live close to us and believed our troubles were over.

However, our father started repeating his old patterns, and we were faced with the agonizing decision of having to take him to court to protect him. Finally, after much prayer, my sister and I knew we had no choice but to ask that we be placed in charge of his finances. The judge overseeing the proceedings agreed with our request.

The scene in the courtroom was ugly that day as our father lashed out in anger at what he saw as his daughters' betrayal. "Why did you do this?" he asked over and over.

"We didn't have a choice," I replied honestly.

Eventually, our father forgave us, but I could occasionally see the hurt and bewilderment in his eyes, an expression that I knew was reflected in my own eyes. I could not reconcile this confused, elderly man with the strong man I had idolized for all of my life.

When he passed away, my sister and I cried together. They were tears of grief, not just for missing our beloved father but for knowing that we had caused him pain.

Those feelings refused to go away. I'd hurt my father, the man I had loved for over fifty years, the man I had looked up to, the man who had served as an example in everything I did. How would I forgive him? How would I forgive myself?

Over the years, I had developed the habit, while taking my walk, of talking to those who had passed. I always had the feeling that my loved ones were close by and were watching over me and my family. I drew comfort from these one-sided conversations.

"Why, Dad?" I asked one morning, tears streaming down my face. "Why did you cause us to have to hurt you that way? It broke our hearts." I swiped at my tears. "I'm sorry we hurt you. I hope you can forgive us."

I had poured out my feelings to my father on other occasions, always to no avail. I was no closer to making peace with him and myself than I had been before.

Then the words appeared in my mind. "I was sick, Jane. I didn't know what I was doing. Please forgive me."

I came to a standstill as I listened intently.

"Please forgive me." The words sounded in my mind once more. "I know you didn't mean to hurt me."

My father was asking for my forgiveness even as I had been asking for his.

Several years have passed since that incident. At times, I still struggle with coming to terms with everything that happened, but I know that my father forgave me just as I forgave him.

Now when I talk with those who have passed on, I make certain that I listen as well.

~Jane McBride Choate

97

Message from an Angel

*As your faith is strengthened you will find that there is no longer the need to
have a sense of control, that things will flow as they will, and that you will
flow with them, to your great delight and benefit.*

~Emmanuel

On a bleak, February afternoon, my father, brother, sister
and I gathered around Mother's hospital bed. We had
just received her test results and were stunned by the
report. Not only did she have a brain tumor, but also an inoperable
tumor between her lungs. With cobalt treatments, she might have
three more months to live. Chemotherapy was ruled out.

"I have always tried to live a good life, but I have committed one
big sin," Mother said, her brown eyes looking up at us. "I love God
so very much. But," she drew a deep breath, and continued, "I loved
my family more."

Sitting up straighter, Mother whispered resolutely, "Whatever
time I have left, I want to use serving God."

My father, brother, sister, and I sought the help of the Divine
Physician. On Palm Sunday, two days after her last cobalt treatment,
we helped Mother out of bed and took her to a Healing Service at
Trinity Lutheran Church in Hagerstown, Maryland. Later, she told us
that she knew "something happened" when Dr. Norris Wogan prayed
for her.

We saw no immediate results. But we believed.

Mother phoned me in June to report that the chest X-ray showed "no signs of any tumor!"

In July, she called to say that her CAT scan showed no evidence of any brain tumor. "The doctor said it has just 'melted away' honey," she said. "God has healed me!"

For the next two years, Mother spoke at many churches, sharing her story, giving praise and glory to Jesus for healing her. We were astonished at her ability to speak before large groups. She amazed us with her energy and joy.

But something happened. Something no one understood. The doctors could find no medical explanation, nor could any clergy; nor could we. Somehow, symptoms began to return. No longer able to walk or take care of herself, she spent the last year of her life in a nursing home. I often visited her and would read the Bible to her. Sometimes I would prop her up in a wheelchair and take her to the Community Room, where I played the piano and sang the hymns we loved.

I could not understand what had happened to her. I prayed, "Dear Lord, if You are ready to take Mom home to Heaven, please let me know." But my faith continued to be strong that she would be healed again. I could not grieve over the circumstances because I could picture the day when she would come home and all this would be like a bad dream.

I thanked Jesus for being with us. I was able to find joy even in those darkest of days. I thanked Him for giving me "the peace that passes understanding." I trusted Him.

During the year Mother had been in the nursing home, she had difficulty speaking and had done no writing. Eventually, she became totally unresponsive. On February 20, 1980, she went home to be with the Lord.

As we were getting things together for her funeral, Dad opened her dresser drawer and discovered a piece of paper on top of her lingerie. All year, he had been in and out of that dresser drawer, taking things to her in the nursing home. The paper had not been there before, and Mother had not been home.

But on this slip of paper, in Mother's perfect handwriting, was a message: "When I die, please have this passage read: I Thessalonians 4:13-18." We rushed to get the Bible and we read:

But we would not have you ignorant... concerning those who are asleep, that you may not grieve as others do who have no hope... the dead in Christ shall rise first; then we who are alive, who are left, shall be caught up together with them in the clouds to meet the Lord in the air; and so shall we always be with the Lord. Therefore comfort one another with these words.

Amazed, we reread the passage.

Smiling through his tears, Dad looked at us and whispered, "An angel!"

~Mary Alice Dress Baumgardner

98

Chicken Soup for the Soul

The Telephone

A sister is God's way of proving He doesn't want us to walk alone.
~Author Unknown

"Sue, listen to me." I pleaded with my twin sister. With tears in my eyes I took another sip of my strong hot coffee and tried to convince my sister once again to contact my neighbor, Nellie.

I leaned forward in my chair facing the floral sofa where Sue often sat when she stopped by for morning coffee. "Remember when I told you about my neighbor, Nellie? Please," I begged. "Go see her!"

Morning conversations with my sister were nothing new. We had been doing this for years. We lived in the same town. So getting together for coffee in the morning was easy.

Many times after taking my children to the bus stop in the morning, I returned to my house and would hear Sue's cheerful voice leaving a message on my answering machine. "Hey Donna, just put the kids on the bus. Thought I'd stop by for a cup of coffee. Give me a call."

We cherished our morning chats. We talked about our families, faith and current events. We shared recipes, home decorating ideas and any concerns we might have. We gave each other advice and comfort.

One morning I shared with Sue an amazing story about Nellie. My friend Denise had shared the story with me. Sue was fascinated. But now she didn't seem to remember Nellie or the story at all.

Sadness filled my voice. I took a deep breath and reminded Sue again, "Denise told me when her mom passed away after a long illness that Nellie, our neighbor, whom I had never met, called Denise on the phone late one night. Nellie said, 'Denise, your mom just came to see me. She wants me to tell you, thank you for taking such good care of her.' Denise told me Nellie was a medium."

"Sue, are you listening to me?" But of course I only heard silence. How could I know if Sue heard me or not when she had passed away two months ago?

I thought back to the morning when Sue phoned me early, canceling our coffee date. "Hey Donna, I'm not feeling well today. I have a bit of a headache. Let's catch up later."

But we never did. Within the hour Sue had a massive stroke and passed away a few days later.

Now I sat alone in the family room and drank the last drops of my coffee. I felt foolish sitting there and talking to an empty sofa and yet I had so much to say.

"Suzy, I miss you so much," I said aloud. "I have so much to tell you. We finished the bathroom upstairs. Remember I was decorating it in a Bermuda beach theme? It's pink, bright and beautiful! I wish you could see it. You would love it."

I continued. "I bought Stephanie a heart locket for her birthday. I had it engraved with 'I Hope You Dance,' your favorite song." Sue had three young children. Stephanie was the oldest who had just turned sixteen. I chose a gift that I imagined Sue would have selected for her if she could.

"I wish I knew if you could hear me!" I began to sob. "Are you there? Are you okay?"

I did not mention to anyone, including Denise, that I was begging my deceased sister to go to Nellie. I really wanted to appear strong for my family and friends. Yet privately I continued to send up this prayer of desperation. My faith had always been strong, but now I needed some confirmation. I needed to hear from my sister!

Exhausted, I got up. I wiped my tears, picked up my coffee mug and placed it in the kitchen sink. I walked through the house and gently picked up my sister's red and black sweater that I kept on my chair. I gave it a hug. It gave me comfort. I could still smell her Vanilla Fields perfume. "I wish you were here, Sue," I whispered.

Later in the week, I was resting on my bed. It had been another rough day of dealing with my grief. "Please God," I prayed. "Help Sue connect with Nellie."

Suddenly the phone rang. "Hi Donna, this is Nellie. You don't know me but I'm a friend of your friend Denise." My heart leaped!

"Oh yes, I know all about you!" I said. My heart was pounding.

"Do you know about my gift?" Nellie asked cautiously.

"I do. Denise told me how her mother came to you. I totally believe in your gift!"

"Well that's good because your sister is driving me crazy." She laughed. "For the past few weeks she has been asking me to call you. I wanted to check with Denise first to see if it was okay. I was planning to call you later today but your sister was pleading with me, 'Will you please call my sister now!'"

Nellie jumped right into sharing Sue's messages. "Sue is showing me a bright pink room. She says to tell you she sees it and it's beautiful."

Ah, the new bathroom. I smiled.

"Your sister is also showing me a locket and says, 'Thank you.'"

My heart filled with joy thinking of Stephanie's birthday locket.

"One more thing," Nellie added. "Your sister is showing me a red and black sweater. She says it is meant to give you comfort."

This message really got to me. Sue was with me when I was holding her sweater.

Finally Nellie said, "Donna, your sister wants you to know she loves you, she's proud of you and is always with you."

I did not hear from Nellie again until the late fall. She phoned me one afternoon with another message from Sue, one I did not understand. "Sue says go ahead and honor her."

I told Nellie I had no idea what it meant. "Honor her? Sue was always so humble." Nellie assured me, "Donna, tuck this message away for later. See what happens."

In early December Sue's husband Bill and I were talking. "The funeral home called. They are having a memorial service for those who have lost loved ones this past year. The kids can make an ornament to honor their mom and place it on their Christmas tree."

Bill was concerned. "Do you think the kids will be okay going back to the funeral home for this memorial?" I remembered Sue's words, "Go ahead and honor me."

I turned to Bill and smiled. "Let them. It will be okay."

The children went to the service and honored their mom. It was one of many steps in their healing process.

I called Nellie to thank her for using her amazing gift to help others. Nellie responded with a humble little laugh. "Donna, I am just a telephone that connects family and friends with their loved ones in Heaven."

Yes, I thought, a telephone... with a great connection.

~Donna Teti

99

The Check

Courage is being afraid but going on anyhow.
~Dan Rather

*a*t age forty-eight, after twenty-nine years of marriage, I was a widow with four sons at home. Tom died after a long battle with cancer. At the end, I bent down, kissed his forehead and whispered, "It's okay, you can go." It was the permission he needed to leave us and end his suffering.

We believed we had taken care of most of the details associated with his death. I had the necessary account information to handle paperwork for Social Security, life insurance, retirement accounts, and the tedious, time-consuming tasks of becoming a single mom. At least that's what we thought.

In the aftermath of numbness, I began the process of filling out forms, sending for copies of the death certificate, and making appointments to "prove" that my husband was gone and life as we knew it was forever changed.

However, one evening as I looked through the information for a rather large, work-related life insurance policy, I found myself a little alarmed. This policy required my husband's membership in an organization that he had belonged to for ten years. The membership fee was paid annually by Tom's employer.

But what I saw in the folder was an invoice Tom had received for the membership fee. He had copied it and passed on to his employer for payment. I would need to contact them for proof of payment.

The next day I called his company and explained my request. His supervisor indicated she would check on the invoice status and let me know. The invoice was dated several weeks before his death so there had been adequate time for payment. Not one given to deceit, I also called the life insurance company and told them I was waiting on this proof of payment.

However, the next day, Tom's supervisor called. "I just cannot find any record that we have paid this invoice. I cannot imagine how it would have slipped through the cracks, but we apparently failed to update your husband's membership. I am so very sorry."

"Sorry" seemed like the smallest possible word for what I had just been told. Tom's driving commitment after his diagnosis was to be certain we would be financially secure when he left us. The income provided by this policy was one of the provisions to make that possible. And I was being told that the company had overlooked his membership payment! That omission was all this life insurance company would need to deny our claim.

Sick to my stomach, I hung up the phone and raged. "God, I thought You were a father to the fatherless and a husband to the widow. You have taken my husband. How could You allow this to happen as well?"

I finally bowed my head and prayed—but not to God. To my husband! I was not in the habit of speaking to the dead nor did I have beliefs that encouraged it. I believed that our loved ones were content in heaven, healed and whole, and we would just have to wait our turn.

But at this point, I needed to hear from Tom and all I knew to do was demand it. "Tom," I urged. "This is a horrifying situation. And I know that you would have never left us if you had any idea this membership invoice wasn't taken care of. If there is any possible way you are able to speak to me from heaven, you need to do it now and tell me what to do."

I don't know what I expected to happen. Probably nothing. But in the silence that followed, a miracle took place. These words came to me: "Go look at the invoice again." Like a robot, I obeyed this order.

Standing there with the invoice in my hand, I read it over and over. Could I really be I missing something?

Then I saw it. At the bottom of the invoice, penciled in, was a four-digit number. Could it possibly be a check number?

I ran to the box that held our canceled checks and record book. Searching through the record book, I found the check number Tom had listed. Yes! It was made out to the organization that carried his life insurance policy—for his membership fee! I sorted through the canceled checks and found the check he had written. It was the proof I needed. The life insurance money would be ours.

Rather than take a chance that his employer would not pay the membership fee in time, Tom had paid it himself and passed on the invoice for them to reimburse him.

As I looked from that invoice with the penciled in number and back to the canceled check I held in my hand, I knew with certainty my husband had clearly led me to the information that I needed. Yes, God is a father to the fatherless and a husband to the widow.

But for one miraculous moment in time, He had allowed my husband to communicate with me from across time and space. This one last message from beyond the grave was an incredible gift that also gave hope and faith to my grieving heart.

~Lettie Kirkpatrick Burress

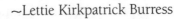

The Littlest Things

Remember, Angels are both God's messengers and God's message, witness to eternity in time, to the presence of the divine amidst the ordinary. Every moment of every day is riddled by their traces.

~F. Forrester Church

One Friday at the end of a particularly hard and stressful week, an employee named JoAnn came to me and wanted to talk. She said she just felt "blah" for the past several weeks.

"It is very difficult to care about anything anymore, not just the little things but even the big things," she said. Little did she know that I was somewhere beyond that same point.

Her statement, though, took me back three months, when our family had lost a close friend. Zella was related to both sides of my family in various, complicated ways, and was like a sparkling extra grandmother to my children. She had a wonderful, hearty laugh combined with a glimmer in her eyes as she smiled. Zella had a hard life, but was positive and wise in her approach to life.

"Sometimes the littlest things make all the difference," she occasionally told me. She saw signs of God in those little, everyday things, whether it be her garden, her rock collection, or the chickens that she raised.

But I found myself beside Zella's bed in an intensive care unit, holding her hand while her children took a break from their vigil. A surgery the day before had revealed a huge mass involving most of her abdominal organs. There was nothing to be done. As Zella and her family hovered in that no man's land between hope and reality, I wanted to impart to her that God cared for her. I asked if she would like a prayer. Zella nodded yes. I had intended to recite the twenty-third Psalm, but realized I could not—I was totally blank! I was able to stumble through one prayer: The Lord's Prayer.

In the past Zella and I had talked about my infamous inability to memorize, and I had told her how I had tried often to memorize the twenty-third Psalm, but had never been able. As I sat beside her, a faint sparkle returned to her eyes along with a weak smile. She squeezed my hand. I knew that in normal times Zella and I would be laughing, in a kind way, about my awkwardness at that moment and how I had botched the prayer. But these were not normal times, and she slipped into unconsciousness the next day and died several days later.

The twenty-third Psalm is familiar to those of us from the Judeo-Christian tradition. It begins with "The Lord is my shepherd…" and is perhaps the most recited Biblical verse. I would wager everyone from that background could think of someone they love or loved very much to whom this verse was important. It is common at funerals, and in times of danger and stress.

I made a renewed pledge to memorize it and tried for weeks. I printed it out in a large font and tried to memorize it while driving each day to work. It was a small miracle that I didn't cause a serious accident. But it just would not stick in my memory.

I became increasingly annoyed and, with disgust, set the prayer aside. Many extra hours at work, the everyday stress of raising children, helping aged relatives and an overly busy life lead to a slow, darkening spiral that I hardly noticed. Over the weeks I became unfocused, and increasing felt ineffectual in many aspects of my life.

So there I was on that Friday night at the end of a long workday, with a woman who needed reassurance, who needed support, who needed motivation. And I was not sure I had any of those things to give. Without great enthusiasm I started one of my standard pep talks.

"You know, JoAnn, it isn't the job that you do that is important, it is how you do your job..." It sounded incredibly trite as I said it.

I encouraged her to care, because with caring comes hope. And where there is hope, there is always a future, a better day. I threw in an impromptu example of how easy it was not to care.

I said, "If you saw a piece of trash in the hallway, it would be easy not to pick it up. You could say, 'it is not my job.' But how much better it is to care. How much more positive it would be to pick up the trash. By thinking and acting positively, you helped a co-worker in a small way, and you helped yourself. Sometimes it is the little things that make all the difference in life."

I was not sure it was a convincing speech for JoAnn and I was certain it didn't convince me. I felt even more tired, more spent. It was as if what little bit of hope, if any, I had given to JoAnn was drained from me, leaving me with none.

I gathered my coat, and walked head bowed and disheartened down the hall. As I turned down a hallway, I passed a small rectangular piece of paper on the floor.

I just kept walking.

I walked about six paces beyond the paper, musing about the irony of the example I had just given my co-worker. But I didn't really want to stop, let alone turn, retrace my steps, and pick up the trash. But I did stop, and stood still for a moment—debating. Sighing, I turned back to the paper.

It was plain white and about one and a half inches wide and four inches long. As I picked it up, I realized it was a bookmark. When I turned it over, in small print, this is what was on the other side:

The Lord is my shepherd: I shall not want.
He maketh me to lie down in green pastures:
He leadeth me beside the still waters.
He restoreth my soul:
He leadeth me in the paths of righteousness for his name's sake.
Yea, though I walk through the valley of the shadow of death,
I will fear no evil for thou art with me:

Thy rod and thy staff they comfort me.
Thou preparest a table before me in the presence of mine
    enemies:
Thou anointest my head with oil; my cup runneth over.
Surely goodness and mercy shall follow me all the days of
    my life:
And I will dwell in the house of the Lord forever.

That was a pivotal point for me. It broke my mood and for some odd
reason, or perhaps some not so odd reason, I was able to memorize
the twenty-third Psalm easily after that day. And that day, and every
day I hear that prayer now, I also sense Zella's twinkling eyes and
laughter.

Every day we are presented with opportunities, some large,
some small, to move forward in life's journey. I can tell you many
times when opportunity knocks at our door, we don't open it to see
what is there. Many times when a gift is placed at our feet, we don't
stop and stoop to pick it up. But I've learned we should, even the
littlest of gifts.

~Dan Reust

Lemon Pie Love

If God had intended us to follow recipes,
He wouldn't have given us grandmothers.
~Linda Henley

Many years after my grandmother passed away, I received a gift in the mail from her. I was about to turn thirty and my mother sent me an envelope. "I know this isn't her famous lemon pie," my mother wrote, "but it is the next best thing."

Everyone eats cake for their birthday, right? Well, not our family. All we asked for was Grandmother's famous lemon pie. This was the one thing she wouldn't teach anyone, not even me. She was tight-lipped with this recipe. When asked what was in it she would say, "A little of this and a little of that."

Inside the envelope was a small index card. My throat tightened as I viewed the handwriting. "Famous Lemon Pie" was the title. Measurements were scratched out and rewritten. Clutching the card, I went to the kitchen to call my mom.

"Where did you get this?" I asked when she got on the line.

"I was cleaning out the attic and found a small box of her things. From the looks of it, she wasn't even sure what she put in that pie," my mother said.

My grandmother was famous in her circle of friends. She was known for her handmade crafts, her acre garden that all the neighbors helped with, but most of all she was famous for her baked goods that she shared with everyone. The best thing about my grandmother is that she taught me everything she knew, almost everything.

When I work on a craft, I feel her words of approval tickle my ears. Tending to my small but rewarding garden, the sun kisses the top of my head and I can feel her happiness wash over me. However, I never feel her presence more than when I am in the kitchen whipping up one of her favorite desserts.

Now I was determined to have her lemon pie for my birthday. I lined up all the ingredients on the counter and began to work. The first pie was soupy and sloshed in the crust when I pulled it out. The second pie began to burn even before it was cooked through.

I made lemon pie over and over, observing every little thing she scratched out and recalculated. By the time my husband got home from work, the kitchen was a minefield of defective pies. It looked as if each and every ingredient had abused me. I lost control when I saw the look on his face.

"What happened here?" he asked.

"I just want lemon pie for my birthday!"

"I will buy you a lemon pie."

He didn't understand. I left the kitchen and ran upstairs with a dusting of flour trailing behind me.

I went to bed that night with the feeling of defeat. Why did my mother have to send me that recipe? I drifted off to sleep with pieces of crust still in my hair and lemon scent on my hands.

My dreams were filled with memories of my grandmother and that pie. I kept trying to see what she was putting in it but she hid it behind her back. "Please tell me what is in that pie," I begged. She smiled as the dream dissipated.

I trudged to the kitchen the next morning and all the pies had been carted out to the garbage. The counters were spotless. It was as if the pie incident had never happened.

The next day would be my birthday and all I wanted was lemon pie. I pulled the ingredients back out of the cupboard. "I can do this," I whispered to myself. There are two things I pride myself on. First, I am the best baker in my circle of friends. Second, I don't give up.

I started mixing the ingredients and when I got to the cornstarch I couldn't scrape enough out of the box for the pie. Doubt was creeping into my thoughts. "I can do this. I can do this," I repeated to myself as I grabbed my car keys.

I stood in the aisle looking at the multiple brands of cornstarch. What was I doing? I felt like I was having a mini meltdown over a pie. I pulled a box off the shelf and rolled it around in my hands as I walked to the register. My eyes settled on the recipes on the back. Lemon pie. Maybe I should use this recipe. I looked closer. It couldn't be.

I rushed home to view the precious index card sitting on my counter. I scanned the ingredients as I looked from card to box and back to the card again. Impossible! Was it this easy? I could see my grandmother smiling as I figured out her secret recipe. It seems it wasn't a secret to anyone who had bought this brand of cornstarch.

For my birthday, I made not one but two lemon pies. I was so pleased with myself as everyone inhaled the pie and dished out the compliments. Now I have a famous lemon pie recipe, but I'm not sharing!

~Helen R. Zanone

Messages from Heaven

~Meet Our Contributors~
~Meet Our Authors~
~Thank You~
~About Chicken Soup for the Soul~

Meet Our Contributors

Monica A. Andermann lives on Long Island with her husband Bill and their cat Charley. In addition to several credits in various *Chicken Soup for the Soul* collections, her writing has appeared both online and in print in such publications as *Sasee*, *Skirt!*, *The Secret Place*, and *Woman's World*.

Linda Apple is the author of *Inspire! Writing from the Soul* and *Connect! A Simple Guide to Public Speaking for Writers*. She is a motivational speaker for writers' groups and conferences. She also serves as the Arkansas Regional Speaker Trainer for Stonecroft Ministries. Please visit her website at www.lindaapple.com.

Suzanne Baginskie lives on the west coast of Florida with her husband, Al. She loves volunteering for the local sheriff's office and her community. Suzanne writes short mystery stories, flash fiction and writing articles. She is currently penning a legal thriller novel. Visit her website at mysite.verizon.net/resv10om.

Dana J. Barnett is a writer and English teacher. Her favorite things to do are writing, reading, hiking, watching movies, junking, and doting on her cats. Currently, among other projects, Dana is working on a children's book. Please send good thoughts her way. Feel free to e-mail her at dbarnett25@gmail.com.

Mary Alice Dress Baumgardner has a B.A. degree from Gettysburg College and an M.A. degree in Studio Art from Marywood University. She writes and illustrates children's books: her latest, *Esther Oyster's Irritation: A Story about Turning Hurt into Beauty*. She and husband, Allen, live near Waynesboro, PA. E-mail her at baumgarm@embarqmail.com.

Linda Benfield lives in Gastonia, NC. She loves God and His creation and enjoys coaching people on living life to its fullest. Having experienced her own share of life's disappointments and pain, she uses these obstacles to help others make better choices to enable them to enjoy life to its fullest.

Margo Berk-Levine went from actress/model to founder/owner of a successful New York staffing company to writer. This is her second appearance in a *Chicken Soup for the Soul* book. Her stories have been in the *Scribblers' Journal*, as well as magazines. Works in progress include a series of short stories and a memoir. E-mail her at mberklevin@aol.com.

Bonnie Beuth received her bachelor's degree with honors in Computer Information Systems and works as an information systems trainer for a law firm in Atlanta. She enjoys travel, writing, playing piano and spending time with her dogs. She hopes to complete a collection of short stories. E-mail her at blbeuth@yahoo.com.

Jeanne Blandford has found her dream job as an editor at Chicken Soup for the Soul. When she is not reading inspirational submissions, she and her husband, Jack, are visiting their two children; working on documentaries; writing and producing children's books or volunteering for OPIN, a local animal rescue.

Sage de Beixedon Breslin, Ph.D. is a licensed psychologist and Intuitive Consultant and an accomplished author. Her latest publications have been written to inspire and touch those who have struggled with life's challenges. Her books, stories and chapters are available on her website at www.HealingHeartCenter.org. E-mail her at Sage@HealingHeartCenter.org.

Debra Ayers Brown, a marketing professional, received her B.A. degree with honors from the University of Georgia and her MBA degree from The Citadel. Visit her at DebraAyersBrown.com and link to her blogs: Slice of Coastal Life, Southern Deb, and My Yellow Bluff. E-mail her at dabmlb@comcost.net.

Marcia E. Brown lives in Austin, TX, and is a widow and freelancer. She loves sharing family stories in magazines, newspapers and anthologies, including several in the *Chicken Soup for the Soul* series. She is now trying her hand at children's stories, especially to please her grandson.

Renie Burghardt, born in Hungary, is a freelance writer with numerous credits. She has been published in several *Chicken Soup for the Soul* books, and other anthologies and magazines. She lives in the country and loves animals, nature, and spending time with her family and friends. E-mail her at renieburghardt@semo.net.

Lettie Kirkpatrick Burress lives in Tennessee where she writes books and magazine articles. Lettie celebrates life with long hikes, lunch at outdoor cafes, clip-on earrings, and chocolate mint! Her favorite people? An understanding husband, five super sons, three daughters-in-love, and six "grand" children. Learn more at www.writingforhim.com.

Barbara Canale is a freelance writer and columnist for *The Catholic Sun* in Syracuse, NY. She has been published in nine *Chicken Soup for the Soul* books. She is the author of *Our Labor of Love: A Romanian*

Adoption Chronicle, and *Pray Your Way Through College*, by Liguori Publications. She enjoys skiing and gardening.

A.B. Chesler is an educator and writer living in Southern California. She enjoys eating, traveling, and spending time with her cats and husband. You may contact A.B. at achesler24@gmail.com.

Jane McBride Choate lives in Loveland, CO, in the foothills of the Rockies. She lives with her husband of thirty-eight years and her cat who believes she is of royal descent. Writing for Chicken Soup for the Soul is a dream come true for Jane.

Jeri Chrysong, a legal secretary, lives in Huntington Beach, CA, with her pug, Mabel. Jeri enjoys writing, photography, traveling, travel writing, and being a grandma to Lucas and Clay. You can visit Jeri at "Jeri's 'You're Worth the Fuss to Fix' Blog" at jchrysong.wordpress.com.

Phyllis Cochran worked for twenty-five years for the telephone company. She turned to writing as a second career and has published two books. Her inspirational stories have appeared in national magazines and in several *Chicken Soup for the Soul* books. Phyllis resides in Winchendon, MA, with her husband, Philip.

Mary P. Collins, LCSW-C, has an intuitive healing practice near Baltimore, MD, offering psychotherapy, life coaching and energy work. She enjoys photography, hiking, travel, and her cats' adventures. She and her husband David Bashoor treasured their spiritual journeys to Maui, their hearts' home. E-mail her at marypcollins@yahoo.com.

Maril Crabtree grew up in Memphis and New Orleans, but has made Kansas City her home for many years. She writes creative nonfiction and poetry. Her work has appeared in numerous journals. She is currently poetry co-editor for *Kansas City Voices*. Contact her through www.marilcrabtree.com.

Diana DeAndrea-Kohn is a freelance writer and small business owner in Washington State. She is married to her husband, Scott, and has three boys, Kenny, Alex, and Brodie. This story is deep in her heart and she is very thankful Chicken Soup for the Soul chose to share it!

Wendy Delaney has a teaching degree from the University of Wisconsin and taught in private and public schools. Wendy enjoys writing and has a story in *Chicken Soup for the Soul: A Book of Miracles*. In addition, she enjoys travel, reading, biking, wellness, and spending time with her daughter, Margaret. Visit her at www.matterofwellness. com.

Terri Elders, LCSW, lives near Colville, WA, with two dogs and three cats. Her stories have appeared in multiple editions of *Chicken Soup for the Soul*. She's a public member of the Washington State Medical Quality Assurance Commission. Contact her via e-mail at telders@ hotmail.com and read her blog atouchoftarragon.blogspot.com.

Susan L. Ellis graduated from Furman University with a B.A. degree in Business Administration. She lives in the Atlanta, GA area with her husband and two daughters. Susan's career is in sales management. She enjoys hiking, reading, travel and gardening. Please contact her via e-mail at dlesle@aol.com.

Joan Eva Engelbart, LCSW, JD, attended the University of Hawaii. She works for a hospice program in California. She is certified in Thanatology and as a Laugh Leader. Joan is interested in medical ethics, enjoys word games and fabric arts and appreciates good grammar. E-mail Joan at j.engelbart@yahoo.com.

Laura Fabiani, the mother of three children, has written articles for *Exceptional Parent* magazine, and a humor blog for their website. Laura loves reading, film, music, and watching the Philadelphia Flyers. She believes life's lessons can be learned from many sources, and counts her children as her greatest teachers.

Norma Favor lives in British Columbia. She is an active member of The Salvation Army church. Her kids, twenty-three grandchildren and two great-grandchildren are the loves of her life. She has written a number of stories for the *Chicken Soup for the Soul* series and other publications.

Denise Bernadette Fleissner is a professional organizer and simplicity coach. After leaving a career in television production to raise her two children, she created Soulfully Simple, a consulting business dedicated to teaching people how to simplify their lives—physically and spiritually. Her company now operates in both Virginia and Colorado.

Lonnie Frock is the owner of Bella Nozze Bridal Boutique. She is actively involved in HTC Writing Group, focusing on personal short inspirational stories. Married for twenty-eight years to a wonderful supportive man, together they have four beautiful adopted children and five amazing grandchildren.

Marilyn Ellis Futrell lives just outside Orlando in Winter Springs, FL, with her husband Glenn. She lost her son, John Robert Woodfin, to an allergic reaction to medication in December of 2005. He was nineteen. Marilyn has had numerous signs from him since his crossing and writing about them has become a major part of her grief recovery process.

Esther Griffin, a graduate of SUNY Geneseo, has been writing since she was a child. After a few published articles, she stopped writing to raise four children, working as a teacher and librarian. In retirement, she has taken writing courses and returned to her early love of writing.

Carolyn Hall received her bachelor's degree from Kansas State University. She and her husband live on a river bluff overlooking the Kansas River. She loves writing about her family, cooking and baking. E-mail her at chall711@gmail.com.

Cathy C. Hall is a writer from the sunny South. Her essays, stories, poetry, and articles have been published in markets for both kids and adults. Come visit her online to find out what she's working on now! You'll find her blog at www.cathychall.blogspot.com.

Chelsey Colleen Hankins graduated from the American Academy of Dramatic Arts in Los Angeles, CA, in 2010. Chelsey enjoys acting, traveling, snowboarding, writing, and directing. She currently resides in Los Angeles and is working on her first book and writing a web series. E-mail her at colleenhnkns@yahoo.com.

Sonja Herbert is the author of many award-winning stories. Her biography, *Carnival Girl*, will be published August 2012. After a two-year stay in Germany, where she was doing research and getting re-acquainted with her family, Sonja returned to live in Provo, UT. Visit her website at germanwriter.com.

Camille Hill is an animal intuitive who communicates with animals in various countries. She writes a pet column for *The Aquarian* newspaper in Winnipeg, Manitoba, and is a contributing writer to *Chicken Soup for the Soul* books. She lives in Kenora, Ontario, Canada with Ed and a variety of animal friends. E-mail her at chill@hilladvisory.com.

Janice Miner Holden, Ed.D., LPC-S, LMFT, NCC, is a professor of counseling at the University of North Texas in Denton. Her primary research interest over the past twenty-five years has been near-death experiences, and she developed and teaches a graduate course on the transpersonal perspective in counseling.

Carol Huff is a frequent contributor to the *Chicken Soup for the*

Soul series. She has also had her work published in other national magazines and currently has a novel on Amazon.com. Her spare time is spent taking care of her thirty-plus animals on her farm in Georgia. Contact her via e-mail her at herbiemakow@gmail.com.

Amy Schoenfeld Hunt is a professional freelance writer and the author of three published books. She is also a costumed historical interpreter at Old World Wisconsin, an outdoor museum that depicts life in the 19th century. She lives in Milwaukee, WI, with her husband and three daughters. E-mail her at AimeeClaire@aol.com.

Christy Johnson, dynamic speaker and author of *Rehab for Love Junkies*, is passionate about sharing the hope of Christ. After a disastrous first marriage ended in adultery and the tragic death of her son, Christy has a passion to empower others to become soul-healthy. Visit her at www.christyjohnson.org.

Mary Potter Kenyon graduated from UNI and lives in Manchester, IA. She has been published in national magazines and anthologies, including three previous *Chicken Soup for the Soul* titles. She writes for the local newspaper and teaches couponing and writing classes. She blogs at marypotterkenyon.wordpress.com. Her author website is marypotterkenyon.writersresidence.com.

Mary Knight has enjoyed a career as a professional writer for over thirty years. She is currently working on an MFA degree from Spalding University and will soon complete her first young adult novel entitled *Unspoken*. She lives in Lexington, KY, with her husband and two cats.

Joanne Kraft is the author of *Just Too Busy: Taking Your Family on a Radical Sabbatical*. A sought-after speaker, with articles appearing in numerous family/parenting magazines, she frequents California coffee shops with her husband Paul and loves being a mom to their four children. Visit her at JoanneKraft.com or GraceAndTruthLiving. com.

Virginia Kroll has had seventy children's books published to date. She teaches folk art at a local youth center. She has six children, two grandchildren, and one great-grandson. She shares her house with many pets.

Brenda Louque received her nursing degree from Danville School of Practical Nursing in 1984. She enjoys traveling, reading, writing, and quilting. She participates in many bereaved parent support groups. Her goal is to someday write a book. E-mail her at brenda419@cox. net.

Tim Martin is the author of *There's Nothing Funny About Running*, *Summer With Dad* and *Wimps Like Me*. He has several novels, including *Scout's Oaf* (Cedar Grove Books) due to be released in 2012. Tim is a contributing author to numerous *Chicken Soup for the Soul* books.

Jeri McBryde lives in a small southern town outside Memphis, TN. She recently retired from the library system and spends her days reading and working on her dream of publishing a novel. Jeri loves crocheting and chocolate. Her family and faith are the center of her life. This is her third story to appear in the *Chicken Soup for the Soul* series.

Heather McGee is a busy work-at-home and homeschooling mother of two children, Justin and Shelby. After working in finance and education, she truly enjoys the fulfilling work of teaching her own children and having the freedom to meander down interesting paths.

Caroline McKinney is semi-retired from the School of Education at the University of Colorado where she has been an adjunct for over twenty years. She spends time with her seven grandchildren and hiking Colorado's trails with her big dog. She enjoys writing poetry for religious publications.

John Miller is a senior technical staff member with IBM, thanks to the encouragement of his friend and manager, Paul Carmine. John and Marie-Therese live in New York's Mid-Hudson Valley and are the parents of five. Marie-Therese is an author of nonfiction books for children and teenagers. Learn more at www.marie-theresemiller. com.

Michelle Close Mills' poetry and short stories have appeared in many magazines and anthologies including several volumes of *Chicken Soup for the Soul*. Michelle resides in Central Florida with her wonderful husband, two great kids, two ornery kitties and three cockatiels. Learn more at www.authorsden.com/michelleclosemills.

C.G. Morelli's work has appeared or is forthcoming in *Philadelphia Stories*, *Highlights for Children*, *Chicken Soup for the Soul* books, *Jersey Devil Press*, *House of Horror* and *The Ranfurly Review*. He is the author of a short story collection titled *In the Pen* (2007).

Michelle Tompakov Muller received her Bachelor of Arts degree in French language and literature from SUNY at Stony Brook and a Master of Business Administration degree in marketing management from Pace University. She teaches English to speakers of other languages at two community colleges in the Baltimore, MD metro area.

Val Muller's fiction has appeared in a handful of magazines and anthologies. Her first novel, *Corgi Capers*, is a middle-grade mystery. You can keep track of her at mercuryval.wordpress.com, and contact her at mercuryval@yahoo.com.

Janice Flood Nichols earned her B.A. degree from Seton Hill College and her M.Ed. degree from the University of Pittsburgh. As the author of *Twin Voices: A Memoir of Polio, the Forgotten Killer* she devotes her time to speaking about the importance of polio eradication and vaccination. Learn more at www.twinvoices.com.

Tammy Nischan is a Christian teacher, writer, and speaker. As the mother of six, two of whom are in Heaven, Tammy's passion is ministering to other grieving moms. Visit her blog "My Heart... His Words" (www.tammynischan.blogspot.com) anytime. She would love to hear from you!

Sally O'Brien was married for forty-five years and has five grown children. She recommends retirement and enjoys the opportunity to spend entire days writing. Her work has been published in two other *Chicken Soup for the Soul* volumes as well as several magazines. E-mail her at sobrien95@msn.com.

Linda O'Connell, a teacher, writes from St. Louis, MO. She believes all things are possible. A blended family of four adult children and nine grandchildren bring tremendous joy to her and her husband, Bill. Linda is a frequent contributor to *Chicken Soup for the Soul* books. She blogs at lindaoconnell.blogspot.com.

Tracey Miller Offutt graduated with a BSN degree, magna cum laude, from Georgetown University School of Nursing & Health Studies. Her clinical practice focused on pediatrics. Previously, she was a journalist and editor. She was married with two children. She passed away in September of 2011 from Crohn's disease. Family can be reached at TraceyOffuttRN@aol.com.

Los Angeles native **Penny Orloff** attended Juilliard, played featured parts on Broadway and sang twenty principal soprano roles at New York City Opera. Her best-selling novel, *Jewish Thighs on Broadway* (available at Amazon.com), is the basis of her long-running solo show. Visit her at www.pennyorloff.com.

Iowan **Kristi Paxton** lives in the woods with her husband and wirehair fox terrier. A former postmaster, she is now a teacher, freelance writer and Mad Housewife Wine spokesmodel. Kristi loves cooking and hates cleaning. For fun, she kayaks, reads and dreams of beaches. E-mail her at kpaxcf@aol.com.

Andrea Peebles lives with her husband of thirty-five years in Rockmart, GA. She enjoys reading, writing, photography and spending time with her family. She has been a loyal reader of *Chicken Soup for the Soul* books for years and now enjoys contributing her own stories. Contact her via e-mail aanddpeebles@aol.com.

Cathy Pendola is a graduate of Northern Illinois University and resides in Flower Mound, TX, with her husband Manny, daughter Francesca and their dog Scooter. She is currently working on getting her first book published.

Cheryl Pierson is the multi-published author of three novels and many short stories, both fiction and nonfiction. She teaches short story and novel writing classes in the Oklahoma City metro area. E-mail her at fabkat_edit@yahoo.com, and visit her Amazon author page at: www.amazon.com/-/e/B002JV8GUE.

Carol Reed is a retired office worker. She enjoys reading, traveling and spending time with family and friends. She plans to write a book sharing her story of her husband's illness and his miraculous road to recovery.

Brianna Renshaw finds inspiration for her writing on daily long runs accompanied by her daughter Makayla, in her jogging stroller, through their neighborhood in Scotland, PA. Every run allows her to see the world in a new way while strengthening her body, mind and faith. Visit her blog at www.pocketfulofplaydough.pageek.com/wordpress.

Dan Reust lives and writes in the Denver, CO area. Contact him via e-mail at danreust@msn.com.

Grace Rostoker writes both fiction and nonfiction, and is fulfilling her ambition to be a full-time writer. She enjoys reading, music, walking, swimming and the California sunshine. Grace lives in San Diego with her mathematician husband and their lively dog. E-mail her at contact@gracerostoker.com.

Lee Rothberg, freelance writer and former nurse, works at the Matawan-Aberdeen Public Library in New Jersey. While a medical staff writer for *The Woman's Newspaper of Princeton*, she received several awards from the National Federation of Press Women. She is currently compiling family stories and recipes for her three granddaughters.

Marcia Rudoff is a memoir writing teacher and newspaper columnist in her hometown of Bainbridge Island, WA. She is the author of *We Have Stories—A Handbook for Writing Your Memoirs*. Her stories have appeared in anthologies, magazines and newspapers. Her personal interests include family, friends, travel, baseball and chocolate.

Tammy Ruggles is a freelance writer, artist, and filmmaker who lives in Kentucky. She is also a mother, grandmother, and retired social worker. Her first book, *Peace*, was published in 2005. Her screenplay, *The Legend of Hayswood Hospital*, was turned into a low-budget horror feature in 2010.

Tara Scaife has a psychology degree from the University of Toronto. She has been writing since the age of sixteen, starting with poetry before branching out into short stories. Tara is current working on her first novel. She enjoys martial arts, scuba diving and curling up with a good book. Tara currently resides in Toronto with her cat, Apollo.

Kim Seeley resides in Wakefield, VA, with her husband Wayne. A former English teacher and librarian, she now teaches handicapped adults part-time. She loves to read, travel, and spend time with her grandson, Evan. She is a frequent contributor to *Sasee* magazine and the *Chicken Soup for the Soul* series.

Jennifer Short attended Trevecca Nazarene University, then graduated from West Virginia University in 1998. Jennifer began writing as a toddler by telling stories to her mother who would then type them. Jennifer loves to read and often reviews books on her blog: jenndiggy. blogspot.com. She also enjoys traveling and her three guinea pigs.

Shirley Nordeck Short has combined her love for writing and guinea pigs and has written numerous picture books featuring one or more of the delightful cavies she has owned through the years. She's been published in *Chicken Soup for the Soul* books, *Reader's Digest* and *Guideposts*. Contact her via e-mail at shirleynshort@gmail.com.

Mary Z. Smith is a regular contributor to the *Chicken Soup for the Soul* series. She also writes for *Guideposts* and *Angels on Earth* and has an inspirational fiction book out entitled, *Life's A Symphony*, available at Amazon.com.

Erin Solej is a language arts teacher and a writer. She is currently writing her first novel, *Visiting Hours*, in memory of Catherine, Henry, and Michael Walsh. Dedicated to: Tomas, Lucas, and Hanna Solej; Joan and Don Woodruff; Teresa Walsh and her children Michael, Kathleen, Teresa, Bernadette, and Patrick.

A former advertising executive, **Sheila Sowder** currently writes from a motorhome while traveling the country with her husband. Her stories have appeared in several editions of *Chicken Soup for the Soul*, and she is the author of *O'Toole's Irregulars (A Neighborhood Bar Mystery)*. Contact her via e-mail at sksowder@aol.com.

A writer and performer, this is **Kim Stokely's** third contribution to the *Chicken Soup for the Soul* books. Her fiction has appeared in *Writers' Journal* and she is a contributor to thechristianpulse.com. Kim has performed a one-person musical, about women in the Bible, in churches throughout the country. Please contact her at www.kimstokely.com.

Deborah Sturgill lives in Ohio's countryside with her husband and their family of parakeets, cats, and an energetic Australian cattle dog. She is an entrepreneur, a Christian Life Coach, and writes books on spiritual and inspirational topics. Contact Deborah at sensitivechristianwoman@gmail.com or visit her website at sensitivechristianwoman.com.

Mary Beth Sturgis, RN, PhD, has been previously published in nursing journals. Working with older adults with acute and chronic illnesses has provided opportunities for spiritual connections and professional growth. Mary Beth is semi-retired, grateful for additional time with her husband, Ed, and her extended family.

Joyce Sudbeck is enjoying her favorite hobby—writing. She also enjoys sharing life with her husband of fifty-eight years and her Chihuahua. Joyce is humbly grateful for all her recent publishing opportunities. She says, "If I live long enough, who knows, maybe I'll get that novel written." Anything is possible.

Annmarie B. Tait resides in Conshohocken, PA, with her husband Joe Beck. In addition to writing stories Annmarie also enjoys cooking, crocheting, and singing Irish folk music. Annmarie has stories published in several *Chicken Soup for the Soul* volumes and many other anthologies. You may contact Annmarie at irishbloom@aol.com.

Nina Taylor is the Editorial Director for Pneuma Books, the book producer for Chicken Soup for the Soul. In between raising her husband, three teenage sons, and a toddler, she edits and ghostwrites books and dreams of finding the time and energy to write young adult novels. E-mail her at nina@pneumabooks.com.

Donna Teti loves her life in Pennsylvania as a wife, mother, aunt, writer and speaker. She also loves being a teacher's assistant to adorable four-year-olds at Goshen Friends School. She has been previously published in *Guideposts*, *Christmas Miracles* and Chicken Soup for the Soul. Her website is donnateti.com.

Jean Vaux is a retreat speaker and life and health coach in Cedar Falls, IA, where she also coordinates an annual writers workshop. She is working on writing two books of her own and also publishing a children's book her mother wrote before she passed away. Contact her at www.jeanvaux.com or jean@jeanvaux.com.

Pat Wahler is a freelance writer in St. Peters, MO. She attempts to balance a full-time job working with juvenile offenders, a family, and writing career with varying degrees of success. Pat has published stories in several anthologies and blogs all things animal at www.critteralley.blogspot.com.

Samantha Ducloux Waltz is an award-winning freelance writer in Portland, OR. Her personal stories appear in the *Chicken Soup for the Soul* series, numerous other anthologies, *The Christian Science Monitor* and *Redbook*. She has also written fiction and nonfiction under the name Samellyn Wood. Learn more at www.pathsofthought.com.

With over thirty years experience in advertising and marketing, **Luann Warner** is a freelance writer. In addition to her contributions to *Chicken Soup for the Soul* books, she hopes to complete her first book in the near future. Luann enjoys photography and spending time with her family. E-mail her at lkwarner3@comcast.net.

Brittini Watkins, a junior in high school, works for Kart Kountry. Brittini attributes her quick-thinking leadership to her four-year rigid training at Louisville Starlings Volleyball Club. Brittini's upbringing molds her into a strong woman. She dedicates this story to her granny, Jean Kinsey.

Janie Dempsey Watts' stories have appeared in *Chicken Soup for the Soul* books, *The Ultimate Gardener*, *Stories to Warm a Grandma's Heart*, and in magazines. Her fiction has been published in anthologies and journals. Please visit her at www.janiewatts.com.

Lisa Wojcik teaches literacy and art to low-income elementary grade children through a Florida public library system. Degreed from the University of New Mexico, Lisa is a science researcher, artist, and writer. Her short stories, poetry, children's literature, and research work can be seen at www.t4studios-bd.blogspot.com. E-mail her at lisawojcik@hotmail.com.

Ferida Wolff is the author of books for children and adults. Her essays appear in anthologies, newspapers, magazines, and online at www.seniorwomen.com. She also writes a nature blog www.feridasbackyard.blogspot.com. Learn more at www.feridawolff.com.

Melissa Wootan resides in La Vernia, TX, with her husband Joey, and son Joshua. Her story, "LadyBug Love," appears in *Chicken Soup for the Soul: Devotional Stories for Tough Times*. She most enjoys writing children's books and loving the two wonderful guys in her life. E-mail her at 4wootans@gmail.com.

Helen Zanone lives in Pittsburgh with her husband and three children. She is on the board of St. Davids Christian Writer's Conference. Helen is active in her writers' group and fulfilling her love for writing. She has multiple stories published in the *Chicken Soup for the Soul* series. E-mail her at hzanone@yahoo.com.

Marilyn Zapata works as a transcriber for court reporters. Her major client is her husband, Art, and after forty years of service, she has achieved tenure and cannot be fired. To view her other, more artistic pursuits, including a four-volume tome of their travels, visit marilynzapata.blogspot.com.

Meet Our Authors

Jack Canfield is the co-creator of the *Chicken Soup for the Soul* series, which *Time* magazine has called "the publishing phenomenon of the decade." Jack is also the co-author of many other bestselling books.

Jack is the CEO of the Canfield Training Group in Santa Barbara, California, and founder of the Foundation for Self-Esteem in Culver City, California. He has conducted intensive personal and professional development seminars on the principles of success for more than a million people in twenty-three countries, has spoken to hundreds of thousands of people at more than 1,000 corporations, universities, professional conferences and conventions, and has been seen by millions more on national television shows.

Jack has received many awards and honors, including three honorary doctorates and a Guinness World Records Certificate for having seven books from the *Chicken Soup for the Soul* series appearing on the New York Times bestseller list on May 24, 1998.

You can reach Jack at www.jackcanfield.com.

Mark Victor Hansen is the co-founder of Chicken Soup for the Soul, along with Jack Canfield. He is a sought-after keynote speaker, bestselling author, and marketing maven. Mark's powerful messages of possibility, opportunity, and action have created powerful change in thousands of organizations and millions of individuals worldwide.

Mark is a prolific writer with many bestselling books in addition to the *Chicken Soup for the Soul* series. Mark has had a profound influence in the field of human potential through his library of audios, videos, and articles in the areas of big thinking, sales achievement, wealth building, publishing success, and personal and professional development. He is also the founder of the MEGA Seminar Series.

Mark has received numerous awards that honor his entrepreneurial spirit, philanthropic heart, and business acumen. He is a lifetime member of the Horatio Alger Association of Distinguished Americans.

You can reach Mark at www.markvictorhansen.com.

Amy Newmark is Chicken Soup for the Soul's publisher and editor-in-chief, after a thirty-year career as a writer, speaker, financial analyst, and business executive in the worlds of finance and telecommunications. Amy is a *magna cum laude* graduate of Harvard College, where she majored in Portuguese, minored in French, and traveled extensively. She and her husband have four grown children.

After a long career writing books on telecommunications, voluminous financial reports, business plans, and corporate press releases, Chicken Soup for the Soul is a breath of fresh air for Amy. She has fallen in love with Chicken Soup for the Soul and its life-changing books, and really enjoys putting these books together for Chicken Soup's wonderful readers. She has co-authored more than three dozen *Chicken Soup for the Soul* books and has edited another three dozen.

You can reach Amy with any questions or comments through the webmaster@chickensoupforthesoul.com.

Chicken Soup for the Soul

Thank You

We owe huge thanks to all of our contributors. We know that you poured your hearts and souls into the thousands of stories that you shared with us, and ultimately with each other. As we read and edited these stories, we were truly amazed by your experiences. We appreciate your willingness to share these inspiring and encouraging stories with our readers.

We could only publish a small percentage of the stories that were submitted, but we read every single one and even the ones that do not appear in the book had an influence on us and on the final manuscript. We owe special thanks to our editors Kristiana Glavin, D'ette Corona, and Jeanne Blandford, who read the stories that were submitted for this book and narrowed the list down to a more manageable number of finalists. Kristi did a fabulous job creating a first manuscript and selecting the inspirational quotes that start off each story, and D'ette did her normal masterful job of working with the contributors to approve our edits and answer any questions we had. Barbara LoMonaco and Madeline Clapps served as our very capable proofreaders.

We also owe a special thanks to our creative director and book producer, Brian Taylor at Pneuma Books, for his brilliant vision for our covers and interiors.

~Amy Newmark

Chicken Soup for the Soul
Improving Your Life Every Day

R eal people sharing real stories—for eighteen years. Now, Chicken Soup for the Soul has gone beyond the bookstore to become a world leader in life improvement. Through books, movies, DVDs, online resources and other partnerships, we bring hope, courage, inspiration and love to hundreds of millions of people around the world. Chicken Soup for the Soul's writers and readers belong to a one-of-a-kind global community, sharing advice, support, guidance, comfort, and knowledge.

Chicken Soup for the Soul stories have been translated into more than forty languages and can be found in more than one hundred countries. Every day, millions of people experience a Chicken Soup for the Soul story in a book, magazine, newspaper or online. As we share our life experiences through these stories, we offer hope, comfort and inspiration to one another. The stories travel from person to person, and from country to country, helping to improve lives everywhere.

Share with Us

We all have had Chicken Soup for the Soul moments in our lives. If you would like to share your story or poem with millions of people around the world, go to chickensoup.com and click on "Submit Your Story." You may be able to help another reader, and become a published author at the same time. Some of our past contributors have launched writing and speaking careers from the publication of their stories in our books!

Our submission volume has been increasing steadily—the quality and quantity of your submissions has been fabulous. We only accept story submissions via our website. They are no longer accepted via mail or fax.

To contact us regarding other matters, please send us an e-mail through webmaster@chickensoupforthesoul.com, or fax or write us at:

Chicken Soup for the Soul
P.O. Box 700
Cos Cob, CT 06807-0700
Fax: 203-861-7194

One more note from your friends at Chicken Soup for the Soul: Occasionally, we receive an unsolicited book manuscript from one of our readers, and we would like to respectfully inform you that we do not accept unsolicited manuscripts and we must discard the ones that appear.

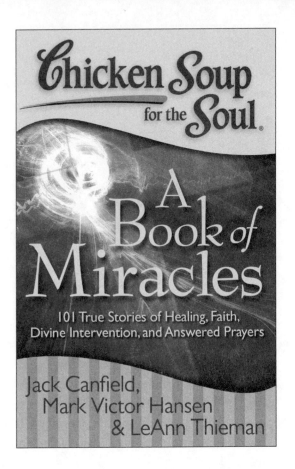

Chicken Soup for the Soul.

A Book of Miracles

101 True Stories of Healing, Faith, Divine Intervention, and Answered Prayers

Jack Canfield,
Mark Victor Hansen
& LeAnn Thieman

Everyone loves a good miracle story, and this book provides 101 true stories of healing, divine intervention, and answered prayers. These amazing, personal stories prove that God is alive and active in the world today, working miracles on our behalf. The incredible accounts show His love and involvement in our lives. This book of miracles will encourage, uplift, and recharge the faith of Catholics and all Christian readers.

978-1-935096-51-1

Miracles!

Chicken Soup for the Soul

for the *Soul*

Grieving and Recovery

101 Inspirational and Comforting Stories about Surviving the Loss of a Loved One

Jack Canfield,
Mark Victor Hansen,
and Amy Newmark

Everyone grieves in their own way. While the hurt and sadness never completely fade, it eases with time. Contributors who have gone through the grieving and recovery process share their stories of what helped, offering guidance and support in this collection of personal and poignant stories. With its stories of regaining strength, appreciating life, coping, and faith, this book will ease the journey to healing.

978-1-935096-62-7

Hope!

Chicken Soup
for the Soul

www.chickensoup.com